MEMOIRS of a
KAMIKAZE

A World War II Pilot's Inspiring Story of Survival, Honor and Reconciliation

KAZUO ODACHI

with **Shigeru Ohta** and **Hiroyoshi Nishijima**
translated **by Alexander Bennett** and **Shigeru Ohta**

TUTTLE Publishing

Tokyo | Rutland, Vermont | Singapore

"Books to Span the East and West"

Tuttle Publishing was founded in 1832 in the small New England town of Rutland, Vermont (USA). Our core values remain as strong today as they were then—to publish best-in-class books which bring people together one page at a time. In 1948, we established a publishing office in Japan—and Tuttle is now a leader in publishing English-language books about the arts, languages and cultures of Asia. The world has become a much smaller place today and Asia's economic and cultural influence has grown. Yet the need for meaningful dialogue and information about this diverse region has never been greater. Over the past seven decades, Tuttle has published thousands of books on subjects ranging from martial arts and paper crafts to language learning and literature—and our talented authors, illustrators, designers and photographers have won many prestigious awards. We welcome you to explore the wealth of information available on Asia at **www.tuttlepublishing.com.**

Published by Tuttle Publishing, an imprint of Periplus Editions (HK) Ltd

www.tuttlepublishing.com

ISBN 978-4-8053-1575-0

Zerosen Tokkoutai Kara Keiji E
© 2016 Hiroyoshi Nishijima, Shigeru Ohta
English translation rights arranged with
FUYO SHOBO CO., LTD.
Through Japan UNI Agency, Inc., Tokyo

English Translation © 2020 Alexander Bennett and Shigeru Ohta

Library of Congress publication data is in progress.

Printed in Malaysia   2105TO

24 23 22 21   10 9 8 7 6 5 4

Distributed by

North America, Latin America & Europe
Tuttle Publishing
364 Innovation Drive
North Clarendon, VT 05759-9436 U.S.A.
Tel: (802) 773-8930; Fax: (802) 776993
info@tuttlepublishing.com
www.tuttlepublishing.com

Japan
Tuttle Publishing
Yaekari Building, 3rd Floor
5-4-12 Osaki, Shinagawa-ku,
Tokyo 141 0032
Tel: (81) 3 5437-0171
Fax: (81) 3 5437-0755
sales@tuttle.co.jp; www.tuttle.co.jp

Asia Pacific
Berkeley Books Pte. Ltd.
3 Kallang Sector
#04-01, Singapore 349278
Tel: (65) 6741-2178; Fax: (65) 6741-2179
inquiries@periplus.com.sg
www.tuttlepublishing.com

TUTTLE PUBLISHING® is a registered trademark of Tuttle Publishing, a division of Periplus Editions (HK) Ltd.

MEMOIRS of a
KAMIKAZE

CONTENTS

FOREWORD

This book was first published in Japanese in July of 2016 and quickly received considerable attention from the media. Although there have been hundreds of novels, documentaries and movies about the Kamikaze, this book is unique. Involved with the Kamikaze Special Attack operation from its inception until the very end, this is a story of young man who joined the Imperial Japanese Naval Air Service aged 16 and was still only 18 when Japan accepted unconditional surrender.

The author kept silent about his harrowing experiences for nearly 70 years, but finally decided to share them in the twilight years of his life. Lucky to have survived, he became a highly respected policeman who never forgot his dead comrades. This book also tells a fascinating story about an important constant in his long life. The author started the martial art of Kendo as a child and still practices actively in his nineties.

Young men and women from many countries were sent to the front and a countless number of them ever came home. The Kamikaze Special Attack Corps may seem akin to extremist suicide bombers who terrorize the world today. It is my hope that the reader will come to view the young Kamikaze pilots who crash-dived into enemy targets as honorable soldiers who selflessly and valiantly sacrificed their lives for their nation and its people. Such martyrdom is surely no different to the sacrifice made by any soldiers caught up in the tragic cauldron of war.

Millions of combatants and civilians on all sides lost their lives in the Second World War. Strong bridges of friendship have since been constructed between former foes, but we must never forget that these bonds are built atop a foundation of bones of those whose lives were ended violently and prematurely.

I hope that this book further augments an understanding of history as seen through the eyes of a young man who somehow lived through the horror, and that it will transcend concerns of nation and generation, reminding us of those who never lived to enjoy a peaceful life after the war.

—Shigeru Ohta

PROLOGUE

A little before noon on August 15, 1945, at an airbase on the north-east coast of Taiwan called Yilan, more than thirty Zero fighter planes carrying 500-kilogram bombs under their fuselages were preparing to take off. They were Kamikaze suicide planes and their mission was to attack hundreds of American ships anchoring off Okinawa. Succeed or fail in their mission, they would not be returning.

Clouds were high in the sky and it was very hot. The propellers sputtered into motion in a haze of smoky exhaust. The Zero piloted by sergeant Kazuo Odachi was in his squadron's first team at the head of the runway, positioned to the left-rear of the section leader's. The moment the planes began to move, an engine-starting car hurtled at full speed down the runway to block their path.

"Abort attack!" a mechanic shouted from the car. Somewhat startled by this sudden postponement, Odachi and the others disembarked their winged coffins and walked back to the command post. Before long, the somber voice of Japan's emperor, Hirohito, crackled from the wireless speakers. It was difficult to hear, but the pilots got the gist of the imperial broadcast. Japan had accepted non-conditional surrender.

In the buildup to the mission, Odachi thought to himself "My time has surely come." It was going to be the last of his eight attempted Kamikaze missions. But this time, once again, his life was miraculously spared. Fighting Grummans in aerial combat, strafed by American fighters when walking down a road, afflicted by malaria, making a narrow escape from Philippine mountains where hope had all but been lost.... He experienced all of this over the course of a year. For whatever reason, death passed him by and he was saved by the skin of his teeth more times than he cared to remember.

Student Draftees and Yokaren Trainees

In addition to footnotes, special columns such as this are included throughout the book to provide contextual information on Japanese history and some details related to Japan's involvement in the Second World War. This is the first such column, and has been included at the beginning to explain why this story is so special.

Most people have heard of "Kamikaze," but few, even in Japan, realize that there were essentially two categories of suicide attacker. This is not referring to the modes or units of suicide attack (planes, boats, human torpedoes, Navy Air Service, Army etc.), as there were several variations, but to the status of the men involved in aerial Kamikaze attacks.

Kamikaze suicide operations commenced around October of 1944. It was a desperate last resort for Japan with its military capacity having been crushed by a series of monumental defeats. Until the final stages of the war, young men studying at university in Japan had been exempted from compulsory military service. With the war situation worsening, however, a new policy to draft students was introduced in the Fall of 1943 to compensate for critical manpower shortages at the front.

Students were considered society's elite, but thoughts of a bright and prosperous future were abruptly cut short for many when they were press ganged into service midway through their studies. A significant number received no more than a few dozen hours of flight training. Some did not even make 20 hours, so only had a rudimentary understanding of flying before being sent to their deaths in one-way suicide sorties.

They wrote long wills and letters to their loved ones. They mentioned the pain they felt about having to die so young, their philosophy of death, their love of family members, girlfriends and wives, and sometimes included private criticisms of the war and its leaders. Many such records were published in a well-known book titled *Kike Wadatsumi no Koe* (Listen to Voices from the Sea). Their moving letters left a deep impression on both Japanese and Western readers. Compared to this and similar books about the Kamikaze tragedy, however, readers will notice a different tone in this volume.

Kazuo Odachi and his comrades enlisted in the Yokaren in their mid-teens, fully aware that their chosen vocation was risky. The Yokaren was the much-lauded Japanese Naval Preparatory Flight Training Program for boys aged 15 to 17. Cadets were originally educated in a three-year preliminary course followed by one-year flight training, but this was considerably expedited by the time Odachi was admitted towards the end of the war.

Compared to student draftees, Yokaren graduates were highly skilled professional airmen. Their training was rigorous, and they were experienced in actual combat with the enemy before the Kamikaze strategy was devised. When they 'volunteered' for Kamikaze missions, their designated targets were enemy fleet ships, especially the biggest prize of them all aircraft carriers. To make the most of their expertise and machines, they had the option of returning to base if engine trouble occurred, the weather turned bad, or a suitable target was not located. Although each mission was embarked on as the last, this is how Odachi miraculously survived seven intended suicide sorties.

Odachi and the other battle-hardened airmen never wrote wills or sent letters back home before their final mission. They had long been mentally prepared to die in the course of duty. In this sense, therefore, there were two kinds of Kamikaze attackers: professional pilots, and amateur draftees. Odachi belonged to the former. That is not to say, however, that the sacrifice of one was greater than the other. Nevertheless, attitudes and expectations were different, and Odachi was one of only a small handful of his peers who came back from the war. That is why his story is unique.

CHAPTER ONE

Kendo and the Yokaren

LEADER OF THE PACK

I was born on December 11, 1926, and raised in a little country village called Kitano Kotesashi in Saitama Prefecture, not too far from Tokyo. I am the second son with three brothers and two sisters. We lived in a big house separated from our neighbors by eight zelkova trees and sheltered by oaks to the south.

My family name, Odachi, literally means "big house." My ancestors can be traced back to the Nitta-Genji clan, a prominent aristocratic warrior family of a thousand years ago. At the end of the twelfth century, a Genji general by the name of Minamoto Yoritomo established Japan's first military government, the Kamakura shogunate. In the fourteenth century, vassals of the Kamakura shogunate enacted a coup d'état to topple the military government and my Odachi ancestors joined them.

A new Muromachi shogunate was subsequently established in Kyoto, but the political situation was far from stable. A split soon formed in the imperial court, and for many decades in the fourteenth century, a northern and a southern court coexisted. The Odachi clan supported the southern court and were thus shunned by the Muromachi shogunate which established the northern court. Eventually the northern court became recognized as the sole imperial authority, and supporters of the defunct southern court were forced to scatter and hide throughout Japan. My ancestors returned to the Kanto plain, and that's where we remained.

I entered Kotesashi Elementary School in April 1933. It was the only school in the village. It had one first-grade class of around 70 students. We were quintessential hale-and-hearty country kids. The younger ones were looked after by the seniors, and we all played together in the fields and at the village shrine every day. Before I took up the traditional martial art of Kendo, I filled my days playing war games or hunting sparrows with the others.

The so-called "bosses" of children gangs were usually fifth or sixth graders. This lofty mantle of authority was bestowed upon me in the sixth grade. After school, I would direct my tribe of urchins to gather at a designated time and place, such as at the shrine gate. I would rush home, gobble down a snack, and then head to the rendezvous point. Homework was never a priority. I called the shots and all the boys in my posse followed my lead. Each tribe had its own patch of turf and gang scuffles were not an uncommon occurrence.

Mr. Kuroda and Kendo

I remember Japan gearing up for war in my childhood days. Physical training started to take precedence over academic classes in schools. I excelled in physical education classes and enjoyed competing. I also joined the village's newly-formed bugle group. Our main task was to regale young men of the village with patriotic compositions at the local train station as they departed for the front.

As the world descended into chaos, we kids were more concerned with our own battles. We fought constantly with children from the neighboring village of Yamaguchi. Mr. Kuroda's house was located between our two villages. Respected by all who met him, he exuded an air of stateliness like a samurai of old. He wore a black jacket with a high collar and loudly recited old poems as he walked to and from school with his characteristic ramrod-straight posture.[1]

Mr. Kuroda was transferred to our school in 1937 when I was a fifth grader. He was 23 years old at the time and had just graduated from Saitama Prefectural Normal School where he trained as a teacher. He was reputed to be a Kendo practitioner of considerable skill. He told us that the style of Kendo he practiced was related to the Hokushin Itto-ryu, one of the predominant styles of classical swordsmanship during the Edo period (1603-1868). It was under his strict tutelage that I started Kendo.

Kuroda-sensei taught Kendo during physical education classes for which we were required to buy a wooden practice sword. Training was harsh. Although prohibited in Kendo today, foot sweeping and wrestling the opponent to the ground was standard. Kendo is usually practiced in

---

[1] Seiji Kuroda devoted his life to teaching. He served on many educational boards including director of high school education and chief secretary of the Saitama prefectural education committee. He also made special efforts to promote Kendo among children and nurtured many famous competitors and instructors.

bare feet on polished wooden floors. Our school did not have a martial arts dojo, so at first he took us through sword forms outside. Alas, in the name of tradition he wouldn't allow us to wear shoes. This resulted in severe grazing of knees and elbows. Torn shirts and bloodied bodies were par for the course. The wounds would become infected because of the grit and sand, and red pee because of the severity of the exercise was not unusual.

My mother was not keen on me continuing, but quitting was not an option. I thrived on the thrill and excitement of it all. In all honesty, I didn't enjoy being dragged across the ground, but resisting all attempts by Mr. Kuroda to grind me into the dirt made me stronger in body and mind. Before long, he was unable to get the better of me.

Eventually we were allocated a classroom to train in, which required moving the desks and chairs out of the way before each session. It sure beat jumping around barefooted on the gravel in the schoolyard. It wasn't until we got the protective equipment that Kendo became interesting. The local government gifted 50 sets of Kendo armor to the village. This allowed us to engage in full-contact sparring using bamboo practice swords.

There were seven or eight members in our Kendo club. I outshone all of them. During the day we would practice in PE class, and had extracurricular sessions two nights a week. Other boys from the area also started Kendo, and Mr. Shimizu from the nearby Army Academy came to help with the teaching. Adults in the village with some experience came to assist Kuroda-sensei as he took us through our paces. Every time we tried to land a strike with our bamboo swords on Mr. Kuroda-sensei's head, he would kick our feet out from under us. It was tough going.

A Kendo tournament was held annually at the local shrine. I entered the competition and remember standing proudly on the winner's podium to receive a prize of bamboo swords for my efforts. I then participated in the prefectural championships when I was in the sixth grade. It was held in a special Kendo hall at a big Shinto shrine in Omiya. Kendo was popular throughout the mountainside regions of Saitama Prefecture, but not so much in the plains area where we were. It was always the mountain boys who prevailed in the major tournaments. They were hard to beat.

The tournament was officially started with a demonstration of sword forms by the legendary Kendo masters Sasaburo Takano and Hakudo (Hiromichi) Nakayama. Mr. Kuroda told us observe them carefully. I was not particularly interested in the exhibition of prescribed forms and failed to appreciate the great men I was watching. I was more captivated by an old Army General with his magnificent moustache in the VIP seats.

As for the matches, my team was knocked out of the competition early on. The individual competition was a different matter. I won my early bouts and made it to the semi-finals. It could have been the first time a plains lad defeated the almighty mountain boys to become the junior champion, but sadly I had to settle for third place.

Yearning for Wings

The bells of war were ringing louder than ever by the time I graduated from elementary school. Junior high school boys wore black uniforms with high collars like priests, and puttees on their legs like soldiers. Schools were transformed into training grounds to prepare youth for battle, and bayonet training was added to Kendo practice. With a military base located near our village, the militaristic mood was perhaps more pronounced than in other regions.

We took great delight in watching the giant mechanical birds landing and taking off at the Tokorozawa Airbase.[2] There were no roads leading to the base, so we walked for an hour navigating blindly through fields and pastures to get there. The airbase was enclosed by barbed wire, but we knew of a small opening in the fence through which we could sneak inside. We lay on our stomachs in the long grass alongside the runway observing the planes circling above. The pilots must surely have seen us. On occasion, soldiers would come by in cars to watch as well. We hid motionless in the undergrowth and waited for them to move along. All I wanted to do from then was become a pilot.

I was 14 on that fateful day of December 8, 1941 when Pearl Harbor was attacked. I heard the news on the radio. "Japan has declared war on America and Britain." Large families were common in those days. If there were three sons, the eldest was expected to remain and take care of family affairs, but the second and third sons were destined for the front. Knowing this, I was determined to enter the "Yokaren" (Naval Aviator Preparatory Course), the elite preliminary training program for navy pilots.

---

[2] The Tokorozawa Army Airbase was established in 1911 as the first in Japan. Captain Tokugawa Yoshitoshi, a descendant of the famous family of Tokugawa shoguns, made the maiden flight from the Yoyogi Parade Ground in Tokyo to the airbase site in 1910. It is a public park now.

I wanted to fight for Japan in the sky.[3]

I told mother of my intention to sit the Yokaren examination. She objected at first, but I persisted and told her that if at least one of her four sons were not prepared to serve, our family would lose face in the village. Mother cried as she realized that there was little choice in the matter. My father said nothing. As it happens, one of my other brothers joined the army. He also survived the war.

The Yokaren examination was tough and consisted of Japanese, mathematics and science. These were all subjects I studied at school, but the examination was of a much higher level. In addition, we were expected to memorize the "Imperial Rescript to Japanese Soldiers and Sailors" as an introduction to the martial spirit of Japan. I studied it every day, and even bought supplemental textbooks to prepare for the exam held in Mie Prefecture's naval base. Thousands of candidates gathered from around the country, including many from Saitama. I was 16 at the time.

I travelled to Mie (just below Nagoya) by train with two friends from a neighboring village—Kinzo Kasuya and Hiroshi Toyoda (see photos). Hiroshi was the dux of his school, and Kinzo was also a smart kid. Other boys in our villages failed, but we three passed. Father, hearing of my success, said nothing. To him it was a matter of course. Mother said with a tinge of sadness, "Good for you...."

Locations in Japan important to the story.

---

[3] All trainees were teenagers who volunteered for service. The "A-Class" Yokaren course was for boys who had graduated from junior high. "Special B-Class" was for boys who had completed elementary school. There was also a "C-Class" which drew from men already in the navy. The eligible age for entry was 14 to 19. Many a young lad wanted to join, but the entrance examination was extremely competitive with a pass rate of around 1 in 80.

CHAPTER TWO

Training Hell

The Kasumigaura "Naval Aviator Preparatory Course" (Yokaren) in Chiba Prefecture was full. A new "Special B-Class" course was established at the Iwakuni Naval Airbase in Yamaguchi Prefecture in Spring of 1943. It was designed as a shorter, more intensive training program, and I was inducted into the first cohort of cadets.

It was an enthusiastic send-off by the villagers, not the usual adieu given to draftees, as I was the first ever Yokaren trainee from our village. This was considered quite an honor and seemed to warrant much pomp and ceremony. Relatives and well-wishers gathered at my home for a big party the night before departure. At 8:00 the following morning, I marched to the Kitano Tenmangu Shrine where the district's traditional protective deity is enshrined. Hundreds of people turned up to wish me luck and walk with me to the shrine. Village youngsters at the head of the parade brandished a big flag emblazoned with the words "Congratulations Kazuo Odachi! Yokaren Trainee." Others performed military songs with their trumpets and drums. I followed the band, and the mayor, assemblymen, and teachers walked behind me. Nearly 200 elementary school pupils also joined in the parade.

We ascended the stone steps of the shrine where I was blessed by a Shinto priest in front of the main worship hall. Returning along the same route to the station we passed hundreds of children in front of the school waving small Japanese flags and enthusiastically shouting "Way to go Kazu-san! Good luck!" I was about to respond in kind but remembered the distinguished gentlemen behind me and thought it prudent to behave in a more adult manner.

Even more villagers were waiting near the station. The mayor entered the station building with trumpeters lined up next to him. They blasted a fanfare, and all gathered turned and bowed in the direction of the Imperial Palace. The mayor then delivered his address. "Allow me to offer a few words of encouragement to our brave young Mr. Odachi who is about to embark on his adventure to fight for Japan...." When he finished, I made a snappy salute and responded in kind. "I thank you all for this send-off. I will do my best to serve with honor and repay your kindness with dedication to duty. I shall now humbly take my leave." I boarded the train amid a flurry of red and white as everybody waved their flags.

My parents did not attend my grand farewell. They were too busy making traditional celebratory food to give to neighbors for their support. The send-off was lavish in every way. I figured that they all secretly thought I'd be dead within a couple of years, and this was my last hoorah. Kinzo Kasuya and Hiroshi Toyoda boarded the same train at the next station. We all set off together as brothers of the so-called "cherry blossom corps."[4] In their case, however, it was to be their final goodbye. They were killed in action a few years later.

Training in Iwakuni

The Iwakuni Naval Airbase was built in 1938, and that was where we commenced our Yokaren training there.[5] Rising at 6:00 each morning, the days started with physical exercise followed by breakfast. Then it was classes and training sessions until 17:30. Evenings were set aside for self-study and revision. We took classes in mathematics and other subjects just as we did at school with the addition of Morse code and English. Flying didn't come until later. Our instructors in the early stages were originally school teachers, but their lessons were severe beyond compare.

Our basic military training consisted of bayonet fighting and marching. We also practiced Sumo wrestling, marksmanship, and various team-building exercises. Rowing was particularly exacting. The oars were thick and blistered our hands, and our backsides became bruised from the hard seats. Everything we did was connected to training. Even walking from one barrack to another was prohibited. We had to run.

We were not allowed into the mess hall when morning classes finished until passing an impromptu test first. An officer would order us to halt. A soldier on the roof then signaled with flags and we had to decipher

---

[4] Cherry blossoms or *sakura* in Japan are cherished for their shirt-lived beauty as the spring wind scatters the pink petals in full bloom. Yokaren trainees were viewed as epitomizing cherry blossoms. A popular song about them goes "You and I belong to the cherry blossom corps. We bloom together in the garden of the fleet...."

[5] Iwakuni Airbase is still used today by the Self-Defense Force of Japan, and by the U.S. Marine Corps.

the code. Whispering our answers into the officer's ear we were given permission to enter the mess hall if we got it right. Otherwise, we would be stuck outside and subjected to a barrage of insults decrying our "lack of military spirit." Insults were one thing but being forced to forgo lunch was the worst.

Every minute of every day felt as if we were in our own small war, but I had no issue with even the strictest instruction. I was determined to never show the "white feather" of defeat as it was a matter of pride. I kept my sights firmly on becoming a fighter pilot. Kinzo, Hiroshi and I chose this way, so failure was not an option.

There were about 1,800 fellow trainees in Iwakuni, and many of the cadets in our first Special B-Class course were outstanding fellows. As more pilots were killed in action, we were sent to fill the gaps and became core aviators in the air fleets stationed around Taiwan and the Philippines. Thrust into the center of the action, our cohort was destined to suffer the largest number of casualties in the war.

One memory I have from that time was the mysterious demise of the battleship *Mutsu* in June 1943. The *Mutsu* was one of the largest battleships in the world. Even though it was anchored in Hiroshima about 20km away from our base, the almighty noise from the explosion was clearly audible. The cause of the explosion remains unknown.

Training in Nagoya

After six-months in Iwakuni, we relocated to the Nagoya base to undertake the midterm training course. The base was on top of a hill near the little town of Koromo. It was appallingly chilly there, and life was bleak. We were taught flying basics in gliders before advancing to the "Red Dragonflies," the nickname for Yokosuka K5Y biplane trainers (see photos). Their color, however, was orange. Four trainees made up one team and we repeated take-offs and landings under the watchful eye of instructors seated in the back.

Typical flight training would go as follows: I would allocate the top of the hill in front as the target. After informing the instructor "Target OK" through the comms tube, I pushed down on the lever to take off. Gradually ascending to 200m, I would call "First turn" and made a 90-degree turn to the left. At the next turning point, I would make one more 90-degree turn to the left, and fly the reverse route looking down on the runway. I would then make a third turn to the left, and then one more before descending to land on "three points." That is, a stable landing on the two wheels attached to the main wings and the rear wheel. After successfully touching down, I would disembark and run to report to the trainer. The next trainee would then head to the cockpit while I returned to the bench to observe his flight.

In addition to this basic training we also practiced more complex maneuvers such as the "aileron roll," "vertical loop," "left diagonal loop," "right diagonal loop," and "hammerhead stall." The "left oblique spin" involved climbing to the upper left, turning over and then descending. The "hammerhead stall" was executed by climbing quickly on an angle, and as the plane lost speed at the highest point, a sudden turn was executed. This technique was an evasion maneuver often used by Zero fighters. Our Red Dragonflies could perform it just as well if not better than Zeros because they flew slowly without the undue stress that resulted in catastrophic structural failure seen in other machines.

Still, the Red Dragonfly was not immune to the occasional mechanical fiasco. I had two frightening experiences with the engine suddenly cutting out. I thought I was doomed, and informed my instructor that I was preparing to crash land on the bamboo below. Fortunately the engine came back to life, and thankfully saved mine.

Trainees also made mistakes. Every now and again the wheel struts under the wings would collapse because of heavy landings. This would inevitably earn a hard slap in the face from the instructor along with a stream of profanities for "taking the piss."

We had three uniforms; a flight suit, practice suit, and formal wear. Our formal uniform was a black, high-collared suit with seven buttons. Engraved on each of the buttons was a small cherry blossom and an anchor. We became known as "seven buttons" because of the uniforms, and there was even a song about us. "The young hot-blooded men of the Yokaren. Cherry blossoms and anchors, seven buttons so smart...."

Our formal uniforms fitted well, but flight and practice suits, and shoes were a different matter. Asking for something in our size would result in being told to "go boil your head" and "make your body fit the clothes instead of whining for clothes that fit your body!" The flight boots were awful. My shoe size was 24cm, but I was issued with 28cm boots making it hard to control the foot pedal in the cockpit. Running around base without tripping up was also a mission.

We wore our practice uniforms most of the time. Referred to as "sailor suits" these were not made to fit either. There were fewer buttons than our iconic formal wear, and the hems of the trousers were overstated bell-bottoms, supposedly making them easier to remove them if we ended up in the sea.

Even bedtime was a test of grit. We underwent a nightly ritual of setting up our hammocks as the trainers timed us. We placed our hammocks on the floor and knelt as we waited for the signal. With the sound of a whistle, we grabbed the metal hooks and attached them to the poles, unwound the hammock cords, placed the pillow inside and shouted "Done!" If the last one in our team took more than 18 seconds we would be scolded for our deplorable lack of enthusiasm and would have our backsides whacked three or four times with the trainer's disciplinary baton dubbed the "Martial Spirit Bludgeon." The time limit was gradually shortened to 17 seconds then 16 seconds.

Life was tough and there wasn't much to enjoy about the experience. Even washing clothes was toilsome beyond belief. Navy boys were expected to look smart and well-groomed. This meant that we had to wash our clothes often, but the laundry facilities were on an exposed hill where the frigid wind and freezing water prevented the soap suds from dissolving. Our hands were paralyzed with cold and it took forever to get our gear clean.

The instructors habitually frightened the living daylights out of us. We found out later that some of them were hardened veterans, but many others were not. The latter were "dropouts" who lacked the necessary skills, or who were not imbued with "the right stuff" to be fighter pilots. As such, these fellows tended to be relentless in their bullying, and were clearly bent out of shape with jealousy.

No good memories were forged in Nagoya. Perhaps the only exception was the sugar biscuits. When we were allowed a little time off training, we purchased packs of biscuits and bottles of cider which we consumed in a special room in the shop reserved for navy men. Munching on biscuits and chattering away in our fleeting moment away from the slog was our only reprieve.

First Time in a Zero

There were 60 trainees in Nagoya at first. All of us wanted to be fighter pilots, but many were weeded out and dropped from the course. The training duration was shortened to three months from the scheduled four, and I was sent to an airbase in Oita as a fighter trainee.[6] At first, we weren't sure why things were hurried along but it became abundantly clear later. The war was not going well, and Japan needed Zero pilots in battle theaters ASAP.

After our basic training, some of us were sent offshore to places like Singapore. I was bound for Singapore at first, but my orders were changed to Oita. This is where cadets were taught how to fly Model 32 Zero fighters. I was dispatched to Oita in January 1944 with about 50 others. Being in a bomber meant you were one of a team of seven, whereas the Zero pilot was captain of his own machine. It was what all of us desired most.

Arriving in Oita, I was dismayed to see three "Military Spirit Bludgeons" hanging ominously in the barracks. Three veterans were sitting in a circle. They stared long and hard at us wondering whether we would be able to hack it. I knew we were in for a difficult time but couldn't let the negativity get to me.

I boarded the fabled Model 32 Zero for the first time. It was markedly different to the Red Dragonfly I was accustomed to. The rhythmic sound of the engine was powerful and soothing. It handled sublimely, and I felt as if vapor from the engine was engulfing my body. The Zero and I were one.

The training Zero came with a back seat for an instructor. We graduated from these before long and flew solo in single-seated models. The Model 32 was very stable. There was one instructor for each trainee team of four. We mainly practiced taking off and landing to start with, then progressed to standard flight drills and finally aerial dogfight maneuvers against other Zeros.

A month passed, and we started to sense a change in mood around base. Instructors would fire us up by screaming that we had no more time to waste in training. "It's time to get where the action is." Before long,

---

[6] Oita Prefecture is located on the east side of Kyushu. The very last Kamikaze sortie took off from this base at 4 p.m. on August 15, 1945, shortly after Japan's surrender. The base was converted into an athletic ground after the war. A stone monument can be found there in which the names of the last Kamikaze pilots are engraved.

we were deployed to operational units. Our original four-month train-ing schedule was concluded in a little over a month. I was transferred to Kasanohara Airbase in Kagoshima Prefecture.[7]

Kasanohara Airbase

There were three naval air bases in Kagoshima: Kanoya, Kokubu, and Kasanohara. I moved to Kasanohara in the middle of February 1944. Na-val Fighter Wing squadrons of the 1st Air Fleet were referred to with animal designations—Lion, Tiger, Panther, and Wolf. Those in the 2nd Air Fleet's 221st Naval Air Group 312th Fighter Wings were named after natural phenomena: Storm, Lightning, and Thunder. I was attached to the 312th Wing in the "Storm" (Arashi) Corps, and this is where the real fighter pilot drills began.

Trainings at Kasanohara started out as usual. After a week or so, a senior officer told us that things were about to get serious. "Your seniors have been annihilated in the Truk Islands. The stakes are higher now. Get ready for hell lads." The Navy had been secretive about the defeat in Truk. The Imperial General Headquarters never disclosed discouraging news, but the details trickled down to us by word of mouth anyway.[8]

With squadrons in the 1st Air Fleet all but gone, the 2nd Air Fleet was called in to bolster air attacks in the southwest Pacific. We trained relent-lessly from morning to night. Aside from on rainy days, we were usually not allowed to sleep in our quarters. Instead, we kipped under the wings of our aircraft outside. There was no bathing or change of underwear. We became scabby and filthy, and constantly beleaguered with itchy skin.

Drills were of a much higher level than before. Taking off and landing on aircraft carriers required pinpoint accuracy. A long line of white linen was laid out on the runway in the shape of a carrier platform. Precise landing demanded careful consideration to the velocity and direction of the wind. If a landing came up short, the instructors would be furious.

---

[7] Kagoshima Prefecture is in the southern part of Kyushu and is famous for its active volcano, Sakurajima. Several naval and army bases were located in Kagoshima. Kasanohara Airbase was established in 1922 but was closed when the war ended. Many Kamikaze sorties departed from Kasanohara. In January 1945, 70 Zero fighters were deployed from there and all were sacrificed in suicide attacks.

[8] On February 17 and 18 in 1944, the U.S. bombed Truk Island. More than 200 Zeros were destroyed, including 100 new models.

"You moron! You just smashed into the stern of the carrier!" Conditions on grass and tarmac runways were also different, so we had to learn to cope with various environments.

For shooting practice, a Zero dragging 200 meters of rope from its tail with a 5-meter streamer attached to the end would serve as the target plane. It took off first with the rope and streamer trailing behind. Four attack Zeros followed suit and fired their 7.7mm machine guns in turn at the streamer. They were each loaded with different colored bullets—red, blue, yellow, or purple—so that hits could be identified.

There were two ways to strike. One method was called the "upper-rear attack" and entailed chasing the target Zero from 1,000 meters above and then descending rapidly from behind on a 45-degree angle to shoot at the streamer at the closest point before pitching away in a "hit and split" maneuver. The other method was called the "upper-front attack." This was also initiated from above at 1,000 meters, but we came in from the front in a rapid dive firing a burst at the streamer just as we crossed paths and suddenly rolling out of the way.

The trainers checked the colors marking the target streamer to identify who was successful. If your color was not there, the insults would fly. Some trainees found the task very difficult and met with little to no success. I wasn't bad but tended to fire a little too deeply.

We also practiced chasing tactics. The lead Zero was piloted by an instructor and we had to keep on his tail being careful to not to get too close. We tried to keep around 200 meters to the rear, but a slight miscalculation meant that the lead Zero would vanish before us.

"Team fighting" and "advantage vs. disadvantage" training was designed to be as realistic as possible. The former comprised of mock dogfights with four vs. four, or eight vs. eight planes. The latter involved four Zeros soaring at 5,000 meters above sea level and the other four flying from the opposite direction at the lower altitude of 4,000 meters. One group flew in formation from the direction of Mount Kaimon, the other from Shibushi Bay. The point of engagement was just above Kasanohara base from where senior instructors watched the dogfights through binoculars. The four fighters at higher altitude were expected to capitalize and take their lower flying prey to task. The disadvantaged fighters, on the other hand, were supposed to somehow escape and maneuver to turn the tables.

Mock dogfights required mastery of rapid ascents, descents, and circling at maximum speed. A Zero that exceeded its speed threshold in rapid descents was in danger of breaking up through stress on the frame. It was crucial to keep speed within the limits and carefully time the climb. The joystick had to be pulled fully back which took immense strength in the arms. The transition into rapid ascent would generate incredible Gs, pushing my body and head back into the seat and distorting my face. I would start to see yellow, purple, and finally black as I all but lost consciousness. It was dangerous but the only way to learn.

Combat tactics also depended on the weather. If we flew under clouds, we risked easy identification by the enemy because of the Zero's distinctive silhouette. On overcast days we flew in the clouds meaning that visibility was non-existent. We flew out from the clouds momentarily to confirm each other's position, and then back in again.

The time frame for each simulated dogfight was only five to six minutes but it was exhausting. Some cadets failed to pull the control up sufficiently and ended up crashing into the hills. There were four such accidents during my time at Kasanohara. Senior officers made us go and recover the bodies. Debris would be strewn everywhere as we clambered up to the crash site, so it usually took some time to locate the pilot's remains. In one case we were unable to find any sign of a body at all. When a body (or its parts) were recovered, everything was taken back for immediate cremation. A funeral was never held. Relatives would come about a week later to collect the ashes.

Flying in formation was another important skill that we were drilled in thoroughly. We practiced keeping 16 airplanes flying neatly in formation, which was not easy especially if visibility was poor. Night flying was the worst. Lights were not allowed so it was virtually impossible to see other planes flying in proximity.

The daily routine varied. We sometimes had formation training right after breakfast, followed by lunch, an hour-long afternoon nap, then battle training, and night flying after dinner. Sometimes we flew before breakfast in dawn exercises. Each day's agenda was posted on a board in advance with our initials placed underneath to indicate which activity we were assigned to.

The food was good. Fighter pilots didn't cook as meals were organized by the mess crew. We usually got milk and eggs for lunch. After flight drills we were given a special bag containing a small bottle of rice wine, tobacco, chocolate, adzuki-bean jelly, caramel and other treats. Every so often we were given time off to boost morale.

It was wise to be considerate to the maintenance staff. They never got treat bags like us, so we shared our provisions with them. This was how we ensured our Zeros got the care they needed. Particularly in the Army, rank-based hierarchy was very strict. Even one rank up was carte blanch to torment juniors. This was not the case among airmen where rank was not as important as how many flight hours you had under your belt. Anyone with 1,000 hours or more was first-class. Although I had only been in training for one-and-a-half years, I managed to accumulate 6 to 700 hours. This wasn't bad going considering the hurry the Navy was in to get us to the front.

CHAPTER THREE

Blooded in Taiwan

Lead-up to the Second World War

The Kamakura period marked the onset of the first samurai government of Japan in 1185. Samurai hegemony lasted throughout the Muromachi and Tokugawa (Edo) periods, finally coming to an end in 1868 with the Meiji Restoration. Following the Meiji Restoration, Japan's new imperial government embarked on a path of rapid modernization to catch up with the West.

At that time, most Asian and Pacific countries were controlled by Western colonial powers. As Japan started to flex its political muscle on the international stage, it came into conflict with the gigantic Qing dynasty of China, and Russia, which was seeking hegemony over China and the Korean peninsula.

Japan won the Sino-Japanese war of 1894, and then managed to subdue Russia in the Russo-Japanese War of 1904-05 with a lauded naval victory in which the Russian Baltic feet was decimated. This result signified Japan's entry as a force to be reckoned in international politics and inspired Asian countries who had long suffered under colonial oppression.

Japanese leaders at the time had experienced the turbulent days leading up to the Meiji Restoration. They were aware that Japan was out of its depth against Russia in terms of its military power and resources. In order to stop the war as quickly as possible, they engaged early on in diplomatic discussions with Russia with American President Theodore Roosevelt serving as mediator. The Japanese leaders were men who embodied the ancient proverb by Sun Tzu, "Know your enemy, know thyself, and you shall not fear a hundred battles."

Nevertheless, Japan's victories made future military leaders arrogant. A couple of decades later, this culminated in Japan's aggressive military, economic and political machinations in China resulting in Chinese antipathy toward Japan and growing distrust among former allies such as Great Britain and the United States, who also had stakes in China.

In the Great Depression from 1929, powerful nations aimed for the formation of a bloc economy. Japan was undergoing significant population growth but lacked resources. Faced with serious economic and social challenges, Japan opted to advance its interests in Manchuria and other parts of China. Although losing 100,000 men and using a massive proportion of the national budget in the Russo-Japanese War, victory enabled Japan to legitimately secure a foothold in South Manchuria. At the time both the Japanese government and her people considered Manchuria to be a "lifeline."

In addition, many Japanese opinion leaders were of the belief that Japan had an obligation to bring independence and prosperity to Asian countries oppressed under Western colonial rule. As the first modern state in Asia, Japan saw itself as the region's leader, and sought to establish a new Asian cooperative scheme to counter traditional colonial powers. Firm in their resolve, Japanese leaders became oblivious to growing anti-Japanese sentiment throughout Asia, and a cruel war ensued that pitted Japan against China and other Asian countries.

Chiang Kai-shek aimed for unity in China and from the early 1920s and began advancing through to the north to subjugate military cliques in the region. He reached Beijing in 1928, causing considerable tension with the Japanese Army in Manchuria. In 1931, Japan sparked the Manchurian Incident in northeast China. The following year, the Japanese Army initiated the establishment of "Manchoukuo" (the State of Manchuria) with the "Last Emperor" Pu-Yi of the Qing dynasty on the throne. This action was heavily criticized by the League of Nations and led to Japan's withdrawal from the organization.

Japan plotted to broaden its interests and influence Beijing and Tianjin in northern China. The main purpose was to cope with the growing influence of Communism exerted by the Soviet Union over northeast China, and to prepare for war with the Soviet Union in the future. Tension continued to escalate between Japan and the anti-Japanese front led by Chiang Kai-shek of the Chinese Nationalist Party, as well as Mao Zedong of the Chinese Communist Party. On July 7, 1937, a confrontation between the Japanese and Chinese armies known as the Marco Polo Bridge Incident broke out in the outskirts Beijing at midnight.

At the time the Japanese Cabinet and Army were divided into factions supporting either all-out war or peaceful negotiation. The pro-war faction looked down on the Chinese Army as lacking vitality and fighting spirit, and assumed that victory could be attained in a relatively short period of time. They took the initiative which led to further repercussions in Shanghai and middle China along the Yangtze River. The Shanghai Incident broke out in August 1937, and military aggression started to intensify. In December that year, Japan invaded Nanjing, the capital of China. Chiang Kai-shek retreated to Chongqing in Sichuan Province to the west of China, thereby establishing a secure center for all out resistance backed by the Americans, British, and the Soviet Union. The second Sino-Japanese War was now in full swing.

The Second World War was fought between the Axis powers (Germany, Italy, Japan) and the Allies. It was triggered In September 1939 with Nazi Germany's invasion of Poland in spite of having had its independence guaranteed by Britain and France. In September 1940, the Tripartite Pact between Germany, Japan, and Italy was concluded under the Fumimaro-Konoe Cabinet. It provoked a strong reaction from the United States and the Allies who enforced strict economic sanctions against Japan such as an embargo on oil and iron exports.

In the spring of 1941 Prime Minister Konoe maximized efforts to negotiate with the U.S. and avert hostilities. A major reason for conflict between Japan and the U.S. was economic competition in China, especially after the Russo-Japanese War. The U.S. grew evermore distrustful of Japan after the Manchurian Incident, and so the crucial issue at the heart of negotiation for the Americans was the withdrawal of the Imperial Japanese Army from China.

In the middle of negotiations in July 1941, the Japanese Army moved into the southern region of French Indochina making the situation extremely volatile. Konoe tried urgently to talk directly with President Franklin Roosevelt. According to the dictates of the Meiji Constitution, however, the prerogative of supreme command for both the Army and Navy was wielded by the Emperor and was completely independent of the Cabinet or Diet. Even the Prime Minister had no mandate to command the nation's military.

Roosevelt and Churchill were already determined to wage war with Japan at that time, and the slow pace of the negotiations under Konoe gave the Americans ample time to prepare for war. Konoe pleaded with Army Minister Hideki Tojo to withdraw the Army from China. His pleas were rejected outright, resulting Konoe dissolving his cabinet in October 1941. Tojo succeeded Konoe as Prime Minister.

Tojo did not jump immediately into hostilities with the United States as Emperor Hirohito still sought a peaceful resolution. In both the Army and Navy, especially in the Navy, there were staunch opponents to waging war against America. It was acknowledged that Japan had neither the military power nor the resources to match the United States in all out armed conflict. Nevertheless, the line of thought that favored immediate military action in order to acquire territories to bargain with in negotiations came to the fore, lest Japan missed its chance and faced absolute defeat in the future.

The catalyst that finally forced Japan's hand was the Hull note ("Outline of Proposed Basis for Agreement Between the United States and Japan") which was delivered to Japan on November 26, 1941. It demanded that Japan abandon its interests and claims in China, not only those which had been acquired by invasion, but also those rights and interests which were legally procured through negotiation after the Russo-Japanese War. It was essentially an ultimatum that Japan could never agree to, and was thus equivalent to a declaration of war.

Commander in Chief of the Combined Fleet, Isoroku Yamamoto, was strongly opposed to the Tripartite Pact and any thought of entering a war against America. Now he was obliged to plan and prepare the Navy for an attack on Pearl Harbor on December 8, 1941. The operation resulted in a spectacular victory and solidified America's resolve for war. Many have since observed that Roosevelt and Churchill actually desired that Japan make the first move to force America's hand.

In the early stages of the war, Japan achieved some outstanding victories on the Malay Peninsula, Singapore, Philippines, etc. It expanded its control over the West Pacific and even closed in on the north of Australia. It was the Battle of Midway in June 1942, northwest of the Hawaiian archipelago that proved to be a major turning point in the war. Japan lost many carriers, aircraft, and experienced pilots.

In February 1943, Guadalcanal in the Solomon Islands was captured by the U.S. after some furious fighting. In February 1944, Truk Lagoon, Japan's main military base in the South Pacific theater, was laid to waste by naval air attack and hundreds of Japanese fighter planes were destroyed. In June to July 1944, Japan's stronghold in Saipan was annihilated in the Battle of Mariana Sea. In October of that year, the Japanese Naval Fleet was routed in the Battle of Leyte Gulf which Odachi participated in while stationed in the Philippines.

In February to March 1945, the U.S. recaptured the Philippine islands which General MacArthur departed with his famous words "I shall return." Shortly after, Japanese military might was decimated in the Pacific following their defeat at the famous Battle of Iwojima. The Japanese mainland was now the target of ferocious air raids. In the spring of 1945, the U.S. began its operation to take Okinawa. The Japanese Army and Navy stationed there were wiped out by June.

Meanwhile, the war in China was also going badly for the Japanese. Supported by the United States, the staunch anti-Japanese resistance led by Chiang Kai-shek was a constant thorn in Japan's side. Japan won most of its battles in China initially, and came to occupy major cities throughout the country but could not make China yield completely. The Americans even commenced with B-24 and B-29 raids against mainland Japan and Taiwan from deep within the Chinese mainland.

On July 26, 1945, the Potsdam Declaration demanded Japan's unconditional surrender. Cabinet, Army and Navy leaders debated furiously about the pros and cons of accepting the conditions. On August 6 and

9, atomic bombs were dropped on the cities of Hiroshima and Nagasaki. The Soviet Union took this opportunity to declare war against Japan and rushed in to take over Manchuria and the northern territories formerly occupied by Japan.

It was with an official declaration by Emperor Hirohito that Japan surrendered to the Allies. At noon on August 15, Hirohito made his official announcement to the Japanese people over the radio. This was just as Odachi's was about to depart on his final Kamikaze mission from Taiwan. Odachi and his comrades fought against Allied forces for around one year, a relatively short period. However, it was the time in which the writing was on the wall for the Japanese. As many veteran senior pilots had died, the now hopeless responsibility of protecting the country fell on the shoulders of Odachi and his friends through the most desperate of tactics—Kamikaze.

Although we didn't know it at the time, the Imperial Japanese Navy 1st Air Fleet had been routed. The gravity of our losses wasn't immediately clear to us then, but it was precisely at this juncture that I entered the war.[9]

I sensed beforehand that I would be dispatched to a base somewhere in the south, either Taiwan or Saipan. In mid-August 1944, we were transferred from Kasanohara to Hsinchu Air Base on the northwest side of Taiwan. New intelligence reported that 11 American carriers were preparing to mount an assault on Taiwan. The IJN's 2nd Fleet was directed to Taiwan to defend. As our carriers had already been destroyed, naval aircraft were only deployable from ground bases.

The 221st Naval Air Group had little more than 60 airmen. We headed to Taiwan separately in four or five squadrons, of which I was in second or third group to leave. We carried personal effects in our blue zippered parachute bags. My possessions fitted in but there was no room left for

---

[9] In the early months of 1944, the U.S. took the offensive against Japan from two directions in New Guinea and the mid-Pacific region. If the U.S. could take control of the Mariana islands, it would enable their heaviest B-29 Air Fortress bombers to raid mainland Japan. Furthermore, taking back the Philippines would cut off supply routes of oil to Japan. With all this at stake, Japanese and American fleets clashed on June 19 and 20 in 1944 in what became known as the Mariana Naval Battle. Japan was soundly defeated with fighters being decimated by the Grumman F6F Hellcat inflicting the loss of more than 400 airplanes and three carriers. Saipan fell to the Americans in July followed by Tainan in August. This led to American control of the Mariana Sea.

the parachute.

I dropped the bag behind the seat and secured it with a cord to stop it falling on me in case of some sudden maneuver. A spanner left in the cockpit by mechanics once smacked me fair in the head.

I was impressed by the majestic mountains of Yakushima and the beautiful coral reefs of Okinawa as we flew overhead. Taiwan came into view before long. I was happy to arrive but there was little indication that we were within spitting distance of the combat zone. I was taken aback when I flew into Hsinchu Airbase with its four long runways forming a tetragon, and one more runway set on an angle. All of them were paved with asphalt or concrete with the zones between the landing strips covered in lush green grass. It was an impressive base of the likes I had never seen before, designed to facilitate landing from all directions in any wind condition. Moreover, several planes could land simultaneously. As it was our first landing, however, we took our aircraft down with extreme caution.

Hopping out of my cockpit, I was once again awestruck by the quality and size of the base. It was so big that I had trouble identifying any of the other crews. All I could see were a few big aircraft parked in the distance. There were several other air bases in Taiwan besides Hsinchu including Taichung, Tainan, Kaohsiung, Yilan, and Hualien. The oldest were Kaohsiung and Tainan, the latter being particularly spacious allowing us to land in any grassy zone we liked. The runways in Kaohsiung and Tainan were paved, but Hsinchu was the best.

Our orders were to intercept B-24 bomber raids, fly patrol, and provide air cover for an Army convoy sailing to Xiamen. When not out on sorties we continued training. Our first taste of action, however, didn't happen until the middle of October.

Gearing Up

New improved fighters like the Grumman F6F Hellcat were making life difficult for Japanese airmen. Faced with such formidable opposition, fewer of our planes were making it back, and our fleets were frequently rearranged to compensate for losses. The airplanes of the 1st Air Fleet were originally tasked with patrolling the southwest Pacific. We were supposed to provide back up when necessary, but with the 1st having been routed in the Battle of Mariana, there were hardly any operational fighters left in the area. It seemed inevitable that we'd be in the thick of it a lot sooner than we had envisaged.

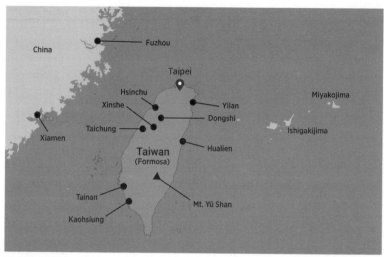

The island of Taiwan.

For the first few months, however, all we did was train in the same format as Kasanohara except for tactical training which involved eight vs. eight Zeros instead of four vs. four. It was as close to real combat as possible so there was no room for mistakes. If information came in that Americans were approaching the east coast of Taiwan, we would fly to Hualien Airbase. If there was intelligence of the enemy somewhere in the south, we would fly to Tainan or Kaosiung. All the air bases in Taiwan became home as we pogoed around the island.

Although we were still officially in training, there was always a high degree of tension. We were never that far from the action and were ready to scramble without delay. We heard about losses being sustained here and there, and flight drills were conducted with the understanding that it would become the real thing at a moment's notice. We were ready. Our senses had been honed and some of our men had already seen combat, even boasting of shots that had found their mark. We were all brimming with confidence, at the beginning....

The completion of a training mission was signaled by the lead plane rocking its wings. One of our planes once veered away to fly under a suspended bridge in a river valley. I mischievously followed suit, and so did the rest of the fighters in our section. Another time we flew close to the river surface causing fishing boats to capsize. We were all aged only 17 to 19 after all. Just teenage lads wanting to have a bit of fun. Rowdy behavior took the edge off our volatile situation.

Taiwan was a bountiful place, and there was always a big basket full of bananas and citrus fruits located at the front of the barracks. Our three daily meals were excellent, just as they were in Kasanohara. The mess staff cooked our meals and took care of menial tasks such as washing the dishes. We often slept outside on the grass protected by a smoldering pyrethrum coil which kept the mosquitos in check. In August and September, the soft breeze at night made it more comfortable than sleeping inside the stifling barracks.

Escorting Convoys

With training concluded, my debut sortie was to the Xiamen channel between mainland China and Taiwan. We were to escort supply ships in what was going to be our first real opportunity to test the fruits of our hard training. We were fired up and determined to deal to any enemy planes unlucky enough to cross us.

We didn't know why the fleet was headed to Xiamen but assumed that the Army was preparing to transfer military units from northeast Manchuria to the south. The fleet headed from the Yellow Sea (located between mainland China and the Korean Peninsula) to the north of Taiwan. The Yellow Sea was relatively stable at the time, but the area surrounding Taiwan was becoming increasingly perilous. Japan had already defeated the Chinese Nationalist Air Force by this stage, so the odds of being intercepted by Chinese fighters were low. Moreover, no U.S. or British fighters had been spotted west of the line between Okinawa and Taiwan. Still, we didn't want to take the Chinese factor for granted. Should they appear, we had no idea what they would be flying. It could be American or Soviet Union-built aircraft, and we had no clue whatsoever about the latter. This element of the unknown kept us edgy and vigilant.

The weather was fine, and visibility was good. We could see scores of ships in convoy heading to the East China Sea via the Taiwan Strait. We flew over them in two formations comprised of eight Zeros each. We circled at around 5,000 meters altitude as the ships cut through the blue sea below. Each escort mission lasted about two hours. When one team finished they would "rock" their wings for the other to take over. Once, I took my aircraft down to about 200 meters to make a pass over some of the ships. The sailors on deck waved up at me. I felt a strong responsibility to keep them from harm's way. As it turns out we didn't encounter any enemy planes on our debut mission.

The B-24s

Taiwan remained calm for a while after we arrived, but we kept an eye on what was happening in the east. The first enemy airplane that we saw, however, flew in from the west. It was a giant B-24 Liberator (see photos). I heard later that they raided Taiwan a few times before we arrived there. The B-24s flew at approximately 6,000 or 7,000 meters as they dropped their payloads on our facilities and then headed westward to their bases. We assumed that they came from Chongqing deep in the west of China. They were certainly capable of traveling great distances.

When news came through from our Army stationed in China that four B-24s were en route to Taiwan we scrambled to intercept. I chased one B-24 at high attitude on its return journey. No matter how much I accelerated I could not close the distance. A little more, a little more.... I kept the pursuit going until noticing that I had almost flown as far as mainland China. I had to give up the pursuit as my fuel was running out.

The B-24s were much bigger than we imagined. We knew that they had four propellers and a wingspan of 34 meters, but they took our breath away when we saw them for real. The airframe was sturdy and covered in duralumin plate. They were completely different to the "Mitsubishi G4M Type-1 Attack Bomber" (Allied reporting name "Betty") which was the biggest plane in the Imperial Japanese Navy. Our planes were smaller and painted a drab grey color. We almost felt cheated.

Another time I intercepted a B-24 and fired into its fuselage. I was sure that my bullets hit home but to my utter surprise the bomber flew away as if nothing happened. I learned later that B-24s were protected by thick resin "armor" around the fuel tanks. We were advised that shooting at B-24s was virtually futile. Even so, whenever we had drinks in the barracks we discussed how to shoot down these giants. Somebody observed, "Their machine gun turrets spin around like this, so it's useless hitting them from this direction. The best way must be to shoot underneath from the rear of the fuselage...." Another pilot mentioned, "Wait for it from a higher position in front, fire at it as you dive and then fly under the fuselage to attack on the turnaround...." These strategies were easier said than done. I was never able to get myself in a position to try them out.

The B-29 bombers (see photos) were bigger than the B-24s and superior in performance. These beasts also ventured into our skies on occasion but wouldn't hang around long. I assumed that they were on recon missions taking aerial photos of Taiwan before returning to base in China. They flew higher and faster than B-24s. We tried to intercept them, but it took too long for Zeros to reach 8,000 or 9,000 meters. At 6,000 meters I would have to put on an oxygen mask while climbing at full throttle, but the propeller would spin meaninglessly at this altitude because the air was too thin. The speedometer needle fluttered near the bottom of the dial and we'd burn through the fuel. The B-29s soon disappeared above us so we no chance to engage them.

We never heard of any B-24s or B-29s being shot down around Taiwan. We were uneasy that Japan's leaders were not developing better planes to match these airborne fortresses. It was all we could do to take off and save our planes when they came to bomb our bases. We attempted to engage if they came within a feasible range, but they mostly flew high in the sky leaving us as helpless spectators while they wreaked havoc on our airfields.

The Zero

The Zero was designed by Mitsubishi Heavy Industry and Nakajima Aircraft Company as a carrier-based fighter for the Navy. It debuted in 1940. According to the "Imperial Calendar" in use in Japan at the time, this was the 2,600th year of the founding of Japan, so the Zero was named after the last numeral of this year. The Zero proved itself to be a highly capable fighter plane in the air battles over China, and it featured prominently in the Pacific from December 1941. Greatly respected by the enemy, it remained Japan's most famous fighter to the end of war. Over 10,400 were produced with ten modified variants. By the end of the war, it was altered again to carry bombs in Kamikaze suicide missions.

The first mass-produced Zero was the Model 21. Its maximum speed was 533km/h, and had a cruising distance of up to 2,530km. It was powered by a 1,000 horsepower engine and was armed with two 7.7mm and two 20mm machine guns. Compared with fighters of other countries, the Zero's cruising distance was relatively good, it had excellent turning ability, and daunting attacking capacity. These capabilities were enabled by a total weight of only 2.4 tons, almost 1 ton lighter than the Grumman F4F Wildcat (see photos). It was half the weight of the later Grumman F6F Hellcat. Its light weight, however, was only possible through compromises. Its defensive ability and the strength of the airframe was sacrificed making the Zero prone to catching fire when hit. There was no plating to protect the pilot, and if it dived at a velocity of 63040km/h, there was a very real danger of the plane disintegrating in mid-air.

Japan failed to develop a viable successor to the Zero, relying on minor tweaks here and there to bolster firepower. This led to gradual increases in weight which in turn decreased its turning ability. By contrast, U.S. fighter capabilities improved significantly with the development of aircraft like the Hellcat.

Solo and Team Combat

Air tactics began to change as the battle in the Pacific intensified. Before my time it was common for three fighters to make one unit. Japanese pilots would fly in formation until the enemy came into view then would break off to assail targets individually in dogfights. The early Zero pilots were very adept at this mode of attack and used a special "twisting-in" maneuver like a corkscrew loop called "*hineri-komi.*" When chased by the enemy, the standard Zero tactic was to climb suddenly at maximum speed then turnover at the highest point to steal the advantage. I heard of one situation where a Zero was chasing an American fighter, with another fighter chasing that Zero, and yet another Zero chasing that fighter all in a chain. This scenario suited Japanese pilot tactics. There was always banter of who shot down how many planes and we would celebrate the feats of "Shoot Down Kings" (aces).

The situation started to worsen for us from around the Battle of New Britain (Rabaul) in 1943, especially with the introduction of the new Grumman F6F Hellcats.[10] They had double the horsepower of the F4Fs

---

[10] The Grumman F6F Hellcat was a carrier-based fighter. The Americans captured a Zero that had made an emergency landing and were able to make a thorough analysis of its airframe and capabilities. Based on their findings, they made many improvements to the F4F Wildcat and developed the F6F Hellcat. It could fly at more than 600km/h and at an altitude of 7,000 meters. It had excellent turning ability and sturdy protection for the pilot. The total weight

and were a superior machine to our Zeros. They hunted in packs of four and avoided individual dogfights focusing instead on team battles. U.S. pilots researched our strategies thoroughly and formulated maneuvers to take advantage of our weaknesses. For example, our famous sharp-turning *hineri-komi* defensive ploy had one major drawback in that the Zero's speed would drop significantly for a few seconds at the point of turnover. One of the four American fighters waiting at altitude targeted this instant and unleashed a spray of lead just as the Zero was about to plunge into the dive. If the Zero was caught in this trap, there was no way to escape.

The Japanese pilots had to adapt to keep ahead of the game, so adopted a similar four fighter team and style of combat. These changes were already being implemented by the time I started my training. We were advised against individual combat and told instead to take the initiative, making concentrated bursts in first contact. This meant that good teamwork was vital. The most effective method was to fly at altitude to spot enemy aircraft in advance, then make a rapid dive toward them and shoot at the crossing point. The difference between winning and losing came down to which side detected the enemy first.

When shooting, I would press the center stick trigger with my right thumb for a few seconds. Any longer and the bullets would run out too quickly. It was often impossible to tell whose bullets hit the target but there were occasions when I knew I had hit the mark. Still, the Hellcat never let on that it was hit as its airframe had been redesigned to mitigate the impact of enemy fire. The only way to shoot one down for sure was to make a direct hit on the pilot in the cockpit.

Rainy days were spent in the classroom. We sat cross-legged and listened to lectures outlining the latest American tactics and discussions led by vets who had survived close run-ins with the improved Hellcats. To hone maneuvers in our four-fighter teams, for example, we were told where the first and second aircraft needed to fly. "When the first turns away, the third must follow behind in cover. Then, the second and the fourth which were here must fly in behind the third...." This was all life-

---

exceeded 4 tons (nearly double the Zero's weight) so the engine power was doubled from 1,000 to 2,000 horsepower to compensate. This contrasted with the Zero which remained at 1,000 horsepower. The only thing that the Zero could match the Hellcat in was turning under 400km/h. The Hellcat was introduced to the Pacific theater in 1943, and more than 12,000 were produced over the next three years.

saving advice, but inevitably required incredible discipline and nerve under extreme pressure to execute.

Some officers were still under the false impression that Zeros were superior to Hellcats. One of them asked an instructor, "Why can't we engage in dogfights to take advantage of the Zero's agility?" The instructor told him plainly: "That's impossible. It's all just empty theory now. Go ahead if you insist, but you'll be the first one to buy it."

Instead, we were repeatedly told, "When you face the enemy, fly straight at him like a game of chicken. Never turn away earlier than the enemy. Go in with the intention of letting your propellers bite into his plane. This is the only way they will show their bellies, and that's when you shoot. They don't have strong hearts like you boys. Go for their guts."

Sliding Maneuver

It was often commented that if two fighters with the same capability and skill engaged in combat, the victor would be the one who takes the higher position. If we found ourselves at lower altitude and needed to take evasive action, the first thing we were taught to do was accelerate into a dive. As the enemy followed, the next move was to press hard on the left pedal while pulling the center stick strongly to the right. This would make the Zero slide forward to the diagonal left. I could also do it the opposite way.

The irregular sliding movement generated air turbulence around the Zero, and in turn affected the trajectory of the enemy's rounds. To successfully perform the sliding maneuver took considerable strength in the arms and legs, and it also induced a lot of torque on the airframe. I could hear my plane creak and was always afraid that it might fall to bits on me.

I had a habit of removing my gloves before any action to stop my hand from slipping off the controls. I also took off my headgear and placed it on my lap because it hindered neck movement and I couldn't look around me. The most dangerous area was to the rear. I liked to assess if there was anything coming from behind. Rear-below was particularly treacherous as it was a blind spot from the cockpit. Even when I was in pursuit of an enemy aircraft I would check right, left, below and behind to make sure I wasn't in somebody else's sights. A surprise attack when engaging an enemy in front would not end well. We were told to watch the front 80 percent of the time, and the back 20 percent.

I could tell when the altitude was 4,000 or 5,000 meters without referring to the altimeter just by the feel to the plane. This is higher than the mightiest peak in Japan, Mount Fuji at 3,776 meters. We were advised to attach our oxygen masks over 4,000 meters, but few of us did. The mask had a long tube necklace which restricted head movement, so we usually held on until 6,000 meters. The air being so thin that high, it was hard to get enough oxygen without it. To compensate, I used to take two deep inhalations followed by one exhalation.

Earplugs were inserted on a rapid climb to protect the ears. I followed this protocol at first but gradually became accustomed to the pressure. High altitude also resulted in pain shooting through my mouth and teeth through sucking in the cold air. There was no heater, but we kept warm enough thanks to the heat of the engine and the exhaust fumes that infiltrated the cockpit.

Landing Woes

Each airbase had a 15 meter pole located in the midpoint of the runway with a streamer attached to the top to indicate the direction and strength of the wind. This was vital for making a clean landing. If the streamer was horizontal, we knew that the wind was blowing hard at about 12 to 13 meters per second. When we made unscheduled landings in different bases, streamers were often absent forcing us to wait until somebody ran out to the runway to attach one.

At bases with grass runways we identified suitable places to land by the flatness of the vegetation. If it was still long that meant it was dangerous to land on because it hadn't been used for landing before. Fuel permitting, we'd do another pass over the base if we weren't certain.

Paved runways with a headwind made for the best landing conditions. The Zero could make a three-point landing and come to a stop in about 150 to 200 meters. That distance increased with a tailwind. A side wind was a little tricky to cope with. The airframe caught the wind and tilted the aircraft so that one wheel touched the ground first meaning too much weight on one point. There were many incidents where planes were pushed to the side this way resulting in the wheels breaking up.

I mitigated this danger by slowing down as I came in to land and moving the rudder the moment of touching down. If the side wind was coming from the left, I would press down on the left pedal to guide the airframe to the front-left, essentially straightening up in the wind. This was a subtle operation requiring careful consideration of how much we could be blown off course and landing slightly upwind and to the side of the runway's centerline. Landing was much more difficult than taking off.

There was a rule for landing called the "mid-air pass." When we approached the runway, we flew 200 meters overhead and passed by first. Banking our wings, the officer in charge looking through his binoculars confirmed by saying "Number such-and-such passed." Only then could we start the landing procedure. Everyone on the ground watched as we came in. Even if they didn't know the pilot, they could assess his skill level by how well he landed. After a successful landing the engine would be revved for a few seconds before alighting the aircraft and running to the command post to report in.

Aircraft landed separately at smaller bases. Runways were typically 50 to 60 meters wide, but planes were prone to swinging to the sides, so as much leeway as possible was appreciated. At large bases four planes could land in unison. We could even do eight simultaneously at the largest. It just depended on the conditions. We relied on hand signals and nonverbal cues to coordinate our approach. The runways on carrier decks, however, were considerably narrower and always a harrowing prospect.

Cockpit Lunches

We had lunch in the cockpit on long flights. This was usually a couple of rice balls wrapped in bamboo leaves made by the mess staff. We stuffed the rice balls in the pockets of our flying suits and looked forward to scoffing them in the cockpit. We never took water bottles for some reason. I don't know why, but I guess it was because we never really got thirsty. No matter how loudly nature called, we refrained from taking a dump or a whiz in the cockpit. Having said that, if our bladders were bursting and peeing was unavoidable, one small consolation was that it dried quickly through the engine heat.

Some pilots tucked into their lunches as soon as they levelled out after take-off. They would move to the front of the formation and let the others know, even though enemy aircraft could appear at any moment. Boys being boys, sometimes pilots would sneak up behind those enjoying their lunches and frighten the living daylights out of them.

Fighter pilots were a special breed in the Navy. Each one was, in a sense, a lone wolf. Flight hours was more significant than official rank, and pilots who had done the hours and proved themselves in battle were treated with respect, even if their rank was low. They were allowed in the cadre's chamber called the "Gun Room" which was off limits even to commissioned officers without enough flight hours.

Under the Commander was the Assistant Commander, Flight Commander, Squadron Leaders, Section and Assistant Section Leaders. The commander was usually a Colonel or Lieutenant Colonel. Under him were 60 to 70 pilots. Promotions came rapidly. I started at the lowest rank of Flight Petty Officer 2nd Class but was promoted to Flight Petty Officer 1st Class within three months, and Superior Flight Petty Officer three months later. Then Chief Flyer to Flyer 2nd Class, and Flyer 1st Class on August 15, 1945. I can't remember when I was made Flyer 2nd Class.

Embroidered Scarf

In those days, most big towns in Taiwan had sugar companies run by Japanese. The factories had clubhouses where wives of employees took good care of us. On the second floor of one such clubhouse, there were five or six Japanese tatami-mat rooms in which we could rest. On the ground floor was a large hall, cafeteria, and a room for listening to music and playing Japanese chess. The facilities were built for company personnel and their families, but we were permitted to come and go as we pleased. These were still relatively carefree days as we didn't know the misery that awaited us.

When stationed at the Hsinchu base, we occasionally visited the local town to unwind after long training periods, or after completing two to three weeks of sorties. Somehow this information always got out and we were greeted by throngs of Japanese girls living in Taiwan. It was quite perplexing when they called us by name. We had no idea who they were. We were invited to their homes for dinner, and ended up going to several houses each night. It was decided who would go where first by scissors-paper-stone. The families welcomed us with delicious food cooked by the mothers. Alcohol flowed freely. We went from one home to the next after an hour, indulging in three full meals in a single night.

One girl gave me a scarf on my second or third visit. It was made of cloth from a used parachute and was embroidered with pink cherry blossoms and a navy blue anchor, the symbol of Yokaren. Brushed onto the silk was a poem composed by a pilot who died at Pearl Harbor (see photos).

For you [your imperial majesty],
if my life is short like scattering cherry blossoms,
then I have no regrets.[11]

The characters were so exquisite, I figured her father must have written it. She gave me another scarf with "221st Naval Air Group Storm Corps, One shot, one kill"[12] and my name stitched on it. I wore it on all my sorties. The others liked to give me a hard time about it. "Hey, fashion Queen!" they would chide. "Piss off!" I replied. I wore this religiously when I sortied. I intended for it to be wrapped around my neck in my final mission as a Kamikaze pilot.

I never saw her again. If letters were not censored the way they were, I might have kept in contact. I will always remember her name though. My wife kept the scarf in a drawer after the war. The color of the stitching was vivid pink, but it faded over the years. I told my wife that I received it from a young girl in Taiwan whose family I became friendly with. She understood its immense value and treated it with the utmost respect.

The Japanese girls in Taiwan must have been happy to have all these dashing young men from the mainland over there to protect them. We received love letters from girls who we didn't know. The content was mostly the same. "Dear So-and-so, thank you for devoting your life in service to the nation. Stay well and good luck." Some of the letters contained beautiful pressed flowers which really lightened our mood. Our superiors told us never to get too close. We all knew that "happily ever after" was an unlikely outcome. We weren't destined to live for long, but we appreciated their kindness all the same.

Formosa Air Battle

On October 12, 1944, news came in that 12 enemy carriers had appeared east of Taiwan. It was time to scramble. Bombers and torpedo planes took off first to keep the American fleet at bay. We were determined to keep the air battle offshore and away from the island itself. Before long, hundreds of Japanese planes not stationed in Taiwan started arriving at our bases to refuel. Losses started to mount.

---

[11] *"Kimi ga tame nanika oshiman wakazakura, chitte kai aru inochi nariseba"*
[12] *"Ichigeki hittsui Arashi-Sentouki-Tai Odachi Kazuo"*

Fifty Zeros departed from Hsinchu in pursuit of the bombers. I was among them. We headed east and could see small dots like speckles of sand contrasted against the clouds to the north. There were too many to count. The dots soon grew to the size of beans and we realized that they were the enemy judging by their direction and formation.

We climbed to 4,000 meters, the optimum altitude for combat in the Zero, but the enemy climbed higher. We gave chase but then the enemy started to dive. We were now disadvantaged as their planes had considerably more grunt than ours. They had spotted us and were heading in our direction. I could tell they were F6Fs because I studied pictures of enemy aircraft every day. Thumb on trigger, I was resolved not to show the underside of my aircraft. We pushed our Zeros into full throttle and charged forward into the fray. We were all of one mind.

The wings of an F6F came into my sights. I knew that he was hunting me too. I was flying at about 350km/h and he at around 400km/h. The Zero had two pairs of machine-guns on each wing. We were approaching each other at approximately 200 meters each second, so I was focused solely on getting the timing right for my burst. I would need to press the button at 500 to 600 meters out, and then veer away at the last second to avoid collision. I was ready spray him the instant he showed his belly.

I held my shot. "Not yet, not yet...." I fired and so did he. Passing each other by in a flash, it was too fast to get a look at his face. We got so close that I thought his propellers might cut into my neck. We were told never to hesitate at that moment, and just aim to carve the enemy with our own propellers. Of course, death was a certainty if this happened but at least we would take the enemy with us. I turned to pursue but he was gone.

The enemy was going too fast to give chase, so we returned to base. Only eight could keep in formation. Of the 50 Zeros in Storm Corps out on this first sortie, 17 did not return. I didn't see any of my comrades being shot down. All I could see was the enemy in front of me. I had no idea how many successes we had. The tactics drilled into us so thoroughly were hopeless against the overwhelming clout of American planes.

This was my first real taste of combat. Those of us who came back sat in a circle drinking in our half-burned barracks. There were 17 empty coffins covered with white cloths in there with us. The sharp metallic sound of the F6F still rang in my ears. I knew we couldn't compete, and I'm sure my comrades thought so too.

My team sortied again the next day, but we didn't encounter the enemy. Our base had been heavily bombed in our absence, and all the barracks were burned to the ground. American bombers destroyed our beautiful airfields while we were out on sortie. If one U.S. carrier transported 80 planes, 11 meant that they had 880! How on earth could we defend our bases against these numbers? Why didn't we have more warning?

We knew in our bones that we had been soundly defeated in the Formosa air battle. However, radio news broadcasts from the Imperial General Headquarters reported that we had won a "marvelous victory." We could not reconcile the fact that Japanese scout planes and submarines missed such a large enemy fleet until it was too late. If we had known what we were up against, at least we could have been better prepared. It seemed to me that we were already defeated before the fight began.[13]

My personal effects, uniforms and pictures were all gone. My favorite photograph of a Zero taken high above the Sakurajima volcano also perished in the fire. The photos I have of this time now are few that I had sent home. The gate of the airfield was the only thing left standing. A young American airman was tied captive to a post with rope. His plane must have been shot down and he bailed out with his parachute. He looked to be around the same age as me and was clearly afraid for his life. I said to him, "It could be me tied up instead of you. We share a similar destiny." Of course, he had no idea what I was saying and stared at me with a searching eye. It did think that such treatment of POWs must be in contravention of international treaties, but I kept my mouth shut.

---

[13] The Americans needed to render Japanese bases in Taiwan and Okinawa inoperable to successfully take back the Philippines. For three days from October 12, 2,500 air planes took off from 17 carriers in the U.S. Third Fleet and attacked Japanese air bases in Taiwan with a vengeance. Japan tried to intercept the bombers but lost more than 300 pilots. About 150 fighters belonging to the reorganized IJN 1st Air Fleet made sorties from the Philippines with about 70 percent being shot down. Japan had completely lost air superiority. Only three American cruisers and carriers sustained damage.

The Imperial General Headquarters still publicized Japan's "great triumph" claiming they had successfully sunk 18 U.S. carriers, three battleships, three cruisers, and badly damaged eight more carriers and 18 other ships. The truth is not even one carrier was sunk. It later came to light that a scout plane observing the battles from above repeatedly mistook the flashing of flames from air-brakes on Japanese planes as explosions on enemy ships. Based on these grossly mistaken reports, the Imperial Japanese Navy and Army believed that the American No. 3 Fleet had been nullified. This error was to have grave consequences later on.

CHAPTER FOUR

Battle of the Philippines

Shortly after the air battles of Formosa ended, the 2nd Naval Air Fleet's Storm Corps received orders to head to Clark Field in Luzon.[14] "Tomorrow, embark for the Philippines" came the directive. Other Air Groups were given the same ultimatum, but we went separately in several waves. Taking off on October 18 or 19, my squadron was in the second or third wave.

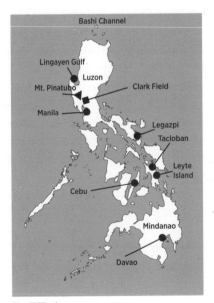

The Philippines.

---

[14] Clark Field was originally constructed in the Philippines by the United States as an army airbase and served as an important strategic stronghold. Clark Field was occupied by the Japanese Imperial Navy from the early stages of the war in 1942. Regaining control of this series of air bases became a priority for the Americans as they fought back through the southwest Pacific. Odachi and his comrades were deployed to Clark Field not long before the Americans successfully recaptured the base.

The air bases in Taiwan had been hit badly in American attacks, and few Zeros were left in an operational state. It took some time to repair the damaged planes because there were no parts. We cannibalized hopelessly wrecked planes for duralumin plate and used it to patch bullet holes in the fuselage. The color was different making the mended Zeros look battle worn and tired.

Once repaired, we were immediately sent to the Philippines in teams of three or five. Who went when depended entirely on the state of repairs. The Model 32 Zero which I had flown since Kasanohara was in good shape, so my departure came early on. My destination was the central airbase in Clark Field. The Americans were already pounding bases in the Philippines and we had to be careful about our time of arrival. It was preferable to land at nightfall to avoid daytime raids.

We flew over the Bashi Channel between Taiwan and the Philippines and headed south to the northern edge of Luzon. A long road running southwards from Lingayen Gulf was visible from the air. I figured that this must be the "Manila Highway." Several lines which looked like landing strips came into view in the distance ahead. I counted nine in total as I approached but couldn't tell if they were runways or just crofts. I soon realized that it was indeed the colossal Clark Field, albeit much shabbier than the fine bases in Taiwan. From appearances alone, my first impression was that it wasn't worthy of its repute as a great stronghold. It was truly massive, though.

On the west side of the Manila Highway was a grass runway interspersed with white pavement. That was Clark's central airbase, the one we were bound for. I chose a line that looked to be in good condition for landing. Although Zeros had spring suspension, the landing felt heavy. The runway was originally made of concrete, but the surface was potholed and uneven because of shelling. The holes were filled with dirt which soon became overgrown with weeds. I knew that I would have to be careful when landing from now on to avoid damaging my plane.

I imagined before arriving that there would be underground shelters given it was referred to as a "fortress." The setup fell well short of my expectations with just a series of grassy landing strips. All of us were left somewhat disappointed. Aircraft parked on the grassy areas outside were always sitting ducks. There were some concrete shelters, but they could only house one fighter each. We kept our aircraft safe by hiding them in the bushes around Clark, covering them with branches cut from trees. This took time and planning.

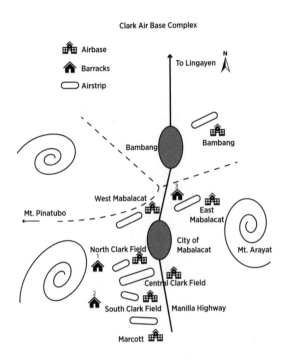

Nightly Bombings

Our quarters were originally built by the Americans in a forested area close to the western edge of the base. The building was raised off the ground with a small flight steps leading up to the entrance. It was spacious and very "Western." Notwithstanding, there were no beds or chairs, so we made our bedding on the floor with a few blankets and looked forward to sleeping soundly in our new home.

This was never to be. From the very first night we endured air raids by American bombers and were abruptly awoken by the furious sound of shells exploding close by. Frightened out of our wits, we grabbed our blankets and rushed down the steps to take shelter under a big tree. Even at midnight, American bombers could accurately target the runways and barracks from high in the sky. This was hardly surprising as Clark Field originally belonged to them. We thought it prudent to take cover some place far away from its facilities.

We "slept" under that tree for the first night. I use the term loosely and we were all dreadfully tired the next morning. The following night was not much better. Again, we fled the barracks and sought safety elsewhere. Some of the barracks were hit and burned to the ground.

To the west of Clark Field was the Pinatubo volcano (1,486m), and Mt. Arayat to the east. Arayat was not particularly high, but it was a beautiful mountain. We called it the "Mount Fuji of Manila." Clark was sandwiched between these two mountains. We heard rumors that anti-Japanese guerrillas were making bonfires halfway up the mountains to guide American bombers in their raids. The constant barrages and incessant worry prevented any hope of peaceful slumber.

We relocated to another airfield to the south in the Clark network. Our new quarters were a small hike from the west side of the base. It was a shabby little cottage of the likes seen in comic books. It didn't take long before bombing commenced in this area as well, and again, we were forced to run for our lives in the dark of night. At times we even slept under the wings of our Zeros. We reasoned that the pinging of bullets hitting metal would alert us to the need to bolt. It was virtually impossible to rest there as well. The bombings continued almost every day, but we had yet to see any American fighters in the skies overhead. This indicated to us that the American carriers were still quite a distance away from the Philippines.

The Battle of Leyte Gulf

Intelligence filtered through that the U.S. fleet with its many carriers was approaching from the east of the Philippine Sea. It was coming to support a large body of troops led by General MacArthur which had landed on Leyte Island in the mid-east region of the Philippines.[15]

---

[15] The U.S. Navy arrived on Leyte Island in its campaign to wrest control of the Philippines from the Japanese. Japan was unable to offer much resistance when around 200,000 troops landed at Tacloban on the northern shore of Leyte. The 80,000 Japanese soldiers stationed there were crushed by the Americans. Many who were not killed by the enemy fell victim to starvation. A well-known Japanese historical novelist, Shohei Ohoka, wrote a book titled "War Chronicles of Leyte" in which he states, "Countless errors and haphazard implementation of strategy made this campaign one of the most disastrous of the war for the Japanese. Both Army and Navy leaders discharged their duties appallingly."

On October 23, 1944, bombers and fighters of the IJN's 2nd Naval Air Fleet made an all-out attack on Leyte Gulf. I wasn't aware at the time, but the strike happened two days after the first Zero Kamikaze suicide attack mission departed from Clark. Ours was not a suicide mission, but was a desperate foray all the same, involving more than 120 planes. Some reports say the number was 250.

My Zero was part of a team tasked with securing air superiority to protect our bombers. We flew ahead at an altitude of about 4 to 5,000 meters, keeping a sharp look out for intercepting fighters. An assortment of bombers made their way in formation below us. There were torpedo bombers and dive bombers to go after shipping, and others to take out targets on land. It was a majestic sight with their wings glittering in the sunlight. Something began to stir inside me. I tightened my scarf and removed my gloves securing them under my legs. I remember the excitement as I scanned the sky vigilantly to my right, left, up, down, forward and behind.

A mass of black storm clouds came into view ahead. This meant heavy rain, thunder and lightning. The inclement weather would wreak havoc on our visibility and possibly result in collisions, so we were ordered back to base. We were deployed again the following day, but my team returned without encountering enemy planes. I heard that some of the other teams didn't have such a quiet time of it.

Arriving back at base, I left my Zero with the mechanics. I noticed a communications officer scurrying around in a panic. I asked him what was up. He moved close and whispered in my ear. "The battleship Musashi was attacked and sunk in the Sibuyan Sea." The Imperial Japanese Navy rarely told the rank-and-file what was going on, so we relied on kernels of information passed down through unofficial channels, or by word of mouth. In any case, I was gob-smacked at the news. Our team had just flown over the Sibuyan Sea and didn't see the Musashi, let alone have any inkling that it was in trouble below. Sure, the ocean is expansive, and we were short on planes so couldn't keep tabs on everything going on. Still, it was hard to believe that the almighty Musashi had been destroyed with nobody to defend it from the sky (see photos).[16]

---

[16] The Battleship Musashi was launched in 1940. It was the second "great ship" of the IJN following the Yamato. Both were 65,000 tons and measured 263 meters from bow to stern. These

"Joining" the Kamikaze Special Attack Corps

I noticed Zeros from other Air Groups flying into Clark Field during the day and night. We could identify where they came from and what squadron they belonged to if they came to our barracks, otherwise we had no idea who they were. At rollcall each morning we saw unfamiliar pilots in our ranks. "Who's that?" we'd ask each other. "He came in last night...."

I remember Zeros flying in from Singapore and Borneo to join us. Squadrons seemed to be coordinated randomly and we never really knew who was in charge. I heard of a strange mix up where the captain of an Air Group originally based in Borneo landed in Clark Field, but his men flew to the airbase in Manila instead. We didn't care about their problems, however, as we had plenty of our own to worry about.

Our planes were changed frequently because of maintenance issues. Each Zero had its own peculiar feel so we needed to take care flying different machines. After taking off I always tested the controls by pushing hard to the right, left, and up to gauge the aircraft's responsiveness.

I came to the Philippines from Taiwan as a pilot in the 2nd Naval Air Fleet's 221st Air Group. Completely unbeknownst to me, at some stage in the proceedings I was transferred to the 1st Naval Air Fleet's 201st Air Group. Most of the original pilots in the 201st had been killed in air battles east of the Philippines in the Mariana islands, Solomon Islands, Rabaul, Palau and so on. Suffering heavy losses throughout their campaigns, the 1st Naval Air Fleet was forced to retreat westward, and its fighters ended up at Clark Field in a last ditched effort to prevent the Americans reclaiming the region. Carriers made up the backbone of the 1st Naval Air Fleet, but its flyers were forced to become land-based as most were sunk at the Battle of Midway. Eventually, it was pilots of the 201st Air Group who filled the initial units of the Kamikaze Special Attack Corps.

A friend inquired, "Kazu, when were you transferred to the 201st? Your name is on the flight roster." I was surprised to say the least. "Really?

---

massive ships were armed with powerful 46cm cannons. Considered the biggest battleships in the world and touted as "unsinkable," the Musashi was pounded by the Americans from 10:00 until 19:00 on October 24, 1944, at the battle in Leyte in the Sibuyan Sea. A combination of tactical errors made by the Japanese and a lack of planes to defend with doomed the Musashi, and it sunk after taking over 50 bomb and torpedo hits.

I had no idea!" (Kazu is short for Kazuo, my given name. There was another pilot who shared the same family name of Odachi. His given name was Umesaku, so we just called him Ume.) The squadron leader and section leader were scheduled to arrive at Clark Field separately, but they didn't show up and we had no clue of their whereabouts. That's why I was never informed of my transfer. The system of command was in a state of utter confusion.

"No.1 Rapid Mission" and Kamikaze Special Attack Initiation

It was widely understood that what happened in the Philippines would ultimately dictate the outcome of the war. The U.S. forces led by General MacArthur moved to reoccupy the Philippines. Fully cognizant that allowing them to land would spell disaster, Japan focused everything at her disposal to prevent the American advance. This was referred to by the Japanese high command as "No.1 Rapid Mission." The basic strategy was to use the Imperial Japanese Navy's last remaining four carriers as bait to entice the U.S. fleet toward the Northern Sea. This would then provide an opening for the battleships Yamato and Musashi to enter Leyte Bay from the west, and attack the huge American convoy transporting troops. The airplanes of both the 1st and 2nd Naval Air Fleets were supposed to attack U.S. carriers defending the convoy. The strategy was a gamble, and it failed. Bad judgment led to the destruction of most of Japan's carriers and battleships, including the so-called "unsinkable" Musashi. Many fighters were also destroyed in the Leyte attacks. With few ships and aircraft left, Japan was unable to take the initiative in campaigns thereafter. It was under such desperate circumstances that the Kamikaze Special Suicide Attack Corps was initiated by Vice-Admiral Takijiro Ohnishi, also known as the "Father of the Kamikaze," who arrived in Manila as the incoming Admiral of the 1st Naval Air Fleet.

Kamikaze Special Suicide Attack missions took various forms. Zeros and other kinds of craft were sacrificed by both the Navy and Army. For example, small manned rockets called "Ouka" were attached to the undercarriage of bombers which flew them towards a target ship. The "Kaiten" was a manned torpedo fired from a mother ship on a one-way trajectory into enemy shipping. Vice Admiral Ohnishi was only in charge of the 1st Naval Air Fleet so there must have been decision makers higher up who formulated strategies that involved both the Navy and Army. Following in the tradition of Samurai warriors, Ohnishi killed himself by cutting his stomach open (*seppuku*) the day after

Japan's surrender. His suicide was presumably to take responsibility for deaths of young men in Kamikaze attacks. He never apportioned any blame to his superiors, and it has not been clarified to this day who was ultimately responsible for the strategy.

Vice-Admiral Ohnishi arrived in Manila on October 17, 1944. Two days later, he visited the 201st Air Group's headquarters in Mabalacat near Clark Field. The town was located about 100km from Manila and was surrounded by several air bases in the Clark grid. Ohnishi met with four 201st Air Group officers including Commander Rikihei Inoguchi and Deputy-Commander Asaichi Tamai. Ohnishi informed them of his plan to form a Kamikaze Special Attack Unit in the 201st Air Group. The officers all concurred.

Tamai immediately set about recruiting 'volunteers' for the first mission. Lieutenant Yukio Seki was appointed captain of the first suicide unit. Tamai then chose other members mainly from among former cadets of Yokaren A-class whom Tamai had instructed. The first Kamikaze suicide mission consisted of four sections with 23 airmen in total.

Inoguchi and Lieutenant-Commander Tadashi Nakajima (leader of the 201st Air Group) published a book after the war called "Documents of the Kamikaze Special Attack Unit." It was translated into English in 1958 as *The Divine Wind*. They described the scene in which pilots were chosen based on Tamai's account to Inoguchi.

"He reviewed the critical war situation when all 23 of the men were assembled and then explained Admiral Ohnishi's proposal. In a frenzy of emotion and joy, the arms of every pilot in the assembly went up in a gesture of complete accord.... They are so young. But though they cannot explain what is in their hearts, I shall never forget the firm resolution in their faces. Their eyes shone feverishly in the dimly lit room.... Theirs was an enthusiasm that flames naturally in the hearts of youthful men."

The next morning on October 20, Ohnishi addressed the chosen ones. He named the four units as Shinpu[17] Attack Unit "Shikishima," "Yamato," "Asahi," and "Yamazakura." Shikishima is a poetic appellation for Japan; Yamato is the ancient name for Japan; Asahi means the "morning sun"; and Yamazakura means "mountain cherry blossoms." The terms were taken from an old Tanka poem by Motoori Norinaga,

---

[17] "*Shinpu*" is an alternative and the original reading for the ideograms used to write "*kamikaze*" or divine wind.

a famous eighteenth century scholar. "*Shikishima no Yamato-gokoro wo hito towaba Asahi ni niou Yamazakura-bama*" (The Japanese spirit is like mountain cherry blossoms, radiant in the morning sun). These four sections made their first sorties on October 21. Another three sections were organized with the designations "Hazakura," "Kikusui," and "Wakazakura" on October 22.

Invited to 'Volunteer' Under the Southern Cross to Die

I don't remember if it was before or after the attack on Leyte. One evening, pilots who had arrived from Taiwan were drinking rice wine in the barracks near the southern airbase. Just as we opened the bottle, somebody shouted two or three times: "Fall in at the command post!" It was not often that such ultimatums were given at night. We threw on our flying uniforms and caps and hurried to the command post under the light of the stars. I recall being in such a rush that I slipped and fell on a grassy slope near the runway.

We lined up as ordered. It was dark because lighting was kept to a minimum, but the stars and moonlight provided us with enough illumination to see what was going on. The command post was a canvas sheet placed over bamboo poles, and it was surrounded by several high-ranking officers. Under the tarpaulin was a bench on which an officer of rank with bright yellow insignia on his shoulders sat. There must have been 14 or 15 officers altogether, and they all looked important. I hadn't been at Clark for long, so was unaware of who exactly they were. Something felt very odd.

Around 50 or 60 pilots had gathered. Some, but not all, were stationed with us in the southern part of the airbase. There were also some former Yokaren acquaintances who had flown in from Balikpapan, Borneo, and Malaysia. I stood in the third line but couldn't identify who was standing in front of me. Those to my rear were not lined up in any particular order.

"Airmen, step forward!" came the command from a mid-level officer. We moved up and then the high-ranking officer in the tent stood and started to speak. He did not say his name. Without delay he relayed the current state of affairs in the war. "The reason you have been summoned here is because the situation is grave. We are running out of aircraft, and the time is approaching where our only recourse to victory is for each plane to be loaded with a bomb, and for you brave pilots to become one with your machines...."

At first, his sermon was rather abstract and difficult to follow. He continued: "In accordance with the burden of duty and loyalty, we ask you to hurl yourselves into the enemy ships. We implore you to become a part of the special attack force." I began to work out what he was saying. "Anyone with objections is welcome to make his protest known. I trust you understand the solemnity of this calling, and can find it in your hearts to assent.... Those who agree, raise your hands.... This is not an ultimatum. You must decide by yourselves...." Now, I understood perfectly.

No one raised his hand at first. Not a word was spoken, there was just silence. The gathered airmen started to fidget. "Those who agree, raise your hands!" barked an officer attempting to elicit a response. I sensed that those in the front row were worrying about what those behind them were doing. Those in the back were watching the fellows in the front intently. Eventually a few in the front reticently put their hands up. Someone raised his hand partway. Others then began to raise theirs slowly, one by one.

Sooner or later all had their hands in the air. Of course, I did too. It just seemed to go up, although I don't know why. I looked up at it and saw the Southern Cross constellation twinkling brightly in the direction my hand was pointing. "How many days do I have left?" I thought to myself. "Maybe one or two. I won't be in this world much longer...." The vivid light of the Southern Cross is still seared into my mind. I have never forgotten that moment, or that image.

An officer piped up. "We are extremely gratified by your willingness. Mission orders will be decided from now." After being dismissed we sauntered back to our barracks in silence. I heard somebody murmur, "So, the time has come...." We continued drinking but I have no memory of what we talked about.

The next day, I was listed as "required personnel." This meant that I was on standby for a Kamikaze suicide mission. Although that was my status, the order never came for the three months I was stationed in the Philippines. I have no idea why the wait was so long but expected the ultimatum to come any moment. Maybe it was because I was not an original member of 201st Air Group. Or, maybe it was my age. I was only 17 at the time.

On the "night of the Southern Cross" we were asked if we were loyal enough to sacrifice our lives in suicide missions. None of us had the audacity to reject this "volunteer proposal" even though we were told it was to be a "personal decision." How could we possibly refuse? We were essentially cajoled into committing suicide. I am probably the last airman alive who can relay this story as it happened that night. To this day, I resent the way we were petitioned by our commanding officers as if we had a choice.[18]

Were Kamikaze Pilots Volunteers?

Pilots in the Kamikaze Special Suicide Attack Corps were officially designated as volunteers. Officers could not order their subordinates to join. The genuineness of this volunteer status, however, has long been a point of contention. Criticisms abound that the mirage of volunteering simply vindicated commanding officers for sending so many young men to certain death. Both Inoguchi and Nakajima were strong advocates of Kamikaze missions in the Philippines and enjoined numerous airmen to make the ultimate sacrifice. Neither of them ever accepted a suicide mission themselves.

As for Odachi's narrative of the midnight gathering in Mabalacat on October 19, there are several other accounts of that occasion. One claims that Tamai screamed at the airmen, twice urging them to accept. The airmen raised their hands slowly and answered "Yes sir" in muffled voices. A squadron leader, Lieutenant Takeo Yokoyama, chronicled how he was ordered by Tamai to handpick the first members from his men. He nominated Shigeo Oguro, a 20-year-old from the Yokaren. Oguro was then rostered in the Shikishima Unit and was killed on the first mission. Yokoyama regretted this decision for the rest of his life.

After following Tamai's order, Lieutenant Seki confessed to a war correspondent before his sortie, "Japan is finished. Killing such an excellent pilot as me? I could drop a 500-kg bomb on an enemy carrier

---

[18] Odachi was originally affiliated with the 2nd Naval Air Fleet's 221st Air Group. The Commander, Vice-Admiral Shigeru Fukudome, initially opposed Kamikaze missions before the attack on Leyte. His superior, Admiral Ohnishi, tried to persuade him otherwise, and it is thought that Fukudome eventually acquiesced after the first successful Kamikaze attack mission was completed by the Shikishima team on October 25. Accordingly, it can be surmised that airmen in the 2nd Naval Air Fleet joined the Kamikaze missions after this date. Odachi's recollection of this series of events seems to indicate that it was earlier than October 25, something that has never been corroborated in previous publications. We analyzed historical accounts to make sense of this discrepancy and concluded that Odachi's account was in fact accurate. The "night of the Southern Cross" occurred before October 25. This illustrates the many holes in our understanding of the history of Kamikaze.

without having to go down with it. I refuse to die for the emperor or Japan. If I must die, then I will do so for my beloved wife, and no other." Other testimonies relay how Tamai and Nakajima became increasingly uncompromising regarding Kamikaze operations, and severely rebuked 'unsuccessful' pilots who returned to base. Such observations are missing from official accounts.

There is no simple answer as to whether Kamikaze missions were truly made on a "voluntary basis" as many factors must be taken into consideration. In the early stages, some officers informed their men that the choice was theirs and encouraged them to submit forms circling their level of enthusiasm to join the Kamikaze Special Attack Corps: "1. Eager to Apply; 2. Will Apply; 3. Will Not Apply." Apparently, many circled the first option.

Some commanders patently rejected the strategy and refused to let their men join this operation to the very end. On the other hand, young airmen often found it difficult to express their misgivings about volunteering. The reasons are complex and include a mixture of pride, sense of shame, and resignation to the fact that sooner or later they would die anyway. They were already prepared to die in combat against enemy planes, but certain death through suicide diving was a bitter pill to swallow. In the later stages of the war, entire squadrons were assigned Kamikaze missions affording airmen no choice in the matter.

Many officers bade their men to take Kamikaze assignments saying, "You go now lad, I will follow you in death." Few of the officers ever did. There were, however, some notable exceptions. As mentioned, Vice-Admiral Ohnishi committed suicide the day after Japan's surrender to take responsibility. Vice-Admiral Matome Ugaki embarked on a Kamikaze sortie himself shortly after surrender, never to return. Of the responsible officers who survived the war, a few went on to enjoy success and status. Nakajima, for example, became an executive officer in the Self-Defense Force of Japan.

Kamikaze operations were criticized vehemently in the post-war period, and the issue of who should take ultimate responsibility is still highly divisive. Many books have been published on the subject, and it is generally agreed that documents or testimonies emphasizing the voluntary basis of suicide assignments were really attempts to dodge culpability. There has been extensive criticism directed at the book mentioned above, *The Divine Wind*, for this reason. Nevertheless, although the motivations and reasons for going were multifarious, the grace and incredible valor demonstrated by the Kamikaze pilots in meeting their deaths was nothing short of remarkable. Disagreement surrounding whether they were actual volunteers or not should in no way overshadow their poise in sacrifice and their dedication to duty.

Farewell Shikishima Brothers

Our second barrack also became the target of bombing, so we were moved again. The building was new and located near Mabalacat Airfield in Clark. One very hot day, we walked down the Manila Highway towards our new quarters. We were wearing our flying uniforms and formal shoes not suitable for hiking long distances. We also carried all our personal effects with us. After walking for a half an hour, we learned that some teams were about to embark on a suicide mission. We entered the Mabalacat Airfield and made a line along the runway to bid them farewell. It was the Shikishima unit led by Lieutenant Yukio Seki (see photos).

This was one of the first Kamikaze Special Attack units appointed by Vice-Admiral Ohnishi. They had volunteered a few days prior to this, and it was our first time to witness a Kamikaze departure. It was not until after the war that I learned the exact date: the morning of October 25, 1944. The Zeros were lugging bombs under their fuselages and took off with escort fighters to assist them through to their targets. I waved my cap as they sped down the runway, knowing in my heart that I would be getting a similar send-off before long.

I had just witnessed the departure of the Shikishima unit in what was to be the first successful Kamikaze attack. As it happens, I was destined to be in the very last team to depart on a suicide mission on August 15, 1945. In the space of ten months, I existed on the precipice of life and death in the Special Attack Corps.[19]

After watching the Shikishima team fly off into the distance, we continued walking to our new barracks. They were shacks made of bamboo with makeshift roofs of palm leaves. The split-bamboo floor was raised about 1 meter off the ground and there was barely enough space to house four pilots. We made use of the blankets kindly left for us by

---

[19] The earliest Kamikaze units, including Shikishima, departed on their first mission on October 21, but returned to base after failing to find any enemy ships. Sorties were repeated until targets were found. The farewell that Odachi remembers here was Shikishima's fourth attempt, and what was to be the first official Kamikaze Special Attack Corps success.

the Americans, but the bamboo floor was uncomfortable. Adding to our discomfort was the perpetual fear of anti-Japanese guerrillas sneaking under the floor and stabbing us through the openings as we slept. We did have guards at the base, but there was good reason to be paranoid at this volatile time.

Word that the Shikishima boys had accomplished their mission reached us that day. The escort Zeros reported that one of the Kamikazes smashed into an American carrier. The direct hit was initially reported to the commander in Cebu, and this was in turn relayed to Clark Field by radio. It didn't take long for the news to spread throughout the massive sprawling base. We weren't sure, but heard that one American carrier had been destroyed, and another carrier and cruiser had been crippled by the attacks.[20] We were ecstatic. "They did it! I will too! Give me a carrier to smash into!"[21]

Securing Bombs with Rope

In the early days of the Kamikaze attacks, assignment teams consisted of pilots originally affiliated to the 201st Air Group, although there were a few from the 221st Air Group as well. One of them was a Flight Petty Officer 2nd Class who we called "Mr. K." I saw him lining up before embarking on his mission and was surprised to see him. Even more surprising was the sight of a 250-kg bomb secured to his Zero's undercarriage with rope. Zeros were originally not meant to carry bombs. In some cases they were fastened with wire onto hooks designed to connect supplemental gasoline tanks.[22]

---

[20] Two of the four teams organized by Vice-Admiral Ohnishi on October 20 moved from Clark to bases in Cebu Island and Dabaw Mindanao Island. Although the Shikishima team led by Lieutenant Seki on October 25 is officially recognized as the first successful Kamikaze sortie, it has been suggested that this was in fact preceded by a pilot in the Yamato Unit who deployed on the same day from Cebu. Yet another theory proposes that an even earlier Yamato sortie on October 21 was the first. The successful pilots in both cases were not graduates of the Naval Academy, whereas Lieutenant Yukio Seki was. It is argued that the Shikishima unit was recognized as the first because the Navy wanted to claim the honor for one of its Academy elites. Seki was 22-years-old at the time of his sortie (5 years older than Odachi).

[21] According to American records, one carrier was destroyed with another severely damaged and two others sustaining minor damage.

[22] An attack strategy called "skip bombing" originally devised by the Americans was also adopted by the 201st Air Group from late August 1944. A 250-kg bomb would be attached to the Zero, which would then fly 10 meters above the sea and release the ordnance about 200 meters out from the target. The bomb would skim across the ocean's surface bouncing a

In normal circumstances, the ordnance was attached to clasps for the simple reason that the Kamikaze could ditch it if intercepted by a Hellcat. Bombs were jettisoned over the sea to prevent exploding on landing if the Zero couldn't find a target and had to return to base. This was not an option if the bomb was fastened with wire. It was incredibly dangerous, and we were lost for words when we saw it.

We waved our caps to send the boys off. Before long, Mr. K's Zero returned to base on its own. I figured that he must have had engine trouble. With the bomb secured as it was, I held my breath expecting the worst as he came in to land. Fortunately, it was a textbook landing and the bomb didn't detonate. Like a man possessed, Mr. K jumped out of the cockpit and yelled for another plane ordering the maintenance crew to reattach the bomb. It seemed that his only thought was to somehow perish this day.

An officer from the command post appeared and instructed Mr. K to forgo his mission. He replied "I promised my friends last night that we'd die together. I can't possibly live alone!" I understood what he meant. He waited impatiently for 15 minutes while the bomb was transferred to another Zero. Once ready, he tucked his scarf in again, hopped into the cockpit and started his engine. With a quick salute to acknowledge us, he took off for the last time.

Mr. K was from the Yokaren C-Class in which cadets were selected from Navy ranks. He was one or two years older than me and was always smiling. A 221st airman, he probably arrived in the Philippines a little earlier than me, but I still wondered why he was selected for a suicide mission so soon.

Following repairs, our 221st Storm Corps came to the Philippines independently of the other squadrons. It was not clear who our commander was when we arrived. This was the case for many other aviators stationed around the Philippines. There were not many Zeros left in the 201st Air Group by now, so more airmen had likely been called

---

few times before slamming into the side of the ship. The Zero would make a rapid climb and escape as soon as the bomb was dropped. Clasps for supplemental gasoline tanks were modified to carry these bombs. In the early Kamikaze missions, some of the Zeros (mainly the later Model 52) had already been modified for skip bombing, so it was just a matter of not releasing the ordnance and diving headlong into the enemy. Those which had not been modified had to rely on rope. Mr. K's Zero was one of those.

in from Taiwan. Due to incessant confusion in the chain of command, it was hardly surprising that 201st airmen assumed that all Zeros now arriving in the Philippines were there to bolster their numbers in suicide missions.

I had nothing but admiration for Mr. K, seeing his determination to die with his new comrades. Still, Mr. K's name is nowhere to be found in the official list of Kamikaze pilot casualties. Those who died in suicide attacks were posthumously promoted two ranks, but this honor was not bestowed upon Mr. K for some reason. I guess he was being punished by vindictive superiors for refusing to follow orders.

The Attack on Tacloban

We were given a mission, not suicide, to strike the American convoy heading to Tacloban in late October 1944. MacArthur's troops had landed there and were constructing an airfield. This was to be our target. The night before the sortie I remember all of us asking where on earth Tacloban is. We had never heard of the place before, let alone that American troops had arrived there in force.

A group of aviators arrived in our barracks. We didn't know who they were at first, but under the dim glow of a flashlight we learned that they were bomber crews for whom we were to provide cover fire. They had come to thank us for saving their backsides in advance. We had drinks together and our casual banter forged a feeling of unity. It was almost jovial.

The scale the Tacloban attack was smaller than that of Leyte Gulf, but we flew in the same bomber and fighter formations. My job was to help secure air supremacy at the vanguard. Looking behind and below me, I could see bombers and torpedo planes in formations of about 20 to 30 planes. Far behind were fighters flying up to 5,500 meters ready to pounce on interceptors.

The distance from Clark Field to Tacloban was about 500 kilometers to the south-southeast. We were instructed to go to Legaspi Airbase in the southern part of Luzon, about half way, should we need to make an emergency landing. Being faster than bombers, we kept an eye on the distance between us while looking out for signs of enemy fighters. I peered to the sides, behind, and below, primed and ready to engage any who dared to cross my path.

I assumed that things would start getting hot about 10 kilometers out of Tacloban. As predicted, land-based enemy fighters appeared from below. They were fewer in number, and we had the advantage at a higher altitude. We shot several down but weren't sure who had made the kills. The way was now clear for our bombers, and they descended quickly to drop their payloads. Thick smoke from the furious anti-aircraft fire impeded visibility, but as it faded I could see what looked like hundreds of ships covering the ocean surface below.

We circled our bombers from above. Zeros were also susceptible to anti-aircraft fire and I had to keep my wits about me to not get hit. The wing of a Zero flying close to me suddenly burst into flames. The pilot opened the windshield of his cockpit, smiled, and waved to me before making a sudden dive. Seeing this, I thought "He's got the right idea. I'll do the same if I get blasted." Being from a different squadron I wasn't sure who the pilot was, but he clearly knew that returning to base was out of the question. The smoke prevented me from verifying if he was able to smash into an enemy ship. We still had air supremacy, however, and our bombers were able to complete their job. All bombers returned to base unharmed. In this sense the mission was a rare success, but we were unable to gage how many target ships had been destroyed because of the smoke.

We made repeated attacks on Tacloban, but the Americans fought back hard. We realized then that American carriers we thought had already been destroyed near Taiwan were still very much in the game.

Strafed by a Hellcat

After returning from the Tacloban raid, I left my Zero in the hands of mechanics and headed to the command post to report in. A horrible feeling suddenly came over me. Doing double time along the airstrip, I instinctively looked back to see a Hellcat swooping in very low from behind. I couldn't even hear the roar of the engine due to the direction of the wind. As I ran, I kept an eye on him to see if I was in his firing line. It seemed that I was, so I leapt out of the way and lay flat on the ground the instant he let rip with his canons. The bullets kicked up clouds of dirt around me. I was very lucky to come out unscathed and resented the Hellcat pilot for shooting at targets on the ground.

I was shot at by another Hellcat some days later. We had been confined to the airbase, so five or six of us decided to head into town down the Manila Highway in our flight uniforms. Again, we sensed something behind us, and sure enough a Hellcat was approaching in attack mode. We kept walking pretending not to notice while carefully estimating the distance between us. One of the boys shouted "Now!" and we all jumped into bushes on the side of the road just as the Hellcat unleashed. Fortunately, the bullets sprayed around us.

There was no time to look as we jumped, and it happened that the bush we took refuge in was a huge cactus. It was a few meters high with needles more than 10cm long. The thorns pierced my face and back, and pain shot through my whole body. I was lucky my eyes weren't gouged out. We had no idea that such big cacti grew in the Philippines and were left mightily pissed off and bloody.

We escaped death because we knew how fighters operated and their range. Machine-guns were fixed to the body and wings. The attacker couldn't follow if the target made a sudden sideways movement. If the target moved too early, however, the pilot would have time to adjust, which is why we kept walking normally until the very last second.

We talked of the need for eyes in the back of our head and never ventured into the township again for that would be a suicide mission in its own right. Like birds of prey hunting alone, American pilots seemed to have no qualms about seeking out easy ground targets. To us, this was dirty fighting. I for one would never shoot at the enemy in such a way, and I never heard of any other Japanese pilots who did. War is full of atrocities and Japan committed its share. But for us, fighting was to be conducted in the air, plane against plane. The samurai of feudal Japan were not afraid of an honorable death in battle. Neither were we. The reality of our precarious existence now was that we might be exterminated at any moment without even leaving a trace. There was no honor in that.

Sortie Days

We made sorties almost every day in the Philippines. I was third airman in my section, and our leader was a Lieutenant who had graduated from the Naval Academy. One section consisted of four fighters, but the number of planes in escort missions depended on the circumstances. Sometimes there would be eight aircraft and sometimes 24. We would circle our bases at 5,000 meters keeping a vigilant eye out for enemy planes or take turns escorting convoys southwards in the western area of the Philippine Sea. We never heard back if the convoys arrived at their destinations, but we did if they had been attacked and sunk after we had done our bit.

If the order came to scramble, we would take off into the wind to get airborne as quick as possible. Sometimes we would have to contravene the very basics of flying if the enemy was in the vicinity, and just getting in the air could be a major undertaking. One time when we received information that Americans were coming to attack our bases, we scrambled our Zeros and headed to the west coast over Pinatubo Volcano. We climbed up 6,000 to 7,000 meters to secure the advantage and hovered in the airspace above our bases ready to intercept the bombers. As soon as we identified the enemy we dove straight at them. They scattered and escaped, but were clearly surprised at being ambushed from above. Moments like these kept our morale up.

Our Ace

We frequently embarked on sorties with other sections. In one of the accompanying teams there was an energetic, distinguished captain with a baritone voice. I asked who he was. "That's Lieutenant Naoshi Kanno."[23] I certainly knew the name. He was a famous "Shoot Down King." He always took the lead when we flew with him and was strikingly aggressive. When young airmen were resting in the barracks, he would sit down on the floor among them and make idle chitchat. "You boys doing okay?" he would ask. "Rest up good, lads!" One time I saw him laughing. "You screwed up because...." He would teach junior pilots with humor and good cheer, and the younger airmen would gather around him with bottles of cider as if they hadn't a care in the world.

I never had a chance to talk to him directly, but he reminded me of the famous samurai hero Isami Kondo of the Shinsengumi.[24] I really

---

[23] Naoshi Kanno was born in 1921. He graduated from the elite Naval Academy and became a feted ace later in the Pacific War. He was affiliated with 343rd Naval Air Fleet which was formed in Matsuyama to defend mainland Japan. Kanno engaged in legendary fights against B-29 bombers in the newly developed fighter Shiden-Kai (Allied reporting name "George"). He died on August 1, 1945 when his canons malfunctioned while intercepting a B-29.

[24] Isami Kondo (1834-68) was the leader of the Shinsengumi, a special police force organized to keep public order in Kyoto during the final years of the Tokugawa shogunate (see photos). In those days, so-called "men of high purpose" were conspiring to topple the government. The

wished to be a part of his team. Among all the Naval Academy graduates, his star shone the brightest.

Lost Zeros

American bombings intensified and we were attacked several times throughout the day and night. They were nervous times for us with hardly a moment when we felt safe. The difference between the might of America and Japan was never clearer. We tried to conceal as many planes as we could in shelters but were forced to hide many more in the forest under makeshift coverings of leaves. It was difficult to hide them all and we had to leave some beside the runway which meant that they were doomed.

After each raid we rushed over to check on our planes. Having been at Clark Field longer than the other pilots, my Zero survived the bombardments because I knew the best spots to hide it. Without the advantage of "local knowledge" aircraft belonging to latecomers inevitably became sitting ducks.

The attrition of operational planes meant that a fair few airmen were without rides. This in turn led to a change in mood in our squadron as it reduced the likelihood of being selected for suicide missions. "Whose turn is it for the next sortie?" "Must be the teams from Borneo or Singapore because they haven't done much of late." The fact that such words escaped our lips was a sign that we were losing our resolve to make that last suicide mission. In fact, any kind of mission was out of the question before long because all our Zeros were wiped out in the bombings....

I was constantly drenched in sweat because of the climate, but there were no baths or showers to rinse away the grime. Not once did I have a

---

group was made up of adept swordsmen who hunted and killed anti-shogunate rebels. After the Meiji Restoration (1868) Shinsengumi members, protectors of the now-defunct shogunate, were forced to flee to the eastern and northern regions of Japan. Isami Kondo was arrested and subsequently executed. Forbidden from taking his own life through ritual suicide in the samurai tradition, he was decapitated as a common criminal and his head displayed publicly as a final insult. Long after the Meiji Restoration, the Shinsengumi gradually came to be seen in a different light. Although they met their end as enemies of the state, their faith and loyalty to the former samurai government, and their determination to never compromise their ideals and duty was seen by the Japanese people as praiseworthy. Isami Kondo and his comrades are still very popular among Japanese people today, and there are many novels and movies about Shinsengumi exploits.

Mount Kaimon, or Kaimondake, is a dormant volcano in Kyushu where Odachi trained as a fighter pilot at Kasanohara Airbase in Kagoshima prefecture. It is also known as "Satsuma's Fuji" for its close resemblance in shape to Japan's iconic Mount Fuji. (Author's collection)

Two surviving pilots, Suzumura Zen'ichi (left) and Nishikawa Osamu (right) from the Taigitai ("Great Cause Taskforce"), the Kamikaze Special Attack Corps. (Author's collection)

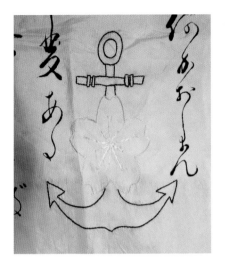

A scarf worn by Odachi embroidered with the Yokaren symbol of a cherry blossom and anchor. (Author's collection)

Part of the scarf which reads "Ichigeki Hittsui" meaning "Take down with one shot." This was a popular motto among Japanese fighter pilots during the Second World War. (Author's collection)

The "Three Birds of Saitama." Kazuo Odachi (back left) Kinzo Kasuya (back right) and Hiroshi Toyoda (front) after passing the rigorous and extremely competitive entrance examination into the Yokaren. Note the uniforms with seven buttons which show the popular Yokaren symbol of an anchor with cherry blossoms. (Author's collection)

Four fighter pilots from Storm Squadron to which Odachi belonged. This photo was taken at Kasanohara Airbase. From the right are Second Class Petty Officer Enoki, Leading Airman Ishimoto, Sub-Lieutenant Kobayashi, and First Class Petty Officer Komori. Enoki was killed during attacks on Shinchiku (Hsinchu) Base in Taiwan. Ishimoto became a member of the Kamikaze Special Attack Group Baika-tai Unit and died smashing into an enemy ship at Leyte Gulf. Komori was also killed in battle near Leyte Gulf. (Author's collection)

Yokaren cadets standing in front of their training aircraft (Yokosuka K5Y, Allied reporting name: "Willow") known by pilots as "Red Dragonfly" because of its color. In the front are cadets Nakagawa (left) and Kondo (right). Standing at the back are cadets Sugiyama, Odachi and Suzuki (left to right). Suzuki was killed on a suicide mission in Leyte. Kondo died crashing his plane into an enemy carrier in Okinawa. Sugiyama was killed in Yilan. (Author's collection)

Forty-seven pilots of the Kamikaze Special Attack Group Taigi-tai Unit.

Grumman F6F Hellcat.

Grumman F4F Wildcat.

Consolidated B-24 Liberator.

Boeing B-29 Superfortress.

A Mitsubishi A6M Zero in the Kure Maritime Museum in Kure, Hiroshima, Japan. (Wikimedia Commons © Z3144228)

A Mitsubishi A6M3 Model 22 flying over the Solomon Islands in 1943.

An old and rare photograph of the charismatic naval aviator Lieutenant Yukio Seki. He was appointed captain of one of the first Kamikaze suicide units.

The Mitsubishi G4M was the main twin-engine, land-based bomber used by the Imperial Japanese Navy Air Service in the Second World War. It was given the reporting name Betty by Allied forces.

Twelve surviving pilots of the Taigi-tai Unit taken in Taiwan, September 1945. Odachi is standing in the middle of the back row wearing a white shirt. (Author's collection)

The aircraft carrier USS *Bunker Hill* burns after being hit by two kamikazes on May 11, 1945. The attack caused 690 casualties including 390 killed, 43 missing, and 264 wounded.

Kazuo Odachi dressed in his flight uniform. This photo was taken when Odachi was stationed in Taiwan. He was 17 years old at the time. (Author's collection)

real shower in three-and-a-half months in the Philippines. We all stunk to high heaven and were constantly plagued by itches because of scabies. There was no medicine to relieve us of the discomfort. One time we decided to tempt fate and bathe in a nearby river during a lull in the bombings. We immersed ourselves in turns thinking it unwise to all go in together. Ignoring the buffaloes soaking in the muddy water close by, we washed ourselves as quickly as we could. It was only ten minutes or so, but it felt so very good.

I had not shaved or cut my hair and looked like a wild mountain man. Some cut their beards unevenly with scissors, but this made them look even more scraggly. Rarely could we even wash our underwear. We just threw them away and made fresh pairs out of old hand towels.

Mr. Takeo Shinmyo

There was a distinguished reporter from the Mainichi Daily News in Clark Field. His name was Takeo Shinmyo.[25] Mr. Shinmyo followed us around throughout the day taking photographs and looking for stories. We became quite friendly with him. He was a kindly man who could connect with the airmen and proffered insights that most of us were oblivious to. He was very attuned to what was going on around him and had the lowdown on all the crews. He was a useful source of information. Being much older than us, Mr. Shinmyo became a surrogate father figure, and we felt at ease opening up to him when he joined us for drinks in our barracks. He would always inquire if there was anything he could do to help. "If you need me to pass on something to your families...." Anybody assigned a suicide mission would go and see dear old Mr. Shinmyo. "I will depart on my last mission tomorrow. So long, Shinmyo-san."

---

[25] Takeo Shinmyo (19081). On February 23, 1944, Shinmyo wrote an article which appeared on the top page of the Mainichi Daily Newspaper. "We cannot win this war using bamboo spears. We need more airplanes." This apparently enraged Prime Minister Hideki Tojo whose government was behind propaganda touting the warrior spirit to incite all Japanese to fight to the very last with bamboo pikes if need be. Shinmyo criticized this nonsense with a well-reasoned article. To write such a critique of government policy took considerable courage, and Tojo ordered Shinmyo's drafting into the military. He was 37 years old and had poor eyesight which made him ineligible for service, so this was obviously petty retribution. The Navy, however, sided with Shinmyo and helped him get an early discharge. Shinmyo was dispatched to the Philippines as a war correspondent for the Mainichi Daily News not long after this incident. Following the war, he wrote numerous articles about the lives and experiences of Kamikaze pilots, appealing to the Japanese public to never forget their sacrifice.

Although there were reporters from other media organizations among us, the only one I remember is Shinmyo-san. The others didn't really show much interest in us, mostly fraternizing instead with the officers who decided on the rosters. We were aware of this and gave them a cold shoulder even if they did attempt to talk with us. Mainly young men themselves they seemed to be indifferent to airmen about to perish for their country.

I saw Shinmyo-san on many occasions after the war. I was coordinator for veterans of the 205th Air Group, and we continue holding annual memorials for our fallen comrades to this day. Although he was never sent formal invitations, not once did he miss a gathering. I believe he was the only outsider who truly understood the hearts of Kamikaze pilots.

Head for the Hills

As if the daily bombings were not stressful enough, I also came down with malaria. With a fever of around 38 to 40 degrees, I trembled uncontrollably for quite some time. Hygiene was bad, and our resistance to illness was low because of poor nutrition. A steady flow of airmen became disease-ridden. Sleeping in shabby bamboo huts or under trees left us susceptible to the vicious mosquitos who injected us mercilessly with their poison. They were much bigger than their cousins in Japan, and the loud buzzing sound was ominous. We had long run out of pyrethrum coils, so it was a smorgasbord of blood for the ferocious disease carriers.

The army physician gave us quinine tablets from his limited supply and told us to take them with water, but that was also dangerous. There was some boiled water but not nearly enough to cater for our needs. We had no choice other than to drink creek water which inevitably gave us bad diarrhea and other ailments. The quinine never worked for me. It lowered my fever slightly but did little else. Still, some of the men didn't take their medicine at all and ended up dying from some horrible disease.

Just as I started to feel better, I would be knocked back again with a high fever. This happened over and over, and I always had the shakes. I hated the nights because I knew that squadrons of voracious mosquitos would be out in force. We were dead tired but there was little we could do to alleviate the suffering. Even the physician threw his hands up in despair. Some Kamikaze pilots embarked on their final missions writhing dreadfully from the effects of malaria.

In January 1945, American troops began to arrive in the Lingayen Gulf, about 200 kilometers northeast of Clark Field. As MacArthur had already landed in Leyte three months earlier, this meant we would be attacked from both the north and south. Many personnel from both the Navy and the Army were now stationed in Clark Field. Most had no choice but to remain as the enemy encroached, so we were ordered to hunker down in the surrounding mountains to fight.[26]

The majority of pilots in Clark Field were dispatched to Tuguegarao Airbase located in the north of Luzon island about 400 kilometers away. They were directed to go by foot over the mountain paths as American troops had already arrived in Lingayen Gulf and were heading toward Manila. The pilots avoided confrontation and traversed the mountains running parallel to Manila Highway. I can only imagine how uncomfortable they were trekking over this inhospitable terrain in flying uniforms. I heard that some of them were picked up by army trucks, but most made the arduous journey on foot with few provisions, and constantly under threat of guerrilla attacks. The ones who made it to Tuguegarao were flown back to Taiwan.

Airmen who succumbed to malaria and other serious maladies remained in Clark Field. I was hospitalized at the base infirmary which was essentially a makeshift tent. We couldn't move, and the quinine was all gone. Being in no condition to defend ourselves, we saw little way out of our dire predicament. Despite our decrepit states we too were ordered to head for the hills when the field hospital was about to be closed. Remaining pilots were instructed to join the ground fighting with the infantry men. I was still crippled by a high fever but had no choice other than to go with them.

It was mid-January, 1945. We headed to Pinatubo Mountain west of Clark Field where a temporary relief facility was set up. Maintenance crew members who had malaria were there also. In all, there were about

---

[26] Around 400 naval air crews were left. Most of the Zero pilots at Clark were experienced vets having seen considerable action in Indonesia, Malaysia, etc. Students of higher education were initially exempted from military service, but with the worsening war situation and shortage of soldiers, students were conscripted from 1943. Many were being drafted into the airbase in Kyushu and trained for a short period solely for Kamikaze missions. Naturally, the pilots based in Clark were significantly more skilled than the students who were not expected to do anything other than die for the cause.

20 of us, and I sensed that we were sent there to try and recover rather than gear up to repel the Americans. After all, we wouldn't have been able to put up much of a fight!

After orders to head for the hills were issued, plane-less airmen became the target of bullying by other soldiers. Maintenance crew and army men were bitter about the "high and mighty pilots" and made us carry the supplies. "Otherwise, you can go ahead and starve for all we care...." They made all the pilots lug heavy bags of rice weighing almost 60 kilograms each, even the ones suffering from malaria. We weren't used to such heavy lifting and ascending the narrow mountain path was a grueling affair.

With no leeway for personal effects, the only other thing I carried was my pistol and a handful of bullets. Mount Pinatubo was covered in thick volcanic rock. It was steep and overlaid with jungle. We climbed a little, rested, climbed a little, rested again. I had a splitting headache and broke into a cold sweat. Totally dejected by this stage, I wondered how many days I had left in me. We were literally on a knife's edge and staring death in the face. I felt utterly defeated.

Somehow, we managed to climb up to around 600 meters, but certainly didn't feel any safer, and the sadistic mosquitos were as ubiquitous as ever. We cut bamboo and laid the branches between rocks to sleep on. All we could do was sleep and eat boiled rice mixed with wheat or other kinds of grain. Our cheeks sunk, our hair and beards were unkempt, but our eyes were still surprisingly sharp. The younger volunteer soldiers were relatively energetic, but the older men in their 30s or 40s were completely sapped.

As time passed, order among the men started to crumble. We didn't really know who was in charge and couldn't operate as an effective combat unit. Amidst the chaos, it was the cooks who wielded the most power as they controlled the food and provisions. It looked as if they were looking after themselves first and giving us the leftovers. Even the cooks, who had always been kind to us, had completely changed in demeanor. One of them came over and said, "You pilots were always arrogant bastards when you had your planes, but you're nothing without them. You're only getting half rations." Some ground crew personnel tried to stand up for us, but others treated us as if we were the enemy.

Machine-guns which had been removed from planes were set up

among the rocks. The problem was that there was little ammunition. The army men had rifles, but maintenance and catering personnel carried nothing to fight with except their spanners rice spatulas.

The pistols that pilots carried were 1939 models, and each of us was issued with two in case we had to fight after crash landing. They had long barrels and were fairly accurate. I inserted them on either side of my belt and kept the bullets in my pocket. More than shooting the enemy, those pistols were useful for hunting birds or animals for food. Wild boars were abundant in the mountains and they made for good tucker. The possibility of having to fight Americans was always in the back off my mind, but I didn't think about the consequences if all my bullets were spent getting food. It was impossible to predict what was in store, but if I was going to die in this accursed war, I just wished it was in the air, not in the mud.

The Narrowest of Escapes

Communication soldiers were neutral to us and provided information. Almost two weeks after taking cover in the mountains, one of the comms officers came to me with some new intel. All airmen were to be transferred to Taiwan. The last transport plane was scheduled to arrive in a few days at midnight. News that only pilots would be flown out reached the ears of the other troops. A strange, almost hostile mood came over them. "You'll get fed well in Taiwan. You don't need any of our grub." "Leave your guns as well."

We weren't sure whether the evacuation planes would make it to our location. If we gave them our revolvers, we would have no weapons to defend ourselves. We ignored them but did leave the blankets we inherited from the Americans. In the end there was no trouble. We felt awkward as we left, and I really hoped that they would escape from the shit storm that was coming. I knew this was wishful thinking.

We were told to wait at the middle airbase in Clark Field for a transporter scheduled to arrive at a specified time. The lift out was arranged to take place in three days, and 15 to 20 of us headed down the mountain with a supply of rice. We hid in a small hut on the west side of the airbase during the day so as not to be made by guerrillas. Late in the evening we walked toward the airbase and found a spot to dig a hole in the ground to start a fire and boil our rice. Surrounding our fire pit with a large cloth to hide the flames we filled up on the rice in what was the first decent meal we'd had for some time. The leftovers were made into rice balls for later, and we hid there for a couple more days until the plane arrived.

With the stars and moon shining brightly, the night of our evacuation was not particularly dark. Still, with no guiding lights on the runway the plane would have to make its landing relying on the natural luminosity, but this would require considerable skill. That issue aside, we weren't entirely sure that the plane would come anyway. We figured it was a fifty-fifty prospect. If it was on its way, we predicted it would come in from the direction of Mount Arayat in the east because the enemy had control of both the north and south sectors of Clark Field, and Mount Pinatubo in the west was too high.

Lying on our stomachs in the grass we strained our eyes toward the eastern sky. Before long, we saw the small lamp of an airplane camouflaged by the stars a little north of Mt. Arayat. Lights on both edges of its main wings were boldly lit up and it headed to the south route as it approached the runway. As the sound of engine became audible someone piped up and said, "That sounds like a Douglas!" The Douglas C-47 was a dual engine transport aircraft which Japan had imported from the United States before the war. It was not armed so if we were spotted by the enemy there would be no way out.

We were in a state of disbelief. "They really came!" we all said in hushed voices. The lackluster drone of C-47 engine was nothing to get excited about normally, but it was music to our ears at the time. It was sure as hell better than the death scream of an enemy fighter!

The middle airbase in Clark Field was located directly to the west of Manila Highway. The plane flew very low and touched down on the landing strip. It reduced speed and stopped on the western edge raising a big cloud of dust as it came to a halt. We bolted towards it as fast as our legs would carry us. The left hatch was opened and somebody inside was screaming at us to hurry up. We jumped in one at a time raising more dust. When the last one was in, someone shouted "Finished!" and the hatch was slammed shut.

The C-47 began to take off at maximum throttle. It was a much slower beast than a Zero and seemed to take forever before we took off. Someone even shouted impatiently for the pilots to get a move on. We were relieved for a moment until we saw several red flashes from the window. It seemed that the Americans had already made it as far as the airbase and had spotted us. They were shooting at us, so the C-47 took evasive action as best it could. This, we thought, was surely the end....

There were no seats. Twenty of us sat cross legged on the floor holding onto ropes for support. There was still a danger that American fighters would come after us, so we kept our eyes peeled looking out the windows into the darkness. The C-47 headed to the east first, then turned north flying over Luzon Island. It was our understanding that the northern region of Luzon had not yet come under American control, but we were forever on high alert. Leaving Luzon behind, we then flew over Bashi Channel which is when we finally felt rescued.

As Japan had offered little effective resistance against the Americans heading south from the Lingayen Gulf, they were able to overrun Clark Field very rapidly. Fortunately for us, by the time we made it out of there they hadn't yet secured all of it. If our evacuation was scheduled any later the C-47 would not have made it. Even another minute would have seen us shot down. We got away by the skin of our teeth.

Finally reaching safety, someone mentioned "They dared to come to pick us up in such dangerous circumstances. It must have cost a fortune. I don't know if this bodes well for us...." Another responded by alluding to an old children's song. "The way out is fine, but the way home is frightening." This light-hearted black humor afforded us a smidgen of inner peace, momentary though it was. We appreciated the rescue operation but at the same time were acutely aware that some heavy burden was about to be dumped on our shoulders. Although our lives had been saved, for the moment, I felt I had aged considerably in the short journey.

The rescue operation must have been mandated at Combined Fleets HQ. Evacuating hitherto forsaken souls was certainly not what our Navy had been known for in the past. The operation was coordinated excellently, and it puzzled us how HQ even knew we were hiding with the others in the mountains. Clearly, they needed Zero pilots meaning the Navy was in even more serious trouble. Most of the experienced ones had already been killed.

About 20 years after war, a Yokaren graduate met up with a veteran from the 205th Air Group at a reunion in Yokohama. It turns out that this fellow was the C-47 pilot who came and got us. Years later, I also met the same fellow at a memorial service at Yasukuni Shrine in Tokyo. Somebody called out to me "Hi Odachi. Know who I am?" I knew at once.

"Guess who hauled your asses out of the Philippines in that Douglas."
"Oh yes, that must have been you," I replied. The last thing on my mind
when we were hightailing it out of there was who the pilot was. Looking
back, it was no mean feat rescuing a bunch of airmen by moonlight in an
unarmed C-47 in hostile territory. I felt truly indebted to him.

Remaining Troops

Admiral Ohnishi of the 1st Naval Air Fleet, and Admiral Fukudome
of the 2nd Fleet and their cadre began the retreat from the Philippines
to Taiwan on January 10, 1945. Naval personnel left in Taiwan were
reorganized and ordered to defend Clark Field bases. It is estimated
that around 15,400 Navy personnel remained. With a severe shortage
of weapons, ammunition, food and medicine, forcing the advancing
Americans back was an unattainable task. The number who survived
this doomed undertaking was a paltry 450 men. The others died honor-
ably with unfaltering resolve against insurmountable odds. A troop led
by Captain Naohiro Sada decided it was futile to engage the Americans
and chose instead to hide out in Mount Pinatubo. After Japan's surrender, the men marched down the mountain in orderly fashion with
a white flag.

The Imperial Japanese Army forces were also decimated. By the end
of the carnage, around 518,000 Japanese soldiers died in the Philippines. Of them, the remains of some 370,000 Japanese military men
have been repatriated to Japan, but nearly 150,000 still rest in the Philippines. It is said that over 1,000,000 people died there, many of whom
were civilians. The United States lost around 15,000 men. These shocking numbers are a stark indication of how lucky Odachi and his comrades were to be rescued, and similarly shows how desperate the Navy
was to procure pilots for Kamikaze attacks in a last ditched effort to
defend the Japanese mainland.

CHAPTER FIVE

Kamikaze Sorties from Taiwan

The C-47 that evacuated us from the Philippines arrived at Kaohsiung Airbase in Taiwan just before dawn on February 3, 1945. Three years and two months before, the Imperial Japanese Navy fleet set sail from this very harbor to oust the Americans. Clark Field was one of the main targets in what was a highly successful campaign enabling Japan to gain control of the region. The situation had changed drastically since then, and Kaohsiung had been ravaged by American bombers.

Filing out of the plane we were guided to a mess tent and served a breakfast of white rice. We poured raw egg over the rice and devoured it without stopping to breathe. The mess crew looked bemused at how ravenous we were. We bathed for the first time in four months, and even managed to take a razor to our hirsute faces. A restful night was spent there before being transferred by truck to Tainan, and then to Taichung Airbase by train. We arrived on the morning of February 5 and ran into pilots who had escaped from Clark to Tugecarao by foot, as well as survivors from Singapore and Borneo. Nobody ever expected to see the lads who disappeared into the mountains, so our arrival caused quite a commotion.

It was like a big reunion, but the gathering was for a very somber reason: we were all inducted as members of the 1st Naval Air Fleet's 205th Air Group. Lieutenant Colonel Asaichi Tamai was appointed as our commander, but I received my orders verbally from Vice Admiral Fukudome, Commander in Chief of the 2nd Naval Air Fleet.

This marked the launch of Kamikaze Special Attack Corps "Taigitai," meaning "Great Cause Taskforce." Kamikaze units were formerly assigned designations before departing on suicide sorties. This was the first and only time that an entire Air Group had been conferred a Kamikaze moniker. From the outset of Taigitai's formation, three naval fleets provided an extra 48 Zeros making a total of 144. We were all placed on immediate standby for Kamikaze assignments from Taichung, Hsinchu and Tainan air bases.

Procuring More Zeros

Although we supposedly had 144 Zeros, the truth is that many weren't operational. Like most other pilots I didn't have my own Zero, so about ten of us were deployed to Japan in the middle of February to procure aircraft for Kamikaze missions. Zeros came off the production lines of Mitsubishi Heavy Industry in Suzuka (Mie Prefecture), and in Nakajima Aircraft Company in Ohta (Gunma Prefecture). We were divided into two groups. I was sent to Suzuka. We boarded a C-47 in Hsinchu and headed for Kasanohara in Kagoshima Prefecture where I had undergone training as a Yokaren cadet.

After landing we immediately went to the command post tent. Our leader saluted the commandant. "We are from the 205th Air Group. Our mission is to acquire new Zeros." Such formal greetings were protocol when airmen visited other bases. There were a few high-ranking officers sitting on a bench. Cross-legged on the floor in four lines on either side of them were about 200 student draftees all with the rank of Ensign.

I knew the squad leader. It was Flight Lieutenant Asai of Storm Corps. Hey, Kazu!" he called out in a loud voice. He came up to me with a broad smile on his face. It had been less than a year since I left this base for Taiwan, but he remained and had been promoted from Sub-Lieutenant to Flight Lieutenant. A graduate of the Naval Academy, he had always been kind to me, and irrespective of his superior rank, I felt that we were friends. Informing him of my experiences in the Philippines, it suddenly dawned on me how much had happened in such a short time.

We headed to Suzuka by train the next day. Staying at an old-fashioned inn in Tsu City (capital of Mie Prefecture), it was the first time in ages that I slept in a soft *futon* on top of *tatami* mats. A luxury car was sent to pick us up the next morning courtesy of Mitsubishi Heavy Industry. It transferred us to the airdrome attached to the Mitsubishi factory. We test flew some brand-new Zeros later in the afternoon and selected ones to fly back to Taiwan.

We jumped in the latest Model 62 Zeros. I began flying in Model 32s, so Zeros had undergone several modifications in a brief period. My first impression of the Model 62 was that it was clumsy on take-off. It took longer to get air born and I needed to pull the center stick fully back to lift off. The Model 32 only needed 30 meters before it started to drift, but the Model 62 didn't get any lighter even after 70-80 meters at full throttle. This was because the weight of the airframe had been increased. The Model 32 was armed with two 7.7mm caliber machine-guns attached to the body and two 20mm caliber guns on the main wings. The Model 62 had one 13mm caliber machine-gun on the body, and two 13mm plus two 20mm caliber guns on the wings. The magazines were also bigger, so these additions in armament made it weightier. The engine stayed at 1,000 horsepower as it always had been, so even though the firepower was greater, the fighter's maneuverability decreased overall. I also noticed that clasps had been added to the undercarriage to attach bombs.

Royal Escort to Shanghai

I think it was February 24 or 25 when we dropped by Kasanohara in our new Zeros on our return trip to Taiwan. The party that went to the Nakajima Aircraft Company in Gunma also came to Kasanohara. Flight Lieutenant Asai was waiting for our arrival and tried to convince us to remain in Kasanohara as flight instructors for student draftees. Although students were highly educated and their military rank was higher than ours, the training period was absurdly short, and they had next to no flying experience.

"We're in serious shit" I thought. We didn't respond to Flight Lieutenant Asai immediately and requested more time to consider his proposal. Sitting as we often did in a circle drinking in the barracks, we discussed what to do. We were all still teenagers, but we had seen some tough fighting in the Philippines and elsewhere. Young though we were, we wreaked of the stench of war. Asai made this unexpected request because there was a critical shortage of instructors. Nearly all the seasoned veterans who would have been perfect for the job were dead.

We were assigned to carry out Kamikaze missions so returning to Taiwan meant certain death sooner rather than later. There was a possibility of surviving this detestable war by accepting Asai's offer. We would be treated well as instructors and even assigned separate rooms. Besides, it was not as if we asked for such an attractive commission. The Flight Lieutenant chose us....

Eventually, however, we had to acknowledge what we knew deep down. One by one, we decided to decline Asai's proposition. "I don't want to be thought of as a coward afraid to die" said one. "They'll think we chickened out after having a few decent meals back home" said another. We unanimously came to a decision to return to our base. After all we had been through, we felt duty-bound to carry out our orders and die for the "great cause."

"Let's return to be with the other guys." "Let's die together." Brave words indeed, but honestly speaking Asai's offer was enticing, and he made a point of asking us openly in front of his subordinates. Sipping our rice wine, we continued to mull the situation over. Someone said, "Kazu, at least you should stay." Another said "Yeah, it was only because Asai knows you that he made the offer." Asai had shown me considerable favor, but there was no way I could go along with that idea. "What the hell?! You think you're going back to Taiwan without me?" Somebody else chimed in to help me out. "We can't leave Kazu here on his own."

As the frank and heated debate about me staying continued, the door quietly opened and an officer wearing an unfamiliar but regal uniform walked into our room. We all turned to scrutinize this mysterious visitor with his prominent silver epaulet. For some reason none of us saw the need to salute him. The officer politely inquired "You gentlemen are returning to Taiwan tomorrow, are you not?" "Yes" we replied. His next statement left us momentarily stunned. "I am Chamberlain for His Royal Highness Prince Mikasa-no-miya Takahito (see photos). The Prince is scheduled to fly to Shanghai tomorrow, but I am concerned for his safety as there are no fighters to accompany him. I have been informed that you are journeying to Taiwan and I wondered if you wouldn't mind escorting His Royal Highness to Shanghai on your way."

We were lost for words. Why would an officer of such noble standing, a Chamberlain to the Prince no less, visit our humble barracks at night and petition us so politely? At last, one of us dared to respond. "We were just discussing the details of our return." "Is going back to Taiwan via Shanghai possible?" It sounded like the perfect excuse to decline Asai's invitation, but our orders were to return to Taiwan ASAP with our new Zeros. We asked the officer to wait while we conferred with each other. He remained in the room as we talked earnestly among ourselves. Our leader reported to the officer that we had no objection but required him to get the go ahead from our fleet superiors. He left our barracks happy to comply.

He came back later to inform us that the matter was settled. "You will escort His Royal Highness to Shanghai before returning to Taiwan via Fujian in China." We don't know exactly what transpired behind the scenes, but these were our new orders. It fell on my shoulders to tell Asai. "We hope for your understanding as this is a request to escort His Royal Highness...." Asai seemed to know already and gave me a wry smile. It was all rather uncomfortable.

The weather the following morning was fine, and two sections making eight Zeros in total got ready for this important task. We took off from Kasanoara and circled above as we waited for the Mitsubishi Navy Type-1 Attack Bomber (G4M) with its imperial passenger onboard to depart from neighboring Kanoya Airbase (see photos).[27]

The G4M caught up with us. We flew in formation in two teams positioned on either side of the bomber as we proceeded to Shanghai. My Zero was Number 3 in the right team meaning that I was positioned closest to our august company.

We crossed over the gulf of Kagoshima and flew out to the open sea turning slightly to the right. Our initial objective was Jeju Island in the Tsushima Channel. When the island was visible in the distance we headed west-south-west in the direction of Shanghai. I think we went via Jeju island first because it was safer than flying directly to Shanghai.

There were several windows on the right side of the G4M. I could see somebody sitting by the third or fourth window. The G4M swayed slightly, and I moved in a little closer about 30 or 40 meters away. The person whom I thought may be Prince Mikasa looked out of the window and smiled as he gave me a wave of his hand. He had a gentle countenance and I sensed that he was grateful for our escort. I reciprocated with a bow and firmed my resolve to get him to his destination safely.

After we changed direction, I noticed the color of the sea below was blue on one side and yellow on the other. I had never seen yellow ocean before. I thought China would come into view soon, but it took longer than I expected. It was only after our arrival that I realized we had flown above the mouth of Yang Zu Ziang River. It was so expansive that I had mistook it for the ocean, but it explained why the water was such an odd hue.

---

[27] Mitsubishi Navy Type-1 Attack Bomber (G4M, allied reporting name "Betty") was the Imperial Japanese Navy's biggest aircraft. Its wingspan measured around 25m, it was 20m long, and was operated by seven crewmen. It is a questionable why Prince Mikasa requested a Navy airplane to fly him to Shanghai from the Navy base in Kanoya when he was affiliated to the Army. This mystery will be addressed later.

Standby Under Wings

The G4M landed first while we circled above on lookout. I could see several people alighting the aircraft and ambling towards a building. We received the signal to make our own landing but never saw our imperial patron in the flesh.

As always, we trotted to the command post to make a formal greeting to the base commandant. He ordered us to "Standby under wings." It was a basic rule to obey any base commandant even if we were affiliated with different branches of the military. "Standby under wings" was a directive for airmen to stay close to their machines, even sleeping under the wings ready to scramble. We received intelligence that an American convoy had crossed the sea between Okinawa and Taiwan and was now in the East China Sea. To our utter disbelief we also learned that there were no naval fighter planes left anywhere in China. That is why we were instructed to remain on standby instead of being allowed to continue to Taiwan.

We watched over the Shanghai skies from early in the morning to night. Four Zeros made up one section, and each took turns doing three-hour shifts of watch duty. We were exhausted. News reached us a few days later that the Americans had sailed out of the region, but we had to keep guard in case they returned. I recall staying in Shanghai for around ten days. We happily visited the Shanghai Navy Club several times while there. It was a beautiful town with its Western-style buildings all in neat rows. It seemed out of place in China.

We returned to Taiwan flying along the southern coastline by way of Fujian province. The bomber that transported Prince Mikasa had already gone back to Japan. We never knew why the prince visited Shanghai, or when he left. Orders to escort a dignitary of this status should have come directly from our superiors. It was unthinkable that a high-ranking officer such as the Chamberlain of His Royal Highness should bid us directly. The fact that he came to our lowly barracks in the first place was extraordinary. Even with the acute lack of operational aircraft, it did not make any sense that a prince was not assigned even a single fighter escort. The whole affair left us with a sense of foreboding, but we did not ruminate on it too long. At the forefront of our minds now was getting back to Taiwan.

After the war, I heard that Prince Mikasa was engaged in activities opposed to the Tojo cabinet. Even so, why would he be travelling at such a perilous time in such a dangerous region? And, as Prince Mikasa was affiliated to the Army, why were naval aviators asked to assist him? Again, why would the Navy provide him with a G4M for transport but no escorts. He was the Emperor's brother after all, so this treatment seemed tremendously discourteous. I still wonder about the whole affair to this day.[28]

The Pacific theater of World War II.

---

[28] We conducted a thorough investigation of wartime records to corroborate Odachi's memory escorting Prince Mikasa, brother of Emperor Hirohito. We came up empty-handed, so as a last resort we ventured to ask Prince Mikasa directly. Aged 99 years old then, in October 2015 we sent him a letter through the Imperial Household Agency and inquired whether he had any recollection of that flight to Shanghai, and what the purpose was. A reply came sooner than we expected. An official contacted us by phone and informed us that His Royal Highness read our letter with the Princess. However, he was "unable to recall" this wartime episode. The Princess looked for any related documents, but all relevant materials must have been burned during the American bombings of Tokyo, so we were unable to validate Odachi's account. Given Prince Mikasa's age it is hardly surprising that he was unable to recall the flight. Nevertheless, if Prince Mikasa was adamant that such a flight never took place, then his wife would not have gone to the trouble to look for records.

    We concluded that Odachi and his colleagues indeed escorted the prince to Shanghai through snippets of circumstantial evidence found in various sources and books. We believe that the purpose of his visit to Shanghai was related to his activities to engage in peace negotiations between Japan and China. Prince Mikasa advocated a peaceful resolution to the conflict and was an ardent critic of the Imperial Japanese Army's conduct in China. He was even associated with a coup d'état to topple Hideki Tojo's cabinet after returning to Japan from Nanking in January 1944. Refer to the Appendix for full details.

Awarded a Short Sword

Not long after returning to Taiwan from Shanghai on March 10, 1945, there was a ceremony held at Taichung for our Special Attack Corps Taigitai. The names of 103 airmen were written on the official roster, and we were all presented with a commemorative short sword sheathed in white wooden scabbard and inscribed with the words "Awarded to Kamikaze by Soemu Toyoda," This was the name of the Commander-in-Chief of the Imperial Japanese Navy Combined Fleet. I considered the sword to be a kind of "alter ego."

Taigitai was made up of relatively experienced airmen, but its stated mission was the defense of Taiwan and Okinawa through suicide attacks, with the primary targets being aircraft carriers rather than convoy ships. Our main base was in Taichung, but units were spread out in Xinshe, Tainan, Hsinchu, Yilan, Ishigakijima and Miyakojima (two islands belonging to Okinawa located just east of Taiwan). We kept ourselves busy as we waited for intelligence on the American fleet and for our suicide mission orders by intercepting bombers raiding from mainland China. We even continued our dogfight training. Sometimes we were called on to courier documents around Taiwan.

Our Taichung base barracks were located about 1.5 meters from the runway. A truck would pick us up after breakfast. There was always someone who held up departures by a minute or so, but once we were all crammed in we were transported to the runway like packages of freight. The truck stopped in front of the command post where a flimsy tent was erected for airmen. Inside were filthy blankets for us nap on or chat until the time came to sortie.

In mid-March, we got word that the American fleet was east of the Sea of Taiwan. The Taigitai transferred its main force to Yilan Airbase on the northeast coast of Taiwan, making Miyakojima and Ishigakijima the vanguard for Kamikaze attacks. I was stationed in Yilan.

500-kg Bombs

The bombs attached to Zeros in early suicide attacks were 250 kg. Over time, however, an impressive 2.5-meter-long 500-kg ordnances became the norm. I remember tapping one ready to be mounted onto the clasps and murmuring to myself "We're going up together."

Model 62 Zeros weighed just over two tons, meaning that the bombs we carried were a quarter of the weight. Maintenance crews used carts to move and attach explosives to the undercarriage. When the carts were slid out from under the bombs, the Zeros dropped down noticeably because of the sudden increase in weight. The suspension and tires strained under the burden and made an ominous creaking sound.

Never designed to carry such a heavy load, the extra stress on the suspension caused Zeros to judder over the potholed runways, rattling us to the bone. We needed 100 to 120 meters of runway when taking off in good conditions against the wind without bombs. With a 250-kg ordnance under our butts we would need 500 meters at full throttle. The 500-kg bombs demanded running the entire length of the airstrip before taking off. I was always afraid I wouldn't get airborne. All I could do was pray for lift off and it took every bit of the Zero's power to get off the ground. Once in the air the climb was painfully sluggish.

The lever had to be pushed forward at full throttle just to reach cruising speed. It barely flew and our range was significantly reduced. The first time I experienced such downgraded maneuverability I doubted if I would make it as far as the enemy. Carrying 500-kg bombs was an impractical and heedless move.

Fleeting Moments of Tranquility

This was my second tour in Taiwan. Although the war situation had worsened somewhat, life there was much better than in the Philippines. We were even allowed to take leave on occasion. Although American raids continued, we still had time to go to town for a haircut. To us, it really felt like Taiwan was a part of Japan and we walked around town dressed casually. I wore a tidy open-necked, short-sleeved shirt and khaki pants when three of us visited a studio to take some commemorative photos. My two buddies both died in Kamikaze missions not long after.

When we were in Taichung before moving to Yilan, a local family offered to make their house our "lodge." This was a term used for private residences that we were free for us to use as a kind of holiday house to get away from the stresses of the base. The owner of this particular abode was a graduate of Waseda University's Technology Department. He was in Taiwan to manage a munitions factory. Most supervisors of Japan-related businesses and factories in Taiwan were Japanese nationals. His daughter was a little younger than us and worked at a local bank.

Four of us accepted their kind offer. Every time we got a pass we headed to our "lodge" first. We would decide beforehand which bar or club to go to that night, and then apprise the family of our schedule, forewarning them that we "might" return late. We rode a bus from base and got off at the stop in front of the Taiwan Bank on the main road. There were always plenty of girls waiting for us there. These were fleeting moments of happiness as we never knew how long we had left.

The Battle of Okinawa and Kamikaze Attacks

After American troops wrested control of the Philippines back, the next push was for Okinawa. The invasion of Okinawa started on April 1, 1945. The American 77th Infantry Division landed first on the shores of the Kerama islands close to the southwest coast of Okinawa's main islands. This was to prepare for a direct assault on mainland Japan, so the Allied forces bypassed Taiwan altogether.

The sea around Okinawa was teeming with Allied ships. It is reported that the U.S. deployed 16 regular carriers, 28 escort carriers, 23 battleships, 39 cruisers, 205 destroyers, and countless convoy ships. There was an unprecedented number of troops with around 450,000 soldiers from both the Navy and Army. Of them about 180,000 were ground force personnel.

Japan had only 120,000 fighting men mainly from the Army. They made Okinawa into a fortress in a do-or-die attempt to repel the invaders and to stall the inevitable invasion of the mainland. Scores of Kamikaze suicide attacks were executed from both the sky and sea.

The hostilities in Okinawa raged for about three months. In the ground battles alone approximately 200,000 people including citizens lost their lives. The number of Americans killed in action is said to number around 12,000. Formal Taigitai records from the Navy have been preserved in the Research Institute of the Self Defense Force in Minato Ward, Tokyo. According to these source materials, 23 Kamikaze suicide missions were made by the Taigitai on U.S. ships from April 1 until surrender in August 1945. Odachi's record shows that he made four sorties as a Taigitai suicide pilot. In addition to these, Odachi recollects three more that are not recorded.

My First Suicide Mission

There were two jobs in Kamikaze suicide missions: human bombs, and fighter escorts. Suicide bombers were chaperoned to their target by Zeros whose duty it was to protect it from interceptors, and to also confirm success or failure of the mission. The escorting Zero essentially served as a shield for the suicide bomber until he made his death dive, so the pilots needed to be highly-skilled airmen. In general, escort pilots were older and more experienced than the Kamikaze pilots they provided cover for.

My first sortie was on April 4, 1945, in what was the fourth suicide attack mission of the Taigitai. A scout plane discovered the location of four enemy aircraft carriers, and we were given a directive to go for broke. My section consisted of two escort Zeros and two suicide bombers. My Zero was loaded with a 500-kg bomb.

We took off from Ishigakijima Airbase at 7:35am and flew toward the coordinates at 10-15 meters above the sea surface to avoid detection by enemy radar. If spotted at this height, there was no chance of escape from interceptors screaming down from above. Even with ample altitude we would still be seriously disadvantaged, but at least we had a chance to dive rapidly to evade machine-gun fire. This altitude meant, however, that evasive measures to the right or left would result in one of the wings dipping into the sea, and that would be catastrophic.

Adding to the precariousness of low flying was the inability to discard the bomb in case of emergency. We would blow ourselves up or be engulfed by the wall of water from the explosion. It was left to our own discretion whether to discard the bomb and fight or avoid engagement and return to base, thereby saving the machine for a dead cert mission. Shedding the bomb required climbing to 200 meters. In short, our only hope was to spot interceptors before they spotted us.

The Zero's altimeters were not very precise, so I kept a very wary eye on the sea surface. This didn't leave much leeway to survey the sky above as a split second of inattention could mean crashing into the briny deep. Flying above the flat blue surface was okay when conditions were fine, but it was a different story in stormy weather when the sea was choppy. Nothing was more frightening than surging waves spattering under the wings. I still have visions of the dark ocean with its white wave crests tickling my undercarriage.

The sea was not so rough on my first sortie, so I managed to keep a careful watch in front and above me. Before long, I saw some little black specks appear 15-degrees to the right, just above the horizon. The other pilots also noticed, so we communicated to each other with hand signals.

They looked to be cruising around 4,000 meters. I leaned forward into the windshield to keep tabs on the dots as I ascended. The specks became bigger, and convinced that they were enemy planes, I decided to engage them in a dogfight. I released the bomb and my Zero suddenly lifted up as if it was delighted to be free of the 500-kg ball and chain. I saw the other bomb-carrying Zero in my section suddenly rise as it also shed its debilitating load. Two bombs exploded in quick succession on the sea surface. I knew that this would give us away.

We climbed rapidly, levelling out every so often to confirm the enemy's position. Four Grumman F6Fs were coming right at us. They were flying around 6,000 meters while we were still only at 2,000 meters. The least I could do was avoid being shot at from above, so advanced directly at the Hellcat prepared to take fire from the front instead. Doing as I was taught in training, I charged the Hellcat so that my propellers would "bite into its guts." If the Hellcat disengaged from this game of chicken and showed me its underbelly, victory would be mine.

Still, the Hellcat was much faster and flying straight at me. I needed more speed, so pointed my nose down in a dive to increase my velocity. The Hellcat still managed to maneuver into the optimal shooting position behind of me. Sensing I was about to be blasted to smithereens, I pushed down hard on one side of my foot pedal while simultaneously pulling the center stick to opposite side as hard as I could. This caused my Zero to slide just as the Hellcat let rip with its machine guns. The spray of lead missed but it was a chillingly narrow escape.

The Hellcat came in for another crack. I have no memory of exactly what I did, but somehow succeeded in fending off the attacks. The aerial combat only lasted a few minutes, and I was left exhausted and separated from the other Zeros. Having been focused solely on surviving the engagement I had completely lost my bearings. I needed to return to base but couldn't be sure if I was flying into enemy territory instead.

I opened the flight map on my left thigh and placed the clipboard with my mission memo on the right. The higher you fly the more likely memory loss sets in, so writing information such as direction down on the memo pad was crucial in finding your way back home. Obviously, this was out of the question when the enemy was coming at you from all angles. I flew around for a while confirming there were no enemy planes, and then set about piecing together my whereabouts with the chart and memos. "Flew 135 degrees around here, engaged here, perhaps two loops at this point, then headed in this direction...." I calculated various points with my compass and made an educated guess, repeating "260 degrees" over to myself so that I didn't forget.

I spotted Miyakojima Island in front of me. I took off from Ishigaki-jima Island but decided to land there anyway. One of the escorts from my section had already arrived. I was informed later that the other suicide bomber had made an emergency landing on Ishigakijima, and his chaperone had made a safe return to base. Fortunately, all of us had survived the encounter. I returned to Miyakojima the same day and discovered that of the other eight Kamikaze pilots who sortied that day, one successfully smashed into a convoy ship.

Consecutive Sorties with Bombs

An American bomber was shot down over Ishigakijima. Among the belongings of a pilot who bailed out was a flight map showing the location of U.S. troop ships. With this information in hand we sortied early the next morning. At 7:20am, a suicide bomber and one escort Zero took off. Three more suicide bombers, including me, and two wingmen sortied shortly after. Our orders were to head to Hateruma Island south of Ishigakijima first, fly 110 degrees to the right for 150 kilometers, then turn to the right again for another 18 kilometers to search and destroy enemy ships.

With a 500-kg bomb under me, I embarked on what was the fifth Taigitai sortie. Almost immediately one of the Zeros had to return to base with engine trouble. Ten minutes later, team leader Lieutenant Takeuchi's engine cut out at 15 meters altitude. Flying to his left rear, I caught a glimpse of him desperately trying to restart the engine. His Zero disappeared into the ocean with hardly a splash.

I met Lieutenant Takeuchi's sisters at a memorial ceremony in Yasukuni Shrine 20 years after war. I told them the details of his demise as official reports always omitted the specifics. They had long been desperate to learn of the fate of their brother, and I hoped that they could find some closure.

Five Zeros became three in the blink of an eye. The second escort Zero flown by Superior Flight Petty Officer Hori took over Sub-lieutenant Takeuchi's role as section leader. The third escort Zero was piloted by my close friend Flight Petty Officer 1st Class Katsumi Kagawa. A few minutes into the flight we spotted a submarine periscope protruding out of the ocean. There was no doubt it was American, and Hori signaled to me with hand signs, "Yes, or no?" Although Zeros had radios to communicate with, they were almost useless. He was asking whether we should take out the submarine. I signaled him back. "No!" as did the other suicide bomber. Our target had to be a carrier, not a submarine. If I was going down, I was going to take a bigger prize with me.

The submarine noticed us and absconded swiftly into the depths leaving a trail of white bubbles. A colleague who went to the United States after the war came across a submarine report in a collection of wartime records. It said, "As we extended our periscope above the surface, we saw Japanese fighters heading straight for us. Had we been bombed we would not have lasted."

We continued flying along our scheduled route in search of a worthy target but came up empty, meaning a return to base to file a "Target not found" report. This was difficult to reconcile, nauseating in fact, as we had already psyched ourselves into a death frenzy.

It was raining hard in Ishigakijima and was too difficult to land, so we diverted to Hualien Airbase located on the east coast of Taiwan. I could see a large school of fish below and ditched my bomb for a safe landing. I asked one of the communications officers about the fate of the Zeros that sortied just before us. They hadn't returned. The Taigitai records state, "Missing after assailing enemy ships." Of seven Zeros that made the fifth Taigitai sortie that day, three did not return.

We were served a mountain of fish for breakfast the next morning. Apparently, our bombs stunned all the fish and they were gleefully scavenged off the beach by local fishermen. I didn't really have an appetite for fish at the time.

In the Barracks

The lights were dimmed in our quarters. Most nights we would sit around a candle and drink. Still young, we weren't exactly hardened drinkers, but the older guys did their best to spur us on. The alcohol lightened the mood and we bonded naturally making plans for our imminent demise together the following day.

Pilots were given a "flight provisions bag" every couple of days which contained a small bottle of rice wine, cigarettes, and some cakes with ingredients to suppress drowsiness. When rice wine and chow was in scarce supply, we would head to the kitchen to stock up. Someone told me to go and get more food. I made my way to the kitchen carrying my two handguns. My pockets were full of bullets bequeathed to me by dead brothers. I went into the kitchen. "Hey chief, how about some more grub." If the cook declined my request, I was going to shoot the ceiling with my revolvers to shake him up. Some of my buddies had already used this tactic to great effect. The cook grudgingly handed over some canned goods. As soon as the cans were opened in the candlelight, three or four pairs of chopsticks plunged greedily into the fare.

Verbal reports of who lived and who died became part of our daily routine. "Two teams sortied. One third came back to base." "Sixteen Zeros sortied today, six didn't make it." This tended to make us even more anxious to get it over with. "I want to follow them in a blaze of glory." Our standard conversation was "Who's going tomorrow?" To which somebody would reply with absolute detachment "That'd be me." We had become indifferent to matters of life and death. Our only concern was making the final moment count.

As we participated in our nightly drinking sessions, we learned who would never be joining us again. We'd say to each other "If you get there before me, wait under the cherry trees of Yasukuni Shrine." Or, "Be sure to fly the 205th Air Group's flag in Heaven while you wait for the rest of us." To be honest, none of us were particularly religious; it just seemed right to say we'd meet up again in the afterlife. We presumed that as we were being ordered to die for our country, at least we weren't destined for hell.

At the end of our drinking sessions we'd all sing. "In the capital of cherry blossoms, Yasukuni Shrine, let us bloom as cherry flowers and meet each other again." There were other Kamikaze specific songs that were sung as well. "To live or to die, we know it's farewell forever, but we take off with a smile as the engine roars." "One friend, and then another, we all perish as heroes; it's my greatest regret that I still breathe." "Beneath the palm tree, I cry alone. Friend, please know my mind is true." We did not sing loud, and we never got drunk. There was always an element of tension that prevented us from completely letting go.

A kind of divination game called "Kokkuri" was a popular pastime among us. Sitting in a circle in the dim candlelight we bound three chopsticks together with string and placed the bundle on the mat. We'd then attach a round lid on the chopsticks and spin it saying, "*Kokkuri, kokkuri,* tell me when I'll die." When it stopped moving and pointed at someone, it meant that tomorrow would be his day. Believing this was to be his grand finale, the usual response was along the lines of "I have a camera and cigarettes in my bag, so you take care of them." I didn't buy into this gloomy superstitious pastime, and I doubt if the others did. We just did it for fun because we didn't have cards or mahjong to fill in time.

Silence Before the Storm

Briefings were ways held before sorties. We'd analyze reconnaissance photos of shipping taken by scout planes and devised the most effective method of attack. The target area for each suicide bomber was decided in advance. "The first Zero should aim for the rear elevator of the carrier. The second, go for the front elevator...." The best crash areas were front and rear elevator shafts on the carrier's deck. These were used to bring fighters up for take-off, or to put them in storage in the hangar below deck. If the Zero could somehow dive into an elevator shaft, it could penetrate deeper into the ship and trigger a colossal explosion by setting off the munitions stowed below. It was the carrier's Achilles heel, and a direct hit would sink it in a matter of minutes. We were taught to identify the elevator by the vivid markings painted around the entrance.

With battleships the tactic was to fly straight down vertically into the chimney stacks. This required pinpoint accuracy but would allow the Zero to penetrate the engine room. The sides of battleships were fortified with thick armor plating and there was the added danger of numerous anti-aircraft machine guns. Failure to crash dive into the designated target, carrier or otherwise, was considered a matter of shame. In spite of our orders, however, all of us really only had our eyes on the carriers.

We were typically informed of assignments around 21:00 the night before. The officer in charge would come to our quarters. "The units to sortie tomorrow are as follows: First bomber is such-and-such, second bomber is so-and-so, escort such-and-such." Hearing their orders, assignees would reflexively mumble "Shit. It's me...." Although we were all prepared for the directive, it still felt like conferral of the death penalty and it was stomach-turning. Even if the alcohol was starting to kick in, this would sober you up straightaway.

"You go tomorrow. I'll probably follow you the next day...." This was the only thing those not assigned could say in consolation. When we heard the footsteps of an officer approaching our room, we would become silent. Nights before sorties were always tinged with melancholy. Those who received the ultimatum would sit in the middle of our circle ever so slightly illuminated by a flickering candle. Only the outlines of their faces were visible. We rarely spoke as we sipped our rice wine. Those whose names had been announced said nothing, and the others didn't have the heart to talk. We stayed like that until we dosed off. When my named was announced, I was no different.

Sometimes, someone would ask "Do you have any personal effects to take care of?" The reply would be "No." The atmosphere was that of a wake, and they continued every day. It's impossible to express in words how we really felt inside. We were all healthy young lads in our late teens who were doomed to die the following day, way before our time, but we were resigned to our fates. Eventually somebody would say, "Let's sleep. We need to be bright and ready for a good showing tomorrow lads." This was our signal to finish the wake and get some shuteye.

After the war, I read the memoirs written by other airmen who found it hard to sleep. I for one had no trouble sleeping, and I imagine that most of my Kamikaze comrades didn't either. Maybe it was because of the booze. I suspect that it was more to do with the fact that we were living as if we were already dead anyway. I was more afraid of being thought of as a coward and never showed any tears. This was normal. Those who had to sortie would board their planes in good spirits; almost, one could say, with expressions of relief etched on their faces.

Cherry Blossoms Scattering in the Wind

Enemy ships were spotted 60 nautical miles south of Miyakojima on the morning of May 4, 1945. The 17th Taigitai sortie departed with 21 bombers and only five escorts. Three teams flew different routes from Yilan Airbase in search of carriers. I was one of the bombers in the second team of four Zeros. We searched in vain, however, and were unsuccessful in locating a target. As we were returning to base, I picked up a Morse code message generated by one of the planes from the group that set off before us. "Chikato Kondo is about to dive." This was followed by another sequence of beeps declaring that Eiichi Hachimura was also about to crash dive into a carrier.

They departed only 20 minutes before us but found their line to glory. We heard later that Superior Flight Petty Officer Tadaatsu Tsunei smashed into and destroyed a carrier. Sub-lieutenant Itsuji Tanimoto and Flight Petty Officer 2nd Class Chikato Kondo successfully crashed into another carrier causing it to catch on fire. Details of their attack were recorded by Kazuo Tsunoda, one of the escort pilots.

"The enemy fleet came into view 45 degrees to the left. I realized that there were four major carriers accompanied by seven destroyers circling to the east. Tanimoto also saw the flotilla and banked his wings indicating that he was going in. He flew straight at the carrier from the front right. The enemy did not have time to react with anti-aircraft fire so Tanimoto was able to penetrate the middle of the deck. His 500-kg bomb exploded engulfing the hull in a ball of fire. Minutes later, the second Zero crashed into the rear of a middle-sized carrier. I flew in low behind the third and fourth Zeros to avoid the anti-aircraft fire. About two minutes later, I think it was the third Zero that smashed into the big carrier to my left rear resulting in an almighty explosion. I lost sight of the fourth but noticed another big explosion about a minute later through the smoke rising from the same carrier. I presumed that this was the fourth finding its mark."

As I departed the hostile zone and the threat of being chased lessened, I was suddenly overcome by sorrow. "Chikato's gone. He's really gone...." I was inconsolable. Chikato Kondo was a fellow "Cherry Blossom" from the Yokaren Special B-Class. We were together in Iwakuni, Nagoya, Oita, and then in the Storm Corps in Kasanohara. We had been through thick and thin together as many of our fellow cadets dropped out of the course. In the Philippines and then in the Taigitai, we had both survived by such narrow margins so many times. He was an honest man, and always obeyed orders without complaining. The brave souls who died in this Kamikaze mission were close buddies of mine. They were all great guys.

It seemed like we were chattering amongst ourselves or playing Japanese chess only moments before. Next minute, we're out on a sortie looking to go down in a ball of fire. This was the ephemeral existence of Kamikaze pilots. Nothing was said when the order to go was given. It was a simple matter of boarding our Zeros and flying into oblivion. So many of my friends died like this. Even now when I see their names on a list somewhere, the faces of each one appears before me exactly as they were in those cheery moments before jumping into our winged coffins. It could so easily have been me who was assigned that route instead of Chikato. It was all so random.

As I approached Ishigakijima, I could see the ground crews were frantically filling potholes on the runway. American bombers had raided our base just after we sortied. There was a small bulldozer available for this task and it was busy all day, every day. One of the ground crew directed me with hand signals toward suitable section for landing. My fuel gauge showed the tank was almost empty and I needed to land in a hurry. The landing was heavy and my Zero jolted violently as I touched down on the pockmarked surface.

Lives Already Sacrificed

We lost friends in every sortie. When any one of us somehow returned from a Kamikaze mission, the standard greeting became "Oh, you're still here." We sat in a circle to burn incense for the souls of our dead comrades and drank in their honor knowing that it was more than likely our turn the next day. It was rather odd how our hearts remained serene throughout these days of impending death. The dividing line between life and death had become blurred beyond comprehension. Oddly again, such feelings had a bizarre effect of elevating our mood. Although we were only 18 years old or so, we had come to realize, to some extent, the meaning of life and what it is to be human. Confronting our mortality every living moment enabled us to gain insights which gave us a sense of poise. I knew I would die in my Zero, and only wanted to get it over with and follow my buddies into the netherworld. I wasn't resentful; just resigned to the inevitable and determined to go as gracefully as I could.

We had been on the receiving end of many hidings by the Americans and knew that we were outdone. There was no way I would shoot down 80 American aircraft in the kind of dogfights Japanese pilots reveled in during the early days of the war. But, if I could dive into the elevator shaft of a carrier, then I could take out the ship, the 80 planes it carried, and its 4,000 crewmen. That, I thought, would be my life well spent.

I knew from the outset that my duty was service to my country and emperor. Notwithstanding, I never truly harbored lofty thoughts of "dying for Japan" each time I sortied. I suspect my buddies didn't either. We were all just reconciled to the fact that death was inexorable. We had an appointment with annihilation as it was our calling. My family and relatives were trying to get on with life back home, and if my sacrifice contributed to their wellbeing even in a small way, then there were no regrets. The only thing I desired was an honorable end to my life as an airman. As such, I did not leave a will and testament, nor did I write letters to my family. Few of us did.

Students drafted into Kamikaze missions from air bases in Kyushu, however, did write to their families. This is understandable. Student draftees, society's best and brightest, were forced into forgoing promising futures with a one-way ticket to a fiery grave. Despite their abysmal lack of training and experience, they were expected to immolate themselves on the lowest hanging fruit. We Yokaren pilots, on the other hand, were always prepared for death from the moment we chose our vocation. We were somehow able to come to accept it as our preordained life mission to crash dive into carriers for the sake of the war effort.

Student draftees were superior in rank than we NCOs because of their higher education. In one fleet, we would sometimes see as many as 20 student draftees wearing the uniform of Ensign or Sub-Lieutenant. Naval Academy graduates were treated completely different to student soldiers even if their rank was the same. They were reluctant to share authority with student draftees, and there was blatant discrimination in the crew quarters. I remember one student sub-lieutenant would come and shack up with us in the NCO barracks rather than cavort with his "equals" in the commissioned officer quarters. More student draftees were killed than Naval Academy graduates, but even more Yokaren graduates died than students. Although we were all on the same side and in the same fleet, elitism was prevalent and highly unpleasant.

The Devastation of Okinawa

I made another sortie on May 18 as a member of the 20th Taigitai mission. I was a bomber in a team of eight Zeros. There were two escorts and Sub-lieutenant Tsunoda was in charge. Our objective was to attack American ships in the seas south of Miyakojima. The weather turned bad soon after taking off, so we had to return to base. In middle of June, however, a decree came out of the blue to cease all Kamikaze missions. We had no idea why, but heard rumors that Okinawa was about to capitulate. This was clearly not good for Japan, but at least we could relax a little now that Kamikaze attacks were suspended.

I figured that with the fall of Okinawa the Americans would be moving their ships and troops there instead of around Ishigakijima and Miyakojima. We also figured that many would be returning to their homeland or to Australia for leave. We heard nothing about any attacks on Taiwan but that didn't mean we were out of harm's way. When the enemy did return, they would be fresh and have their tails up. We, on the other hand, were completely shattered.

The few Zeros that still survived were all damaged and covered in patches. Our bases were constantly under attack by B-29s coming from China, and they were clearly scouting Taiwan also. They flew at around 7,000 to 8,000 meters from where they dropped their payloads on us. The bombs were not so big at around 60 kg or so, but they released 100 to 150 on our heads each time. We monitored the flight direction of the B-29s to gauge whether we were in danger or not. If they came directly over us, we knew it was okay because the bombs would fall on angle and miss. It was a different story if they let go 30 or 40 degrees before us. Still, nothing was certain. When I was in Yilan one time, bombs suddenly fell out of nowhere. I leapt into a shelter just as one exploded 30 meters away. Another close shave.

In Yilan we concealed our precious Zeros in a small village located about 400 meters from the base. We rolled them into the village and covered them with foliage or carpet as camouflage. The Americans refrained from targeting planes hidden in villages to mitigate collateral damage to the inhabitants. They probably realized that destroying airstrips would suffice and knew that we had virtually no operational Zeros to worry about anyway.

We took the Zeros we did have out on patrol every so often, and even did combat training to keep our skills honed. The problem was that high-quality fuel was now unobtainable and we had to make do with low purity gasoline. This meant the engines lacked power and would sometimes cut out completely. Intercepting and chasing enemy fighters was not an option.

Dance of the Fireflies

The temporary cessation of Kamikaze missions soon came to an end. I was assigned to the 24th Taigitai mission organized a few days before August 15, 1945. Our orders were to carry out a suicide attack on enemy shipping around Okinawa with all available operational planes. It had been almost two months since our last Kamikaze sortie in the middle of June. To be honest, the suddenness of the order was flabbergasting. Stranger still was the fact that there was no information indicating carriers were in the region. Nothing seemed right.

In any case, intuition told me that my time had come for sure. I was in Taichung at the time, and we were ordered to relocate to Yilan the next day for our final sortie. Four of us went to a tavern in a small village near the base. We walked through the rice fields on the south side of the barracks carefully negotiating the narrow paths. As darkness consumed the landscape, we saw masses of fireflies flitting over the rice plants. There were so many that they crash dived into our bodies and faces as if to repel intruders trespassing their domain. The fireflies were much smaller than the variety we were used to in Japan. "They must be rice-bran fireflies" somebody observed. The fireflies that swooped through the air in my home village of Kotesashi were much bigger. I had a flashback of how I used to catch them in my childhood. The swarm of fireflies that appeared before us that night was something to behold. "There are so many," I thought, "but I will never see them again." We could make out faint blue and white streaks as they flitted haphazardly before us. The life of firefly is short. I felt a close connection with them.

There was only one drinking hole in the village. We took the room in the back and sat on the straw mats. We opened the window and gazed at the wild dancing of the fireflies while sipping rice wine from our cups. We didn't talk much. Although we had been drinking most days, the *sake* that night tasted particularly good. I said to the fireflies, "Hey, come on in and join us!" Some of them really did. "Farewell to you fireflies, for tomorrow I will not be of this world."

I remember downing one big bottle of *sake* that night, but we were not overly intoxicated. We kept drinking until 2 or 3 in the morning then walked back to base as we sang Kamikaze attack songs, legs slightly unsteady as we stumbled through the paddies. It was the first and last time I have ever seen fireflies dancing the way they did that night. Morning came, and we flew to Yilan ready to die.

August 15, 1945

The established objective for Taigitai sorties was to pummel the U.S. fleet, especially targeting big prizes like carriers if at all possible. We were usually not encouraged to dive into convoy ships, even if they were sitting ducks in the ocean below. This time, however, we were ordered on a one-way sortie to do as much damage as possible to anything that took our fancy. All of us had bombs strapped to our bellies, and there were no escorts. Our order was simple: Die. Every single remaining Zero in Taiwan gathered in Yilan and some transferred from there to Ishigakijima in preparation for a massive concerted attack scheduled for August 13. I was ready to die and had no doubts in my mind that this would be the end.

The sortie on August 13 was postponed because of the weather. The next day we received new orders to sortie on August 15 and were briefed of the formations in which we would fly. To our surprise, the leader of our squadron, a graduate of the Naval Academy, was to lead us in the first Zero even though he had never been rostered before. It was all very bizarre.

Attacks by U.S. bombers had ceased, and something was very amiss. Some airmen complained there was no way decent targets can be located without intelligence on the enemy's whereabouts. "Do they really expect us to dive into convoy ships?" "They're taking the piss!" We were all prepared to die if ordered to do so, but now I was supposed to compromise the value of my final moments on this earth by scraping the bottom of the barrel. If that was the way it was going to be, then I'd just have to smash into the biggest convoy ship I could find.

August 15 came. It was scorching weather shortly before noon. The green body of my Zero was so hot to the touch that it burned my finger. One pilot boarded his Zero wearing a light shirt intending to put on his flight uniform after reaching altitude. Others didn't even both wearing their flight caps.

Although the order was for all available Zeros to make this last ditched one-way sortie, there was only a paltry 30 machines altogether. When the Taigitai was first formed there were about 150 Zeros, but many were destroyed in air raids. I boarded my Zero with a feeling of frustration and futility as I am sure the others did, like carp on a cutting board.

A flimsy tent was erected beside the runway as a command post. Officers and maintenance crew lined up next to the tent to bid us farewell although I don't remember seeing any high-ranking officers. The grassy runway was parallel to the coastline and was only 1,000 meters long. The width of the runway was about 70-80 meters. The surface was cratered from bombing raids. Maintenance did their best to smooth the surface, but it was going to be exceedingly difficult to get air born with 500-kg bombs. We were to take off to the south with the beautiful Pacific Ocean glistening to our left.

About thirty Zeros were going to depart in teams of four. I was in the front line piloting the third Zero of the first section. I took my position to the left rear of the leader. The raucous whirring of engines pounded our ears and blew dust into the air. The leader signaled departure by opening his hands to each side to which the ground crews removed the stoppers wedged under the tires. The first Zero started to crawl forward.

Taking this as my cue, I released the throttle and my Zero lurched into motion. At that very moment I noticed a vehicle hurtling toward us. A soldier in the car seemed to be shouting, not that he could be heard over the howling engines. He made a big cross with his arms. Perplexed at the sudden intrusion, I stopped my Zero just behind the leader's. "Abort attack!" The vehicle slid to a halt in front of the principal Zero to block its path. A mechanic jumped onto my wing and told me that the mission had been cancelled.

We were ordered back to the command post so we jumped in the truck. We had no idea what was happening but were notified in the commotion that an important radio broadcast was due to start any minute. The reception was poor, and it was barely audible, but there was no mistaking the blue-blooded voice of the emperor emanating from the crackling speakers. Japan had accepted total surrender. I heard somebody murmur, "Ahh.... It's over...." We were dumbstruck at first, and then, as if to confirm that we had heard the announcement correctly, asked each other if the war was really over. "Does that mean that we don't need to fly Zeros again?"

I initially thought that the war had "ended," rather than Japan had been "defeated." It also hit me that my life had, for some reason, been spared. I would live to see another day after all. Before long, however, various doubts began to cloud my mind. "What the hell would happen to Japan?" "What's going to happen to me?" "I can't get back in my Zero, so I suppose I'd better get out of my uniform. But, then what?" "Can I go home?" I was confused. Adding to my agitation was the fact that we were stopped as we were coasting down the runway. Had the vehicle come even a minute later, I would not be alive to relay this story.

It was in October 1944 when I "volunteered" as Kamikaze pilot. Ten or so months had past, and I had already turned 18. It felt as though I had awoken from a bad dream. When the dust settled, we were instructed to return to our fleet and flew from Yilan to Taichung. This time, instead of preparing to meet our deaths in a blaze of glory, it felt like we were taking a leisurely sightseeing excursion.

The Taigitai's Last Hoorah

A formal Taigitai report outlined what happened in the lead up to this fateful moment:

"On August 13, an order was issued for a one-way Kamikaze sortie to destroy enemy shipping around the main island of Okinawa. In accordance with this ultimatum, all Taigitai airmen were marshalled and put on standby, some in Ishigakijima and the rest at Yilan Airbase. The sortie was suspended, however, as scout planes were unable to locate the enemy, and because the weather was deteriorating.... Although Commander Tamai ordered sorties until this time to obtain more leverage for negotiating conditions of surrender, he was doubtful if Kamikaze missions would have any import after Japan assented to the Potsdam Declaration. Tamai was pressured by his superiors to deploy the Taigitai on August 15. Just before the mission commenced, the Emperor's announcement of surrender was broadcast and the order was revoked."

It has been noted that in the final days of the war Japan's leaders adopted a strategy referred to as "One more attack, then negotiation." This was to elevate Japan to a better position to parley terms with the Allies by showing that they still had much to lose. The fundamental flaw with this strategy was that Japan had not the means to make any substantial offensive operations. The adoption of this tactic was subsequently criticized as delaying the peace process and causing unwarranted suffering and hardship. Ordering Kamikaze suicide missions was an act of absolute futility, but those responsible for persevering with this approach have never been brought to task.

As for the Taigitai, from the first suicide mission on April 1 through to the last successful one (23rd mission) on June 22, a total of 245 Zeros sortied resulting in the deaths of 46 pilots. Of the casualties, 76 percent were Yokaren graduates. The rest were student draftees. Furthermore, 88 percent of the suicide bombers were airmen of low rank.

In terms of the damage caused to Allied shipping, three vessels were destroyed (one small carrier, two convoy ships), 10 sustained heavy damage (four large carriers, four middle-sized carriers, one small carrier, and one destroyer), and over ten aircraft were shot down.

The Order of Nightmares

Even now, I still have bad dreams about that final order to sortie. I cannot reconcile what it was all for. Why were we, a squadron specially organized to attack U.S. carriers, told to attack convoy ships anchored off the sea of Okinawa? Nobody has been able to answer this.

I suspect that Tamai knew Japan was going to accept the Potsdam Declaration before August 14.[29] Yet, he still ordered all his airmen to use the remaining operational planes in a last ditched assault on convoy ships. I believe that Tamai and the other brass cared little about our lives. Why could the terms of surrender not be concluded with Kamikaze still pilots alive? Was it their intention to inform the Americans that all Kamikaze suicide bombers had perished? My gut tells me that this was the motivation for sending us to our deaths. Otherwise, I cannot comprehend why we were dispatched to destroy such trivial targets.

I don't know who decided to send us to our graves without escorts. I want to believe that our superiors were in the fight with us, if not in body then at least in spirit, and would not sacrifice us lightly if there was any other way. We talked amongst ourselves conjecturing that this heartless

---

[29] On the evening of August 10, 1945, a broadcast by NHK (Japan Public Broadcasting Corporation) delivered news to the world that Japan's Ministry of Foreign Affairs had agreed to the terms and conditions of the Potsdam Declaration. Enraged Army and Navy officers stationed outside Japan pressured NHK to suspend further transmissions. Notwithstanding, word was out, and it is highly likely that chiefs in Taiwan, including Tamai, knew of or even heard the NHK broadcast.

mandate must have come from the Combined Fleet HQ in Tokyo rather than those directly above us. My fury over this unconscionable directive has never abated.

Saved by Radio Waves?

There was a huge difference in radio technology between Japan and the Allies. Often, we would fly into an area where sightings of enemy shipping were reported only to find there was nothing there. If they had been there, by the time we reached the area they had already moved out of range. On other occasions we encountered enemy fighters even though scout planes reported that the skies were clear. I figured that the Americans were keeping tabs on our movements by radar or with their submarines as we were taking off. They always seemed to be a step ahead.

Our air bases also had radar equipment. I had seen them in use once but the scrawling white lines on the monitor were impossible to make head or tail of. The operator told me that Japanese radars were practically useless. I sensed that Japan was lagging way behind the Allies not only in naval and air superiority, but also with its radio technology. Ironically, this may have been a factor that allowed me to survive the war.

Saitama's Distinguished "Trio of Birds"

There were three cadets in the Yokaren B-Class referred to by everyone as the "Three Birds of Saitama."[30] The three were Kinzo Kasuya, Hiroshi Toyoda, and me. Kasuya was the eldest son of prominent farming family. Toyoda was the second son of fish monger. Both had excellent grades at school, and Toyoda was head boy of his class. The three of us took the Yokaren entrance examination together, and became close friends prepared to die together as "Cherry Blossom" brothers.

Both Kasuya and Toyoda were killed in the war. I was the only one left of the trio. Toyoda was posted from Iwakuni to Borneo where he undertook combat training. Fuel supplies were dwindling at the time so some Yokaren graduates were sent overseas where there were enough fuel reserves to train. In the middle of October 1944, shortly after my arrival in

---

[30] "Three Birds" is a common Japanese idiom used to express three outstanding people who excel in a given field.

Clark Field, I heard Zeros coming into land one evening. I went out to see who it was. A few airmen alighted their planes and among them was Toyoda. "Hey there Toyoda!" "Hi Kazu!" It was a happy reunion as we had not seen each other since Iwakuni.

Happy though it was, the get-together was short lived. I visited his barracks the following morning to catch up, but he had already gone. I never heard anything from or about him after this chance meeting but assumed that he was alive and well somewhere. It was not until a few years after the war when I learned of Toyoda's death. It seems that he had flown to Manila that morning. From there he sortied as a Kamikaze suicide bomber, but the base was destroyed in an American raid shortly after his departure so there were no details of what happened to him. I assume he was triumphant.[31] His two-rank posthumous promotion suggests this was the case. Those killed in action were usually promoted one rank. Those who died with distinction, such as Kamikaze pilots, were promoted two ranks.

Kasuya sortied from a base in Kyushu in a Shidenkai[32] and smashed his aircraft into a B-29 in May 1945. I heard afterwards that he intercepted a formation of B-29s heading home after a bombing run. Kasuya dove into a B-29 above Takeda city in Oita Prefecture. The B-29 crashed but the crewmen bailed out with parachutes. Kasuya somehow managed to exit his plane but his parachute failed to open, and he fell to his death on property owned by the Kuboyama family. A daughter of the family saw him falling from the sky and ran out to help but he was dead on impact. I believe he was awarded two ranks posthumously. In 1980, Mr. Kuboyama erected a stone monument for him. A memorial ceremony was held in which former American soldiers also attended. Unfortunately, I was unable to go.

---

[31] According to records, Toyoda sortied in February 1945 as a member the of Kinshitai Kamikaze Attack Unit. They took off from Manila Angeles Airbase. It is recorded that his place of death was "in the skies of Manila" while combatting a B-24.

[32] The Kawanishi N1K Shidenkai (allied reporting name "Rex") was first produced in January 1945. It was not a carrier-based plane like the Zero but designed as a Naval land-based fighter. As the Zero lost its combat advantage and numbers had been decimated along with Japanese carriers in battles in the Pacific, the Imperial Japanese Navy needed to develop strong ground-based fighter to intercept American airplanes attacking the mainland. The Shidenkai was bigger and more powerful than the Zero and engaged in ferocious combat missions against American planes above mainland Japan in the final stages of the war.

Monument Inscription

Late in the spring of 1945 in the last stages of war, as the battles in Okinawa raged, major cities in the mainland were constantly being blitzed by American bombers. The war situation had become desperate and the Japanese were preparing for the impending invasion and death in the defense of the motherland.

On the morning on May 5, a fine day, a formation of B-29s which had completed a bombing run on cities in northern Kyushu appeared in the sky overhead. A Japanese fighter plane from Omura Airbase in Nagasaki intercepted and dove into a B-29 at full speed. It was a brave and bold move. The silver wings of the B-29 folded as it erupted in fire and crashed into this hill.

The Japanese fighter also crashed in a deep valley. The aircraft was a Shidenkai, one of the finest in the Imperial Japanese Navy. The pilot was a young man of 19 named Kasuya. His remains are enshrined in the village hall. He hailed from Migashima village (present day Tokorozawa City) Iruma County, in Saitama Prefecture. His soul rests to this day in the valley. Thirty years passed when we decided to erect this monument in memory of his sacrifice to our nation's future. His precious life is a rock in its foundation.

March 1980

An earlier monument was erected near the resting place of the B-29. The inscription reads as follows:

In May 1945, Japan looked close to losing the war and her people were undergoing severe hardship. The mainland was bombed incessantly by B-29s, and the battles taking place in Okinawa looked to be utterly hopeless for the Japanese. One hundred million Japanese people prepared to defend the country with their lives. A little after 8am on May 5, 1945, a Japanese fighter plane chased a formation of B-29s returning from an attack on Tachiarai Airbase in the outskirts of Kurume City. It battled ferociously in the skies above Naoiri County in Oita Prefecture (this area), and crash dived into a B-29. The B-29 exploded in a ball of fire and plummeted to the ground. The Japanese fighter fell from the sky and the airman, a young Navy pilot, was found dead with a letter to his mother in his chest pocket. Twelve American crewmen bailed out of the bomber and landed safely with their parachutes. They were subjected to violent abuse by enraged villagers, and some of the airmen were killed. Eight more died in human experiments conducted at the Imperial University of Kyushu. We think back on this tragedy of 33 years ago, and the dreadful fates of these men still weigh heavily on our haunted consciences. Here, we erect this monument and remember them in a ceremony that transcends emotions of affinity and enmity. We pray for the souls of all the deceased and dedicate this monument to their memory in the deep felt hope that such a tragedy never be repeated.

May 5, 1977

Kasuya and Toyoda were both cheerful, nice lads. Seven or eight of us visited Toyoda's house and grave after the war. I heard Kasuya's older sister took over the family household following his death, but I felt hesitant to visit out of a sense of guilt. We did not think Japan would lose the war when we entered the Yokaren. As the situation deteriorated and the fighting became desperate, we all managed the adversity with grace and dignity. The war brought the best out in us, but it was truly heart breaking for we who happened to survive. We vowed to perish together with our brothers.

Shortly after the war, I arranged an annual memorial ceremony for the 205th Air Group veterans. Each year for 30 years we met and stayed at a hotel near the Yasukuni Shrine where we drank and talked until dawn. It was through these reunions that I learned what happened to my two wonderful friends, Toyoda and Kasuya.

I also sortied many times with Katsumi Kagawa. He was with me in the 5th Taigitai mission when we signaled to each other to forgo crash diving into the submarine. We boarded the same train from Kagoshima to return home following repatriation after the war. He lived in Hiroshima, so would stay at my house after our yearly reunions before making the long trip back by train.

I had an opportunity to go to Hiroshima on Metropolitan Police business in 1971. I suggested that we meet up. He was married and driving taxis then. We stayed up till late and talked for hours, but hardly ever mentioned the war. We mostly chatted about news of mutual friends. Some things that were just too painful to revisit, and we still embraced a simmering rage about what went on at the end of it all.

Those who attended the 205th Air Group reunions were mainly Yo-karen graduates and some student draftees. Chikanori Monji, author of *Sora to Umi no Hatede (Beyond the Ends of the Sky and Sea)*[33] was a student draftee and secretary to Vice-Admiral Ohnishi, Commander-in-Chief of No.1 Fleet. He attended without fail every year.

Of our superior officers from those dark days Vice-Admiral Ohnishi committed suicide by *seppuku* to take responsibility. I think that he was indeed responsible. It was he who ordered us to sacrifice our lives. I heard that he said to those close to him "I too, am no longer alive." He killed himself the day after surrender.

As for Tamai, Commander of the 205th Air Group, instead of killing himself to atone, he took up the tonsure and became a Buddhist priest. He dedicated the rest of his life to placating the souls of his dead men.

I think their decisions show a stark difference in life philosophy and conscience. Some of our superiors sent young men to their deaths saying "You go first! I will follow!" Many of them did not follow through. I wonder how most of them lived with themselves after the war.

Kamikaze Casualties

Kamikaze suicide attacks met with some degree of success around the beginning in October 1944. Both the Navy and Army utilized this tactic continually at the front in the Philippines. At the battles in Okinawa, many suicide planes took off from bases in Kyushu and Taiwan to target Allied troopships. Not limited to Zeros, almost all Navy and Army aircraft were used for Kamikaze attacks. In the final stages of hostilities, even canvas covered training planes were commandeered. Most, however, were shot down by intercepting fighters before reaching enemy ships. Those which managed to evade interceptors were often shot down by high-performance anti-aircraft machine-guns on the ships. Nevertheless, it has been estimated that around 11 percent (another source claims 16 percent) of Kamikaze airmen successfully reached their intended targets.

---

[33] This book is Monji's wartime memoir. He served Vice-Admiral Ohnishi throughout his tour of the Philippines, and he describes in careful detail the initiation of the Kamikaze Suicide Attack Corps led by Ohnishi. It is one of the fairest and more reliable records concerning the Kamikaze.

It is true that the Kamikaze caused more damage than conventional attacks. Approximately 3600 Army and Navy aircraft were used in Kamikaze attacks in the ten months from October 1944 to August 1945. There is varying data concerning the number of Kamikaze casualties. One official document recognizes the names of all those who perished in Kamikaze attacks: 2,517 Navy and 1,440 Army personnel, making 3,957 in total.

As for the damage caused by Kamikaze missions, 34 ships were sunk with around 300 sustaining damage. Among those sunk, 3 were escorting carriers, 13 were destroyers, and 18 other types of vessel. The 300 that were damaged included 16 regular carriers, 20 escorting carriers, 15 battleships, 15 cruisers, and 101 destroyers.

The Navy already started developing various weapons for suicide missions before the commencement of Zero Kamikaze attacks. Among them, Ouka was a kind of single-man rocket carried to its target by a Type-1 Ground Attacker. The Ouka was released when approaching the target and hurtled into the enemy ship. The Kaiten was a small one-man submarine with a warhead located at the front. It was transported by a destroyer and fired at the enemy, which is why it was called "Human torpedo." The Shinyo was a small motorboat loaded with explosives that was driven into enemy shipping. All of these weapons were deployed in battle, and more were in the process of being developed when the war came to an end.

According to American sources, suicide missions did succeed in delaying the U.S. advance in the Philippines and Okinawa. Prominent Japanese novelist Shohei Ohoka (1909 – 88), who himself was drafted into the Army and served in the Philippines, published a famous book titled *War Chronicle of Leyte* (1974). In it he writes the following:

"Although it was touted that Japanese victory was imminent, by this stage of the war none of the commissioned officers believed it. They were strung along by the illusion that even one more victory would benefit Japan's position in the peace negotiations. They acted to save face and concealed their true objective with the guise of 'strategy.' More abhorrent was sending young men to needless deaths in Kamikaze suicide operations all in the name of 'eternal Justice.'

Nevertheless, of the more than 400 who sortied from the Philippines, and more than 1,900 in Okinawa, 111 missions were successful in the former, and 133 in the latter. Almost the same number met with partial success. The suicide pilots were men of whom Japan should be proud. Enduring mental anguish and distress that falls beyond our powers of imagination, they were able to see their missions through to their fatal conclusion. Their feats should not be equated with the insanity and corruption of Japan's war leaders. The strength of will these young men embodied seems to be lacking in the youth of today as it could only have emanated from the desolation of war. Such a demonstration of willpower should offer Japanese a sense of hope."

By the day Japan surrendered, about 2,300,000 soldiers from the Imperial Japanese Navy and Army were killed in action or had died of disease and starvation. In addition, approximately 800,000 citizens perished in the merciless bombing of Japanese cities. In total it is estimated that 3,100,000 Japanese died in the war.

CHAPTER SIX

Return to Japan

From Zeros to Nothing

We heard all manner of news after returning to Taichung following the cancellation of the last sortie. There wasn't much of a mood for resistance even though we knew of some diehards who stubbornly opposed surrender. We heard that Chinese troops under Chiang Kai-shek were coming to occupy Taichung. The remaining Zeros were to be handed over to the Chinese Army. Their soldiers wore what looked like laborer's clothes with bamboo hats. They carried long poles on their shoulders from which wicker baskets were slung to transport personal effects. We were quite taken aback by their casual appearance.

The commander in charge of Japanese disarmament was a Lieutenant-General in the Chinese Army, a graduate of Japan's Army War College. We repaired the damaged planes and surrendered them as ordered. Upon taking possession of the remaining Japanese aircraft, they asked us ever so politely how to fly the machines. We taught them basic techniques for taking off and landing. The Chinese soldiers were strangely courteous, even referring to us as "honorable teachers."

The Allure of Taiwan

After surrendering all the Zeros, we were directed to a village in the east of Taichung. It was located at about 500 meters above sea level, and close to the entrance of a mountain range that extended the length of Taiwan. The village itself was about 2 kilometers long from east to west, and several hundred meters wide. There were rice fields aplenty making for lush green scenery. The village mayor built three straw-thatched houses for us. Each was about 3 to 4 meters wide, and 12 to 14 meters in length. We settled into the huts and began farming chores under the villagers' guidance. They were very kind and came every day to teach us how to use and repair the tools.

It was a completely different world to what we had experienced in the Kamikaze Corps. As the days went by the dreaded feeling of imminent death started to dissipate. We worked the fields in bare feet and it almost felt as if we had been transported back to our childhood days. Our main tasks involved cropping sugar cane and cultivating vegetables. It was the middle of September and stiflingly hot. We were always caked in mud and sweat, and our faces were tanned dark brown.

By November, the vegetables were ready for harvest. Even though Taiwan was much smaller than Japan, the climate was always warm which meant crops would reach maturity faster and could be reaped a few times each year. Not as much land was needed to sustain the population compared to Japan. It has very high mountains where even apples could be grown. Every kind of fruit found in Japan could be cultivated there. Taiwan truly was a wonderful place to live.

In the evenings, villagers came by our huts to chat with us. The adults and children all spoke Japanese to varying degrees. On rainy days, a former student draftee who specialized in Chinese at college in Japan taught us the rudiments of the language. Our interaction with the villagers was going so well, we began to think about a future there. We discussed amongst ourselves our fears of being arrested or even executed by the Americans if we returned to Japan. We were anxious about what the future had in store for us.

The village mayor suggested that we stay put. He even offered us land and promised to find us wives. He was rather plump man and could speak a little Japanese. "We can harvest rice twice, and vegetables four times a year. You don't even need to work here. Life's easy. If you go back to Japan, you'll not be treated well, so stay with us." He was unbridled in his enthusiasm to keep us in the village. I guess he thought that if we married local girls, it would bring vitality to the village and change the mood there.

We had no inkling of what was happening back in Japan and discussed his offer almost every night. In the end, 15 or 16 of our group decided to accept. I was one of them and was quite happy to spend the rest of my days there. In the middle of December, however, American troops came to the village with an ultimatum to repatriate to Japan. The mayor was quite disappointed, and we felt bad for him.

The Return to Kagoshima by Boat

In late December 1945, we were moved to Keelung port to board a Japan-bound ship. We bid the good villagers farewell having cherished the pleasant experience living among them. Preparation for return was a hasty affair, and before we knew it, we were waiting at the quay in Keelung among rows of warehouses. There were 40 of us gathered there. Most were Zero pilots with a few maintenance crewmen. For some reason, I remember melted sugar falling into sea from one of the warehouses. We were subjected to body searches, and handguns and other items deemed unsuitable were confiscated. I managed to hide the short sword awarded to me by the Commander in Chief of the Combined Fleet.

We boarded a U.S. Navy coastal defense ship and informed we were bound for Kagoshima. We were told in advance that we'd be boarding a Japanese ship, so this sudden change made us nervous. I was afraid that we'd be taken to America instead of Japan, and someone even suggested that we'd be executed and our bodies chucked into the Pacific. Most of us were having second thoughts about boarding, but reluctantly we did.

It soon became dark and the sea was rough. The further out to sea we went, the more blustery it became. The vessel itself was not big at around 1,000 tons so it rolled violently in the storm. Some of the waves were twice the height of the ship, and they smashed us sideways into the ocean. We all got horribly seasick and vomited nonstop.

We weren't keen to have anything to do with the American crewmen. It was the first time we ever had direct contact with our former enemies. We hated them. They kept their distance from us as well, probably thinking that we were unstable maniacs. The whole idea of Kamikaze suicide attacks was such an absurd concept to them, they must have reckoned us to be a bunch of insane freaks who despised life.

The ocean became beautifully calm after the second or third day. When I was looking out to sea from the deck, I could make out the shape of a cone-shaped mountain on the horizon. It had to be Mount Kaimon.[34] I saw it almost every day when I was a Yokaren cadet at Kasanohara Airbase in Kagoshima. The others also saw it and all let out hoots of delight. "Japan! It's really Japan!"

The city of Kagoshima had been burnt to the ground in relentless air raids. We assembled in a classroom of some elementary school

---

[34] Mount Kaimon (924 meters above sea level) is a beautiful mountain located on the southern edge of Satsuma peninsula in Kagoshima Prefecture. Its shape resembles Mount Fuji which is why it is referred to as "Satsuma-Fuji" (See photos)

left barely intact. An American officer told us that we were to return to our hometowns immediately and find jobs. "If you turn into drifters and don't find work," he admonished, "you'll be locked up." I knew nothing about America's new role in Japan as I had no access to newspapers or the radio, but I thought he was over the top considering the war had ended.

They made us write down our final destinations. A Japanese official gave me a train ticket and told me to disembark at Tokyo Station. Some of the Japanese officials sported civvies and others wore their old military uniforms. Everything went smoothly in the end, and despite my annoyance with the American officer, I understood that we were being treated with special consideration.

We stayed a night in Kagoshima and then boarded the train for Tokyo at 7:00 the next morning. Kagawa-san, with whom I had sortied many times, got off at Hiroshima. We were aware that Hiroshima had been obliterated by an "atomic bomb." I stuck my head out the window and looked at the charred ruins of the city. We had already passed through burned cities and towns after departing Kagoshima but Hiroshima was something else. In the other towns I saw half-burned buildings and a few houses still standing. But Hiroshima was flat for as far as the eye could see. It was the most dreadful sight. I asked Kagawa-san if he had any place to go to. He replied "I don't know. I'll have to go and see what I can find." I was worried about him. All I could say was "Well, be seeing you someday." Hiroshima impressed upon me that the war really was over.

Leaving Hiroshima behind us, we started talking about how we were supposed to pick up from here. Somebody mentioned that we'd have to make our own way from now. We were all still young and had always been part of a close-knit group, but now we were going to be alone for the first time in our lives—a strangely worrying prospect. My priority was to get home and find a job lest I be interned by the Americans for being a "drifter." Everybody felt the same, but the chances of finding gainful employment in the confines of our hometowns was surely going to be slim. Born the second son, taking over the family farm was out of the question for me. I just couldn't see what I could possibly do.

Kazuo Tsunoda was on the same train to Tokyo. He was eight years my senior and an excellent pilot. He married when the war ended but was forbidden from taking employment in public office due to the GHQ

"Purge." He fell on hard times for quite a while after the war, as many of us did.

New Year's Eve Homecoming

The train arrived at Tokyo Station at 7 or 8 on New Year's Eve, 1945. I transferred lines and got off at Nishi-Tokorozawa Station, the very place I received my grand send off to the Yokaren two years and eight months before. I dropped in to see a close friend who lived near the station. He and his family were sitting around a *kotatsu*[35] chitchatting when I entered. "Hey!" He looked at me in utter disbelief. "You're alive!" They served me a cup of tea, but I excused myself because my clothes were teeming with lice. I didn't want to infest the *tatami*.

They warned me that an Occupation soldier might arrest me given my appearance, and lent me a bicycle to get home. They were referring to my flying uniform. I jumped on the bike and peddled as fast as I could down the dark roads with no lamp to light the way. I saw car headlights coming from the opposite direction so immediately leapt off my bike and hid. An American jeep passed by without noticing me. I was lucky. It might have been troublesome had they seen me.

It was a little after 10pm when I arrived home. "Hi, I'm back" I announced in a loud voice. Relatives happened to be visiting. They were stunned and rushed to me. "It's Kazu-san!" I stopped short of entering the room because of my foul-smelling, louse-ridden clothes. My mother couldn't stop staring at me. She was lost for words, and then tears began to fall from her eyes. The last contact I had with my family was ten months ago. I sent a postcard home when I returned to Japan to pick up the new Zeros. My family had no idea what fate had befallen me after that, or whether I was even alive.

I turned 19 that month. Two years and eight months has passed since I left to enter the Yokaren. It all seemed surreal. Mother asked me why I wouldn't come inside. "I am covered in lice, and haven't bathed for ages...." Although it was very cold, I stripped naked in the garden and then went inside to take a bath. Soaking in the tub, I talked for a long time with mother who was busy stacking firewood next to the stove. I

---

[35] A *kotatsu* is a low, wooden table frame covered with heavy blanket and a table top placed over it with a heat source underneath.

don't remember what we talked about, but I avoided the subject of the war entirely. Mother boiled my clothes the next day to kill the lice.

I sat near the warm sunken hearth after my bath. I finally felt at home. I took out the short sword I received from the fleet commander and threw it on the fire, thinking "I don't need you anymore." Two days later, a local policeman visited to our house. "You've brought back something dangerous from the war, have you not?" "Oh yes, here it is," I replied and handed him a burned clump of steel.

CHAPTER SEVEN

Metropolitan Police

The Postwar Blues

I slept for most of New Year's Day. In the afternoon I could hear voices coming from outside. People heard that I had returned and were coming to see for themselves. A relative who lived next door, a former professor at Tenri University, came and said in genuine disbelief, "Kazu-san, you really came back?!"

As I lay in my *futon*, I figured that the best plan of action was to wait until things had settled down before looking for a job. Although we were told by the Americans to find work forthwith, Japanese society was in such a discombobulated state that it was not really an option. Before long, my old classmates dropped in to see me as well. I asked them what they were doing. Most had been employed in some capacity in the arms industry, but the companies had closed shop and they were left jobless.

I had no idea what I wanted to do. For a start, I was oblivious to how much Japan had changed while I was away fighting. At least I had some savings to fall back on as there was nowhere to spend my pay at the front. Money was not an issue for the time being, so I squandered my days doing pretty much nothing at all. Most of my friends were unemployed, barely managing to eke out a living by selling household items, helping neighbors with chores and the like. Some of them were making money under the table by acquiring and selling goods on the black market. They would deal in pilfered factory or military equipment, and some stole crops to sell. These were destitute times, and Japan was verging on the state of collapse.

I began to resent this state of affairs. I was prepared to forgo my life for the good of the country and was disenchanted to see how truly crestfallen Japan was. The more I thought about the sacrifices Kamikaze pilots had made the more incensed I became. My brothers died to protect their families and the nation, but their gallant martyrdom had been forgotten as people busied themselves trying to get their hands on a bit of food here, and some extra cash there.

Defeat and Utter Despair

I was no exception. Frittering my days away, I started to think that subsisting like a bum was okay as long as I didn't bother others. It was hard to be upbeat, but deep down I knew that this attitude was wrong. I needed to get back on my feet and appease the souls of my dead brothers. They didn't make the ultimate sacrifice so that Japan could turn to shit. I certainly didn't go around advertising this belief but knew that I had to find a way to inject some positivity in people around me. Anything would do. To this end, I decided to revive the Kagura performance at the local shrine.[36]

Cheering Up the Community

The Kitano Tenjin Shrine in our village had a spacious yard. It was where my purification ceremony was conducted before heading to the Yokaren. At the annual festival held on March 21, it was once customary to erect a stage in the yard for Kagura performances or for small circus groups to entertain the villagers. These festivities had long been suspended due to the war. I reckoned the village youth could get involved and coordinate the first Kagura event in years. Most villages in Japan had Young Men's Associations, and I was sure it would cheer everybody up if we went ahead with the project. I consulted one of my friends, Arahata, who had been a junior pilot in the Army. He willingly agreed to help, and we set the wheels in motion.

First, we had to persuade the president of the Young Men's Association. He was about three years older than me. We went to his house late January in 1946. I asked him for some ideas to bring some joy to the community. He admitted that he had none, so I told him of our plan. He was not particularly keen, however, citing how everybody was too busy trying to get food to survive, and it was not the right time to call on the other members. "Even if I put the word out, I doubt if many will come."

The anger welling up inside me was too much to bear. I exploded when I heard this cop-out. "President, do you have any idea what the hell you are saying?! As young soldiers, we didn't fight tooth and nail to defend such a sad bunch of sourpusses. It's the time for the Young Men's Association to get off its ass and stand up, now!" Hearing my impassioned

---

[36] *Kagura* is a traditional form of Shinto theatrical dance performed to appease the deities.

plea, his mother and other family members seemed a little uneasy as they peered through the sliding door. The president quickly changed his tune and apologized. I suggested he didn't need to shoulder the burden. "We'll take the stand for you. We already devoted our lives to a bigger cause once." He consented, and we put our plan into action as a Young Men's Association undertaking.

Next, we had to convince the shrine's priest. He was also a history teacher at the elementary school I once attended. "We survived the war, as you can see, and we have an idea to help the community. We'd like to bring the Kagura performance back for the upcoming festival." "Who's going to do it?" he asked. "We want to do it as a project of the Young Men's Association. We'll need to learn the moves and the instruments though." He was very receptive. "Excellent idea boys. Please, be my guest." We needed a place to practice. My relative, the former professor of Tenri University, had a large room on the second floor of a warehouse. He was happy to let us use it.

Apart from the dance itself, we also had to study the traditional music called "*ohayashi*" that accompanied Kagura performances. There was an old couple revered as masters of Kagura living in a small hamlet about a kilometer away. We knew how they lamented the demise of Kagura, and the fact that there was no young blood to continue the tradition after they were gone. Arahata and I paid them a visit. They were in their seventies and were delighted with our undertaking.

With all the necessary patrons now onboard, we composed a written appeal to members of the Young Men's Association. A little over 20 fellows from the village agreed to join us, and practice began in earnest. Coming by foot along the dark road every night after work the old couple taught us *ohayashi* and dancing. At first, it was difficult deciding who would perform the Oyama role in which a man plays a woman. "You do the Oyama." "Are you kidding?" In the end, we brought it all together and performed with singleness of mind.

A good crowd gathered on March 21 despite the depressed mood that permeated the village following years of hardship. Even those who had married and moved to other parts of the country came back for the festival. The old couple was pleased, and the priest showered us with praise. It was a raging success.

Recruited by the Metropolitan Police

A man from the Tokyo Metropolitan Police Department (TMPD) came to the village one or two weeks after the festival. His purpose was to recruit me. Public order in Tokyo had deteriorated considerably with many "rampaging foreigners [Koreans] attacking public offices or robbing supplies." Thin newspapers were obtainable back then, but much of the content covered the latest news about foreigners causing havoc in places like Shinbashi and Shibuya in central Tokyo. During the war Koreans were badly treated, and this escalation of violence was a reaction to years of oppression. I was told by my would-be recruiter that the police were currently powerless to control the chaos. He informed me of the drive to bolster police numbers, and he wanted me to consider joining. The police desperately needed recruits to bring some order to Tokyo.

He explained what police work entailed, including the "rotation work system" in which policemen were given time to practice Kendo or Judo in their off-duty hours. He added that every police station was equipped with a Kendo dojo. Only in the Army or the police could Kendo be practiced during work hours. Of course, the Army was not an option anymore but the thought of continuing Kendo in the police was greatly appealing to me. "If I can practice Kendo in the police, then sign me up." I was still 19 but the entry age requirement turning was 20. I would turn 20 in December so took the exam in November and joined the Metropolitan Police Academy in February 1947.

Police departments were prefectural bodies. As I lived in Saitama, not Tokyo, it seemed odd that a Tokyo Metropolitan Police recruiter would come out to see me. I assumed that that the Occupation forces kept tabs on where the former Kamikaze pilots were and furnished the police with that information. Otherwise, how would they have any idea where I lived? From the Occupation force's perspective, "fanatical" Kamikaze pilots were still more of a threat than the burgeoning extreme left and must have thought we were better engaged in maintaining public order than left to our own devices and going where the wind blew us.

CHAPTER EIGHT

Life as a Cop

I was employed by the Tokyo Metropolitan Police Department for 36 years. Retiring in 1983, I saw firsthand many notable incidents during my career. The following are a few that have stuck in my mind and demonstrate how Japan changed after the war.

Taro the Tosa

I underwent four months of basic training with around 60 new cadets in February 1947. The Police Academy was in Minato ward, but was relocated to an old military building in Kudan. Graduating in July, I was assigned to the Waseda Police Station. My first duty was to man a small community police box. I have fond memories of my time there thanks to "Tosa-ken Taro." It was located near Waseda University. Gakushuin Women's College was also about 300 meters away. Close to the rear gate of the station was a large house that belonged to some company executive. It was a propitious building that somehow escaped being damaged in the air raids, and the family that lived there owned a big Tosa dog called Taro.[37]

They let Taro run loose at night, something that would be unimaginable now. Taro always came to our police box and sat submissively in front of the doorway. He really seemed to like policemen. I gave Taro a call when I patrolled the town in the evenings, and he would jump to attention and follow me dutifully. Many strays roamed the streets in those days as their owner's homes had been destroyed in the bombings. When walking the beat alone, I was frequently accosted by growling mutts and had to scare them away with my nightstick. Things were different when Taro accompanied me. He was a big dog, and the strays kept their distance. The majestic Taro always kept his cool and never responded to

---

[37] Tosa-ken is a breed of dog that specialized in fighting. Dog fighting as a form of entertainment in Japan extends back to medieval times and gradually came to be modelled on sumo wrestling. The Tosa dog of Kochi Prefecture is referred to as the "grand champion" or Yokozuna of fighting dogs, with the heaviest of them weighing around 100 kg. (See photos)

their goading snarls.

Returning to the police box another constable would be ready to take over and Taro would obediently go out on patrol again. He walked most of the night with us and slept all day long. The owner was delighted with Taro's voluntary police service. After all, there was no need to take him for a walk.

While on patrol one day our belongings in the station were stolen by some cheeky villain. We were meant to be safeguarding the community but clearly needed to protect ourselves as well. The streets were not well lit, and we patrolled most of the time in darkness. Our patrol grounds had been devastated in the air raids and only a few buildings remained intact. I made door-to-door visits to become acquainted with the locals, and regularly came across families living in air-raid dugouts in their gardens.

Taro proved his worth in many ways in this environment, especially when questioning suspects without backup. Such interrogations could be hazardous as reinforcements were not on call like they are today. Once, I spotted some fellow acting suspiciously and had to find a street lamp to question him under. He was never going to do a runner with the formidable-looking Taro at my side. Taro sat behind the man as I grilled him about his activities and whether he was in possession of something he shouldn't be. The mere presence of Taro convinced the suspect to answer my questions compliantly. Although I only worked at that station for a relatively short time, I was awarded the Metropolitan Police Superintendent-General's Prize two times for my arrest record. This was largely thanks to Taro. He deserved the accolades as much as me.

There was a bakery situated about 300 meters from the police station. Depending on wind direction, the delicious aroma of freshly baked bread would waft into the station early in the morning. I would tell Taro to stay put as I jumped on my bike. I bought loaves of bread for my breakfast and asked for leftovers to give to my trusty partner. The shop owner was generous and furnished me with plenty of crusts which Taro gulped down without even chewing. Other eateries in the area also sponsored Taro's policing with scraps of food.

These were unsettled times and stray dogs were known to attack people in the street. Taro was worth his weight in muscle as a much-valued bodyguard enabling us to do our jobs. The day I was scheduled to leave,

Taro came to the station and sat at the doorway as always. I gently stroked his head and rubbed his neck. "Thanks Taro. You really were an amazing help. I have to leave but keep helping the other patrolmen protect the community." He responded by wagging his thick tail. I informed the owner how appreciative I was to have had Taro as a partner. The family was very proud of him.

Patrolman to Junior Detective

In the spring of 1948, I was made Chief of Traffic Control. I figured it was because I had been a pilot. The Metropolitan Police held a training course for driving techniques, and I was admitted half way through. The cars being used were all American, Dodges and the like, and were borrowed from the Occupation Force. The first time I drove one I felt the power of the engine and its stability. I toured around many areas in Tokyo during my month of training and was soon certified for traffic control duty at the Waseda Police Station.

Not long after this transfer, however, I was reassigned as a detective and relocated to the Criminal Division of Waseda Police Station. I attributed this assignment to the Superintendent-General awards I had received. My superiors thought I had an aptitude for detective work.

I was immediately thrown in the deep end and ordered to go and "pick up a few criminals." One time I went to Asakusa, a popular area in downtown Tokyo with a famous old shrine. I arrested a bag snatcher who happened to be a foreigner, and he was not happy about being apprehended. He started to yell, and before I knew it, I was surrounded by his dubious peers keen on getting him back in their fold. Fortunately, a few policemen were on hand to assist me. I cuffed him and boarded a streetcar to escort him to Waseda Police Station via Akihabara.

Another time in Ueno Park I busted a thief who stole money offerings from the shrine on the hill. Again, I took him to the police station by streetcar, and discovered that he had his fingers in several other crimes. In any case, arresting felons kept me very busy but was no easy task.

Becoming a detective certainly was a step up. Promotion or not, I was not impressed by the measly portions of food. I was only given one day off a month which I used to stock up on supplies. I grabbed my backpack and headed to the public distribution center to exchange provisions for food stamps. The official there greeted me and handed over potatoes and corn powder. "Is this all I get?" "Sorry, that's all for this month" she re-plied. This was hardly adequate considering the rigors of my work, not to mention the Kendo and Judo training I was doing in my off-duty hours.

I would collect firewood at a lumber mill near the dormitory. Putting the paltry morsels in a pan, I made a fire and cooked it all on a small stove. It was all an extra burden when trying to get to grips with the ordeals of detective work.

Women's Medical College Dorm

I shifted from the Waseda Police dormitory into a Tokyo Women's Medical College dorm located in Shinjuku. There were around ten dormitories on campus, and the university had requested that the police send several reliable young officers to keep an eye on the students residing there. In the autumn of 1947, myself and five colleagues found ourselves living among a whole lot of women.

The students were diligent and stayed up into the small hours studying. I lived there for nine years, and there were incidents at the beginning. Late at night, some nefarious individual scaled the university wall and sneaked into the dormitory with the intention of molesting the inhabitants. Instead of sexual gratification, all he got was a jolly good clobbering by us and arraignment for his troubles.

The wife of Lieutenant Yukio Seki (see page 57), the fellow who made the first successful Kamikaze attack in the Philippines, also studied at this college after the war. I heard that she became doctor, and I was very happy to hear of her success.

Police Kidnapping

In the middle of June 1951, I was promoted to sergeant and assigned to the Motofuji Police Station beat. The station's territory was quite expansive and doing the rounds to the many police boxes dotting the area there was taxing work. There were two 18-year-old rookies and I was asked to mentor one of them. This was the first year that anybody straight out of high school, and under the age of 20, had been employed by the police.

The prestigious University of Tokyo was in Motofuji Police Station's precinct. Although one of Japan's most esteemed universities, things were spiraling out of control there with the student movement being increasingly influenced by radicals. One day, my rookie partner was abducted at Yasuda Hall, the big tower that symbolizes the university. He was kid-napped by leftist students from the police box I sent him to.

Apparently concerned that the students were going to take his hand-gun, he let off a few warning shots into the ceiling. As luck would have it, nobody was injured but the situation had turned very messy. Police cars rushed to the rescue with their sirens screaming. I ran to the police box and found that it had been trashed. It was evident that the rookie had been stormed by the students and there was little he could have done.

After this incident, police officers of a more timid disposition avoided entering the campus. I ventured in anyway, completely undaunted by the leftist students. I once walked down a bus thoroughfare leading through the university. Wearing my police uniform I was quickly spotted by some antagonists. Several of them holding wooden staffs surrounded me and demanded I tell them who I was and what the hell I was doing there. They suspected I was gathering intelligence on their movements. "What do you mean who am I? I would have thought that was pretty obvious con-sidering I'm wearing a uniform." Reacting to my sarcasm, one of them curtly pointed out that the university was "no place for a copper to be." In reply, I declared "I'm a public servant. You are not my enemy. This road is public, and it leads to a hospital which citizens travel to by bus. I will pass, like it or not, so get out of my way." They stepped back muttering profanities under their breath. This was a sign of things to come and the following year in 1952, the infamous Tokyo University Poporo Incident erupted.[38]

Pulmonary TB

A shadow was found on my lungs at an annual medical examination in 1954. I was diagnosed with pulmonary tuberculosis. Although I showed no symptoms to speak of, and was working and practicing Kendo every day, I assumed that my condition was due to a lack of nourishment and exhaustion. The work roster for police back then was arduous with the

---

[38] The Poporo Incident was one of the most controversial legal cases in postwar Japan. When students belonging to the leftist theatrical company Poporo were performing at the Tokyo University hall, they discovered undercover officers from Motofuji Police Station among them and a violent altercation ensued. The students were later indicted, but at the high-profile trial the court ruled that police presence at the national university was an infringement of aca-demic freedom.

second rotation lasting for 18 hours from 4pm to 10am. We were not even allowed to sit down while on duty. This system was taking a leaf out of the American book, but they were still well-off compared to us because at least they were being fed properly.

I was hospitalized right thorough to spring of 1957, spending a total of two-and-a-half years in the Tokyo Women's Medical College Hospital. The disease was a common affliction back then, and there were two ways to treat it: medicine or operation. It was a difficult choice to make. An operation would cure it quicker, but three ribs would need to be removed making Kendo out of the question. I talked with the physician in charge and told him how I wanted to continue Kendo. He responded by saying "I can't tell you which option is best, but medical technology is advancing all the time." In the end I chose medication. I was unable to get my hands on the best medicine, Streptomycin, because it was too expensive. I wasn't too concerned. Given my career history, making it through to 60 years of age would be a miracle anyway, I thought.

Not long after my hospitalization, Jiro Kageyama paid me a visit.[39] He was Director General of Metropolitan Police No. 1 HQ. About five years before, when I temporarily belonged to a task force specializing in Kendo training, he was the Director General of No. 5 HQ located in the same building. That's how we got to know each other. He told me that Kuniyasu Tsuchida suffered from the same affliction but recovered after six months of Zen meditation.[40] Apparently, Tsuchida-san was also going to pay me a visit. I never imagined that such high-ranking superiors would come to check up on a mere sergeant like me.

Mr. Tsuchida was chief of the Public Security Department at the time. I got to know him well through his visitations. After he was promoted to Superintendent-General of the Tokyo Metropolitan Police, he would often drop by to say hello. He snapped his Achilles tendon once when we

---

[39] Jiro Kageyama graduated from the University of Tokyo. He served as the Superintendent of Kumamoto, Saitama, and Kanagawa Prefectural Police Headquarters, and Director General of the Kanto Police Headquarters. He practiced Kendo since his student days and was appointed president of Tokyo Kendo Association and the All-Japan Kendo Federation.

[40] Kuniyasu Tuchida was also a graduate of Tokyo University. He served on the battleship Musashi as a naval cadet in the war. He was the 70th Superintendent-General of the Metropolitan Police, and 4th Principal of the Defense Academy. When he was the Director General of the Metropolitan Police General Affairs Department, his wife was killed by a letter bomb sent to his house by an extreme leftist group.

were practicing Kendo together, so I was able to reciprocate his kindness and visit him in hospital.

Although I had contracted tuberculosis, I showed no subjective symptoms or hemoptysis. I spent my days in the hospital playing Japanese chess, reading samurai novels, or composing Haiku poems.[41] I sometimes submitted my compositions to the Yomiuri Daily Newspaper and received several awards for my efforts.

"Akibare no hate ni, hirogaru Kumo-no-shima"

(On a fine autumn day, I gaze at bands of white clouds, swelling in the blue sky above)

There was no remedy for TB back then. Patients exchanged information hoping to be rid of the disease as soon as possible. They compared notes on which medicine was most efficacious and who the reliable doctors were. I also wished for a speedy recovery but didn't enter in the conversations. I couldn't stop thinking about my comrades who had their lives cut short in the war. Fast recovery or not, the fact that I was still here was a wonder in itself.

Quite a few patients were anxious about losing their jobs if they languished in hospital for too long, but I really didn't care about that either. Getting back to Kendo training and somehow making a small contribution to society was my priority, but I was in no hurry. To build my strength I walked around outside at nights or used rolled up newspapers to practice Kendo techniques on my own. I was not supposed to exert myself. When busted for flouting hospital rules I simply told the nurse that I was rehabilitating my legs. In any case, this covert light exercise proved to be good for my recovery. It took a little over two-and-a-half years, but the shadow on my lung gradually dissipated and I was finally discharged.

Autopsy Training

I was not assigned to any taxing work for a while following my liberation from hospital. I recovered well, and in 1960 was assigned to security work at the Diet Building. It was a time characterized by zealous activism by diet members, students, citizens, and leftists against the Japan-U.S.

---

[41] Haiku is a form of traditional verse comprised of 17 characters in 5-7-5 form. It expresses the beauty of nature or human emotions.

Security Treaty, so we were always kept on our toes. I passed the promotion test for Lieutenant, and when waiting for a new assignment to some police station, I was given an opportunity to study the science of autopsies as an assistant to the medical examiner, Masayoshi Iwata. This was a repulsive but invaluable experience.

Dr. Iwata was a renowned medical examiner, and the best in the business back then. Around 50 to 60 corpses resulting from "unnatural deaths" were discovered each day in Tokyo Metropolitan Police precincts. When bodies were uncovered by officers in the field a report would be delivered to Metropolitan Police HQ.[42]

Although most turned out not to be the result of foul play, at least 3 or 4 would be deemed suspicious. Each time a report came through, Dr. Iwata would announce that it was time to go. I would grab his bag and follow him to the car. Dr. Iwata's examinations were nothing short of outrageous. He never used rubber gloves, preferring instead to examine the corpse with his bare hands. If the victim had long hair, he would rub his fingers over the cadaver's head to detect injuries not obvious to the naked eye. He painstakingly caressed the body from the top of the head to the tips of the toes looking for clues.

After a while of on-the-job learning, he gave me a wink to indicate it was my turn. The point of autopsies was to ascertain whether death was the result of a crime or natural causes. If I found a wound, I inserted my finger to examine the width, depth and direction. I could then tell how the weapon entered the body and if the death was suicide or murder. Dr. Iwata would say nothing as I worked my way over the body. He just observed me with a grin on his face and would laugh a little when I told him my verdict. This usually meant that my assessment was correct.

Even if the corpse was decomposing and foul-smelling, Dr. Iwata never washed his hands after an autopsy. He merely wiped them off with a towel because we examined bodies outside where there wasn't any water or soap. His notebook was stained with blood and gore from the many corpses he examined. He even ate meals holding chopsticks with his sullied hands. I did as he did, but when I picked up some food and brought

---

[42] The Metropolitan Police is the biggest of the prefectural police forces in Japan. Its jurisdiction covers the Tokyo metropolitan area. At present, there are about 100 police stations under the headquarters located in Sakuradamon near the Imperial Palace. These police stations are divided into 10 blocks, and each block has a sub-HQ.

it close to my mouth, the revolting stench on my hands was too much to bear. A truly repulsive experience though it was, it turned out to be useful when I became Director of the Crime Investigation Division. I served in this position at three police stations over my career. My aides typically lacked experience in conducting autopsies, so I had to rely on my own field knowledge to find evidence.

When I was Investigation Director at the Honjo Police Station, we would find three or four victims a day who had expired through unnatural causes. The newly assigned Station Chief was annoyingly pedantic, and routinely rejected autopsy results reasoning that they "were not precise enough." I would then go to him myself and make a supplementary report.

An old woman's body was found one year on January 4, my first day back in the New Year. She was discovered dead, sitting at her little *kotatsu* table. We estimated that she had been dead for a few days. The switch on her *kotatsu* was still on and her remains were starting to decompose. I examined the body and declared that she died of natural causes. There was no indication that a third person had entered the house. The shutters were closed when the body was found, although they were opened by a neighbor afterwards, and the entrance was blocked by a spider's web. It was clear that no one had been in or out of the old lady's abode, and that she died alone.

Even so, the Chief was disinclined to approve my initial findings. I took him down to the scene so that he could see for himself. The putrid smell was sickening. The old woman was suspended in a death pose with her head slumped on the table. I lifted a corner of the *kotatsu* blanket and the atrocious odor of decaying flesh wafted out. The Chief made a quick exit shrieking "That's enough, enough already!" I told him "Sorry Chief. We've got to take a good whiff to determine the degree of decomposition. This indicates that she died three or four days ago, sometime on December 31." He hardly heard a word I said in his haste to vacate the scene.

We took the corpse to the lab for a more formal autopsy. Indeed, her death was due to natural causes, a brain hemorrhage, as I had already concluded. Our squeamish, and now less-pedantic Chief was more than happy to accept my findings from then on.

Job Brokering Gangsters

Following my foray into autopsies, I was appointed Section Chief of the Criminal Investigation Division at Totsuka Police Station in February 1964 and was put in charge of organized crime. The police had just started to crack down on gangsters. The public was particularly concerned with illegal job brokering run by the *yakuza*.[43]

Nishi-Toyama park was spacious public area where 400 to 500 day-laborers gathered at the crack of dawn to find work. Contractors and construction companies were also there to hire laborers for whatever projects they had on that day. They may require five to ten men, for example, but needed permission from gangsters. Unauthorized recruiting would invite the ire of these violent thugs.

Company trucks waited in line in an orderly fashion while a gangster stood on the roof of some pretentious car with his tattoos on display for all to see, shouting things like "Ten root cutters! Ten root cutters!" A "root cutter" was a digger, so this meant that some company required ten laborers that day for excavation work. When ten men had been assembled for the task, the company truck edged forward so that they could jump in the back.

Then the gangster shouted "Ten tidying. Ten tidying! One short. Anyone?" The next company needed ten men for clearing up a building site. Another gangster shouted from behind "Hey you! Don't look away. You're up!" When ten laborers grouped, the gangsters shouted to "bring 'em out" as if they were commodities and not human beings.

This vociferous haggling continued until all the trucks had departed carrying their load of workmen. It used to begin around 3:30-4:00am and finished about 7:30-8:00am. During these hours the park was unruly and noisy, and there were all sorts of characters thrown in the mix. As work started after breakfast, there was always a demand for meals. Some vendors made fires and cooked bowls of rice with highly suspicious morsels chucked in for taste. Others set up small stands and hawked illegal home-made alcoholic beverages. Some men bided their time gambling. There was a flophouse district near the park where hundreds of laborers bedded down for the night ready to get to the "recruiting ground" first thing in the morning. One never sees such scenes in Japan today.

---

[43] Term for Japanese mobsters.

The commotion was exasperating for residents who lived around the park's periphery, and they complained vehemently to the police to get something done. The gangsters in charge of the operation belonged to a sub-chapter of the biggest crime syndicate in Tokyo. Their office was located near the park and we knew the associates involved. Some oversaw the directing of company trucks, while others led laborers to their assignments. Illegal job brokering was a lucrative source of income for gangsters. What should have been a direct transaction between contractors and the laborers was instead handled by mobsters who would pocket a percentage of the laborers' wages. Not only did they purloin a proportion of the men's hard-earned cash before handing it over to them, they also ran the flophouses where most of them stayed, and the canteens where they ate and drank. By the end of the day, almost all the money found its way into gangster coffers.

At the time there were huge construction projects underway in and around of Tokyo. The Tokyo Olympic Games of 1964 demanded all manner of facilities, and there was a boon in highway construction. Laborers were in great need and huge sums of money were being thrown around. There was plenty of work then. They used to say, "If you haven't got a job, just go up the hill." "Hill" was the term used for daily recruiting spots like the park. Job brokering, however, was illegal. Helping job-seekers was the responsibility of municipal employment agencies, not dubious private syndicates. We countered this unlawful activity by instituting the "Job Stabilization Law" requiring all those involved in the recruiting business have an official permit. We had grounds to arrest gangsters once this law had been enacted.[44]

Making the arrests took careful planning. If we went to the park in mufti we would still stand out because we weren't tanned like laborers. We smudged charcoal on our faces and wore filthy old working clothes to blend in. We persuaded a construction company to hide us in the loading space of their trucks under tarpaulins to get into the park undetected. I rode in the passenger seat and told the driver where to move the truck.

---

[44] In many countries, arresting a suspect without a warrant is usually permitted in a public space even if an illegal act is not being committed at the time. In the case of Japan, however, other than when a felon is caught in the act, or in some exceptional cases, a warrant is requisite for taking suspects into custody. Making an arrest in Japan can be quite complex as strict protocols must be observed.

Approaching the place where gangsters were plying their illicit trade, we feigned engine trouble and stopped so that I could observe what they were up to.

Another detective pretended to be a laborer seeking a job. He hid a tape recorder in his backpack and moved as close as he could to record gangsters barking orders. Tape recorders were big machines back then, not like the concealable devices of today. Fortunately, the gangsters didn't suspect anything because all the laborers carried personal belongings around in backpacks.

When we had enough evidence to make arrests, I gave the okay for my task force guys to reveal themselves. They dropped their disguises and nabbed around ten gangsters in one swoop. We took them to the police station along with a few laborers as eye witnesses, sat them in four lines, interrogated them, and took statements.

This style of operation had never been attempted by the Japanese police before, so we were pioneers in a sense. We made similar crackdowns several times afterwards and put a big dent in gangster enterprises. The Tokyo District Prosecutor's Office was delighted with our success and lauded our efforts as a first for Japan.

Until this point, the only way we could mitigate gangster activities was by making individual arrests for extortion or gambling etc. Although job brokering was not particularly sinister in the traditional mobster sense, it reaped them huge sums of cash used to fund other illegal and more menacing activities. We couldn't allow them to get too fat.

The "White Bike" Motorcycle Unit

After serving in the Personnel Division in HQ, and then as the Director of Criminal Investigation at the Honden Police Station, I was assigned to a new post in August 1968 as Vice Commander of the Police Motorcycle Unit. This unit came under the auspices of the Tokyo Metropolitan Police Traffic Department, and our patrol area the "No. 8 Block" covered Tama, Hachioji, Tachikawa, and other areas in the west of Tokyo up to the border with Yamanashi Prefecture.

I happened to have a motorcycle license which was a rarity among detectives. I supposed that was why I was assigned.

There were 182 officers divided into six teams in the unit, and 234 motorcycles. As protests against the Japan-U.S. Security Treaty died down, the economy began to improve and life in Japan became more prosperous. Private car ownership proliferated rapidly, and so too did traffic accidents. Although there was still a need for crowd control with ongoing treaty revisions, the Metropolitan Police deemed it prudent to transfer officers from the Riot Squad to Traffic Control. Riot Squad officers in their twenties with an aptitude for riding motorcycles were selected and trained in a facility rented from the Professional Bicycle Racing Association in Shizuoka Prefecture (see photos).

The "White Bikes," as police motorcycles are referred to, were formerly 300cc Hondas, or outdated Kawasaki and Suzuki models. Young punks roamed the streets and highways on bikes far superior to the ones we had. The department splashed out and furnished us with models more befitting of officers of the law. This did wonders for morale. We received news that Honda was going to supply us with 200 new 750cc bikes, the biggest in Japan at the time. We jumped for joy when we saw them parked neatly in rows. Honda outfitted more bikes after this, while Kawasaki and Suzuki followed suit with 600cc and 500cc models respectively.

Overloaded Trucks

The operations we put considerable effort involved speed control and clamping down on overloaded trucks. The latter was particularly welcomed by public and municipal authorities. With rapid economic growth, Tokyo and its surrounds were enjoying a construction boom. To meet demands for building materials, companies cut into mountains and hills in the west of Tokyo, around Hachioji and Ome, and loaded their trucks with excessive cargos of gravel for transportation to building sites. They put 15 tons of rock in trucks when the limit was 10 tons, or 22 tons in 15-ton dump trucks.

With overloaded trucks constantly traversing the thoroughfares around Ome, the side of the road leading into Tokyo started to sink and was was much lower than the other side taken by empty trucks from Tokyo. Dozens of laden trucks drove away from the quarries each morning with a deafening roar.

The winter months saw the arrival of even more drivers from the provinces who wanted a piece of the action. Not familiar with the routes to their destinations in Tokyo, they ran in convoys so as not to lose their way.

The noise was a significant public nuisance, and the damage caused

A kamikaze about to hit the USS *Missouri* near Okinawa on April 11, 1945.

Named after the ancient Japanese province of Japan, the *Yamato* was constructed to counter the numerically superior American fleet. The Yamato and her sister ship, *Musashi*, were among the largest and most powerfully armed battleships to ever sail.

The Japanese battleships *Yamato* and *Musashi* anchored off Truk Islands in 1943.

Ground crew enthusiastically waving farewell to a kamikaze pilot about to embark on his final mission.

Mission log of the 205th Air Group. A section of the text reads "Escort required for aircraft carrying His Royal Majesty's Chamberlain." (Ministry of Defense Archives)

Devastation in Hiroshima after the atomic bomb was dropped, August 6, 1945.
(Wikimedia Commons © M M)

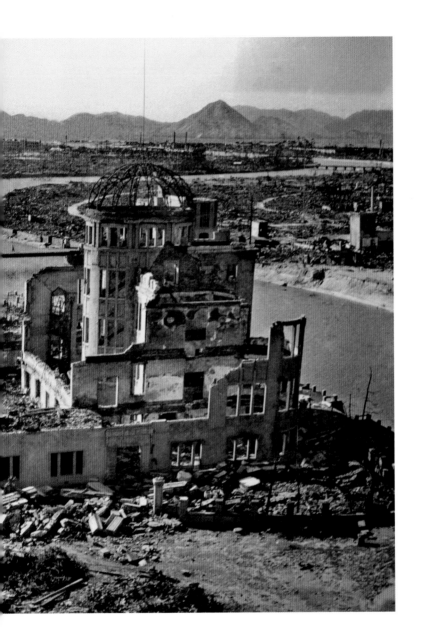

Prince Mikasa-no-miya Takahito Shinno (1915–2016) was fourth and youngest son of the Taisho Emperor. His older brother was Emperor Showa (Hirohito). Prince Mikasa-no-Miya served in the Japanese Imperial Army but was viewed with suspicion by the militarist government because of his anti-war sentiment and strong desire for peace. He became a scholar and part-time lecturer in Middle Eastern studies and languages after the war. (Public domain/Arquivo Nacional Collection)

From fighter pilot to police officer protecting the peace in postwar Japan. During his long career in the Tokyo Metropolitan Police Department, one of Odachi's many roles was to lead the "White Bike" traffic officers in their formative days. He saw many parallels with this duty and his time as a fighter pilot. (Author's collection)

A Tosa dog. Tosas are a breed of dog originally from the Kochi region on the island of Shikoku. They are famous as fighting dogs and are sometimes dressed up like Yokuzuna grand champions in professional Sumo wrestling. (Wikimedia Commons © Pleple2000)

Odachi kept meticulously detailed diaries of his daily activities in the police. They provide a fascinating window on Japan's growing pains in the postwar period and are a valuable record for many notorious criminal cases that he was involved in solving. (Author's collection)

Odachi's police diaries.

An example of Odachi's police notes outlining a case in perfect detail.

Chutaro Ogawa is one of the most famous postwar Kendo masters. Odachi became acquainted with him when he trained in Kendo professionally in the TMPD. (Photo courtesy of Kendo Jidai)

Kondo Isami, (1834–1868) was a famous swordsman of the late Edo period towards the end of the Tokugawa regime. Although originally of peasant stock he became the fourth master of the Tennen Rishin-ryu style of swordsmanship and is famous for his role as the leader of the Shinsengumi.

Second from the right stands Moriji Mochida (1886-1974) receiving his champion prize at the prestigious Emperor's Kendo Tournament in 1929. Mochida was awarded the highest ranke in Kendo of Hanshi 10th Dan. He was only one of five men to ever receive this rank. Odachi has fond memories of training under this great master when he trained in the Kendo Division of the TMPD. (Photo courtesy of Kendo Nihon)

Moriji Mochida fighting in a demonstration match. His teachings are still referred to by Kendo practitioners today. (Photo courtesy of Kendo Nihon)

Kazuo Odachi trains several times a week at the morning sessions in the Tokyo Metropolitan Police Department Dojo in Sakuradamon. Each time, he takes swordsmen many years his junior through their paces.

In his nineties now, Odachi is a highly respected Kendo instructor in the TMPD Dojo. Here, he is instructing students in the Kendo Kata forms.

Shigeru Ohta, Alex Bennett, Kazuo Odachi and Hiroyoshi Nishijima after participating in a Kendo training at the TMPD dojo.

One of Odachi's greatest joys in life is passing on his Kendo knowledge to young students. He has been teaching children at the local school for over three decades and always finishes training with a sermon on how Kendo can help them overcome them overcome adversity and make the most of the gift of life. (Author's collection)

Odachi facing off against an opponent in full Kendo armor demonstrating the steely nerve and equanimity that has served him well throughout his life.

serious financial problems for municipal road management offices who needed to raise hundreds of millions of yen to repair the wear and tear on the roads. The thoroughfares around Ome and Koshu became so rickety, authorities had no idea how to cope. The main highway running from Yamanashi Prefecture to Tokyo came under our jurisdiction, and it was in a terrible state. I gathered leaders from each of the six teams in our unit and explained the situation. This was something that we had to tackle, but how?

The most challenging issue was deciding on a suitable place to weigh the trucks. It would require specialized equipment at strategic points along the road, and there would have to be an area to discard excess cargo. There was a vacant lot next to Yokota Airbase. I visited the base administrator and requested that we be allowed to use the space. He agreed, but but because of the sheer volume we still needed several more places to dump gravel, so I negotiated with landowners in Ome, Fussa, and Hachioji.

They were reluctant at first, but I persisted. "We don't mean to deprive you of your land. This is a matter of safety for the people of Tokyo." It took almost three days, but eventually they consented, and we were ready to go. "Assemble your teams at 11pm tomorrow. Don't tell them why. Just say that there is 'some kind of emergency.'" The last thing I wanted was for my plan to be leaked before implementation.

When the big day came, I explained my master plan for dealing with the problem. I told my men to get ready from 3:00-3:30am. The main piece of equipment that needed setting up were the special scales designed to go under the truck tires. Once in place, we pulled Tokyo-bound trucks over and guided them onto the scales. As predicted, it turned out that many were overloading in excess of 5 to 10 tons each. We made the truckers dump the excess, but some pleaded with us to cut them some slack. We didn't. They ditched tons of gravel and rock, which meant a lot of their projected profit was being tipped out.

We worked through the night, but there were still 20 to 30 trucks waiting in line by morning. We appropriated their licenses to prevent them doing a runner.

In total, we conducted four checkpoints. The first was in autumn of 1969, and the second was the following winter when it was very cold. The officers worked hard and were not particularly happy about the conditions, but we managed to get through it all in good cheer.

Those in breach of weight regulations were fined. Some complained that they had already received fines, but of course this fell on deaf ears. "It's entirely your own fault if you don't have any money to send to the missus. Don't blame us."

One highway checkpoint was near a parking area in Hachioji. Five trucks evaded the checkpoint and bolted. The drivers were found smoking in parking area rest house. The trucks were clearly overloaded and when we inquired who they belonged to, the drivers pretended not to know. "Well, we're not sure. We saw some drivers a little while ago but don't know where they went...."

I directed my officers to make sure nobody left the parking area. The offending drivers took the situation for granted expecting us to give up and move on. "Keep them under surveillance until they come down on their hands and knees begging. They didn't come on the second day. Nor did they show on the third day either. As the trucks stood idly in the parking area, the tires started to flatten under the weight.

On the fourth day the drivers came to me and begged forgiveness. "You've spent the last few days resting, smoking, and eating. I went and watched you myself, so I know who you all are. You are idiots for thinking that we'd give up and let you go. Shame on you." We let them move their trucks, but they swayed precariously from side to side with the tires already distorted from the weight. They were not allowed to dump the excess gravel in non-authorized spots, and had to come to where the scales were set up. By this stage, their wheels and suspension were so bent out of shape that even dumping the excess made no difference. They had to tip the whole lot out and return empty to do repairs. Their companies lost a lot of money.

After the first crackdown word spread among drivers and companies and it wasn't long before all of them stopped overloading. It seems that they learned their lesson, but in truth I did feel a bit sorry for them. After all, they were just trying to make a living. Still, proper management and maintenance of roads was no small matter in terms of expense and safety, so our inflexibility was warranted.

We reported the results to local government offices and more requested that we do the same for them. The locals were appreciative, and housewives even used to make us cups of tea. Anybody who wanted to stock up on gravel were welcomed to come and take as much of the dumped rock as they could handle. And come they did with wheelbarrows in hand.

The Safe-breaker

In the spring of 1973, I was appointed Director of the Crime Investigation Division of Honjo Police Station. We had numerous notable cases to attend to there, one of which concerned a unique stealing incident. I was resting at home one Sunday when I received an urgent call about a safe that had been lifted from a company office. I asked about the room and floor. "It's tiled, and people remove their shoes before they enter." I told my subordinate to make sure nothing was disturbed until I got there.

I conducted a thorough inspection of the scene. The safe was heavy and the tiled floor was clean, so there was a decent chance that the criminal left footprints somewhere. As expected, I found a nice set of prints for us to process. I concluded that the criminal must be a known serial safe-breaker, and he became our designated "Hoshi." Hoshi literally means "star" and is the term detectives use for suspects.

I sent a team of detectives on stakeout and reminded them to keep a careful watch out for evidence to match the footprints at the scene. Big men have long strides, while men of diminutive stature walk in shorter steps. Everyone has their own distinctive gait and such details must be taken into consideration when evaluating footprints. Our number one Hoshi lived in the same apartment so there were bound to be more matching footprints in the building. Proving to who they belonged, however, was no easy task.

In any case, the stakeout took a long time. We parked near the suspect's apartment taking care not to use the same car all the time. We rented cars from private companies with their names inscribed on the side to avoid suspicion.

One day, our Hoshi finally showed up. He entered the apartment building and walked through the corridor. The detectives followed scrutinizing his footprints before he came back out of his room. We compared the footprints to the ones we managed to get off the floor of the crime scene. They were a perfect match, so an arrest warrant was issued. It turns out that our Hoshi was indeed a star in the criminal world with around 300 crimes later attributed to him.

Another big case was the burglary of a condominium belonging to a Geisha. She was very popular and well to do, and her celebrity status made her a target for theft. Similar burglaries had taken place in other wards of Tokyo, but no suspect had yet been identified. I went to her condominium with my men from the Criminal Investigation Department. We examined the scene, but there was no indication that the thief entered from the ground floor or via the neighbor's balcony. We finally concluded that he must have come in from above.

I ventured up to the rooftop with my staff and found a spout that ran down from the roof and past her balcony. It was now just a matter of retrieving fingerprints left from his climb down the spout. Even if he was wearing gloves he would have undoubtedly removed them for a tighter grip as he descended. The fingerprints that we found matched a known criminal. We arrested him and discovered that he also had around 300 other crimes to his name. His modus operandi was so distinctive that his dishonest exploits were featured in an inhouse police manual.

The Leftists

In the mid 1970s inter-factional fights between extreme leftist groups were frequent occurrences. In particular, the Kakumaru and Chukaku factions were embroiled in hostilities that resulted in a few murders and vicious acts of violence.

Before dawn on December 16, 1974, I received an urgent report of a nasty skirmish between leftists on the 6th floor of a condominium building located in Sumida Ward. I ran to the scene and it certainly appeared to have been quite a fracas. According to one of the neighbors, "I heard a big sound like on a construction site. I saw lots of people on the balcony breaking windows with hammers, then they started fighting inside. It was totally brutal. It was like I was watching the raid on Kira's residence by the 47 Ronin."[45]

Apparently, seven members of the Kakumaru faction had smuggled a radio transceiver into one of the upper rooms of the condominium. More

---

[45] The witness was referring to the famous Chushingura story. In the Edo period, Lord Asano Takumi-no-Kami injured Lord Kira Kozukenosuke with his short sword in the corridor of Edo Castle after being insulted. Asano was immediately sentenced to death by *seppuku* (slitting his belly open) for his transgression. His loyal 47 retainers, led by Oishi Kuranosuke, made elaborate plans for revenge, and raided Kira's residence and assassinated him two years later.

than ten members of the rival Chukaku faction assaulted the room from the rooftop with hammers and steel pipes and tried to smash their way through the window from the balcony. The Kakumaru members defended themselves furiously and some were badly hurt. The police stormed the condominium and arrested five members of Kakumaru with a further three men being hospitalized. By the time I got there, the place was in a real mess. I directed my men to waste no time in carrying out a crime scene investigation.

The injured suspects were hospitalized separately, but three days later each group raided the hospitals and escaped with their comrades without release permission from the doctors. We soon discovered that one of the Kakumaru casualties had checked into a different hospital, so immediately procured an arrest warrant. On the afternoon of December 24, more than ten Kakumaru associates converged on that hospital too, and escaped before we could apprehend them. The next day, Chukaku supporters did the same for their injured cronies.

Bey and by, yet another fight broke out. Around 8pm, I received another urgent report that Kakumaru and Chukaku members were at it again in a building connected to Kinshicho Station. They were jumping in and out of the elevators in a department store trying to beat each other into submission. We chased and arrested one, and another was seriously injured.

Such brawls were common and sparked by bitter hatred that festered between groups of the extreme left. Although they were adherents of the same communist principles, they irreconcilably parted ways over differences in interpretation. They never sought police intervention whenever they suffered at the hands of rival groups, and refused point blank to cooperate in our investigations, but it was evident to us that the leftists were on the verge of collapse.[46]

---

[46] In the early stages of opposition to the Japan-U.S. Security Treaty around 1960, protests were generally peaceful. They were led or supported not only by leftists but also by citizens with no particular political leaning. Later, leftists divided into two factions: one was that of the Communist Party-led movement, the other affiliated with new-left movements which pursued communist revolution through violence. Even among the new-left factions, conflict was rife and they fought amongst each other with ruthless resolve resulting in many murders. The hostilities were not limited to Tokyo but occurred throughout the country. This led to the radical new left movement losing popular support.

The Serial Thief

My last assignment in the police was as Vice Director of the No. 3 Criminal Investigation Bureau in the Metropolitan Police HQ. I worked there from autumn 1977 to spring 1983, after which I retired. This division specialized in theft, but if the felon committed homicide, we investigated this as well.[47]

When a serious crime occurred in any given precinct, an investigative HQ would be established at the local police station under our guidance. We dispatched experienced detectives from our bureau to help the station and this proved useful for young detectives to learn the ropes of managing difficult or high-profile cases. It was not unusual for several investigative HQs to be set up by us at various police stations at the same time.

I worked at my department in the morning and then headed to the police station investigative units in the afternoon or evening to offer my expertise. We solved more than a few noteworthy cases in the six years I spent in the bureau and received about ten awards from the Commissioner General of the National Police Agency and the Superintendent-General of the Metropolitan Police. The following is one of the more famous cases I was involved with.

From 1977 to 1979 we investigated a series of crimes which finally led to the arrest of a serial crook who racked up more than 300 larcenies over his clandestine career. The suburbs of Azabu, Roppongi, Akasaka, Shinjuku, and Shibuya in downtown Tokyo are home for the rich and famous. There are scores of magnificent houses owned by company presidents, movie stars and celebrities. With such opulence on display, these areas provided rich pickings for thieves.

Judging by the methodology of the crimes in question, we surmised that they were committed by the same lawbreaker. We established an investigation HQ at Akasaka Police Station and thoroughly reexamined all the previous crimes. I took one of my subordinates and visited more than 30 crime scenes which enabled me to ascertain the thief's tendencies, preferences, and routines for entry.

---

[47] The Criminal Investigation Bureau consisted of four departments. No. 1 probed violent crimes and robberies etc. No. 2 was for white collar crime, and No. 4 focused on organized crime and gangsters.

It seemed that this particular "Hoshi" focused on large old houses. He would sneak through windows on the second floor rather than picking locked doors and windows at ground level. He would then turn the place over in search of cash, but never jewelry, and escape through the same second-floor window without leaving a trace.

We identified houses he was likely casing based on these characteristics, and found a candidate that was occupied by the branch manager of a European bank. Preempting this as his next attempted conquest, we envisaged that the Hoshi was spying on the house each night looking for the best opportunity to break in. I went to see the branch manager with a translator and explained the situation. I asked him if we could place two detectives in his garden each night. He agreed straight away, but it became apparent that stakeouts in his country were only for a couple of hours, not from late evening to morning for a whole month! He was unaware that it was going to be such a big undertaking.

Two detectives concealed themselves in his garden each night. Orders were to not kill the plants, so they took a bottle in case they needed to take a pee. The maid even brought them hot coffee around 10pm each night, but by the end of the month they were gaunt and thin through fatigue. Despite our trap, the house was not targeted in the end, and the hitherto frequent burglaries in the area suddenly stopped.

Undeterred, we looked at similar cases in different prefectures and found that comparable housebreaks were occurring in Matsudo City in neighboring Chiba Prefecture. Clearly our Hoshi had moved his operation there, so we followed suit. Visiting the Chiba Prefectural Police, we outlined the case and asked for approval to set up our investigation there. Being rather territorial, we assumed that they might be uncomfortable with officers from another police department in their midst, but they agreed all the same.

As we continued our inquiries the breaking and entering suddenly ceased there as well. Instead, a similar pattern of burglaries popped up around Fuchu City in the west of Tokyo. The stop-start style of offending suggested that the criminal would desist for a while after stealing a decent sum of cash, and then re-offend when he ran out. Depending on the amount of cash stolen we were gradually able to gage how long the interval would last before re-offending commenced. Our hunches of where he would resume his criminal endeavors, and even the most likely house, started getting closer to the mark. Our detectives were able to enter the Hoshi's mind, and could tell straight away if any reported break-in should be attributed to him or not.

Upon revisiting the burglaries committed in Fuchu and Chofu, we managed to narrow down his next likely target. One evening when we were certain he would strike, I ordered my detectives to conceal themselves around the house. Sure enough, the occupant made an emergency call to report a burglary in progress. I gave the order to pounce, and all the detectives rushed in and detained the crook who was taking cover in the garden.

He was a young man of around 20 years. Born on some isolated island, he was an experienced boxer which explained his remarkable agility. The game was up, and he confessed to all his previous crimes, over 300 in eight months. Most of his offences could be corroborated by evidence we uncovered in our investigations. He worked at a gas station in Fuchu during the day and robbed in the evening.

It turns out that our outlaw had fallen in love with a cabaret hostess and plied her with gifts and money. After a while, he changed his usual pattern and started taking jewelry to give her. Some of his plunder was incredibly valuable with necklaces and rings worth around 4 to 5-million yen each. When we noticed this change I knew that our Hoshi must have a mistress. The reason why he moved from Matsudo to Fuchu was because the hostess had changed to a different cabaret. The power of love....

The Fraudster

Another notorious case involved a remarkably resourceful swindler. In November 1978, an incredibly upset elderly lady living in Shibuya ward came to Yoyogi Police Station. "I deposited 36,800,000-yen in a safety deposit box at the Hatagaya branch of Tokyo Mutual Bank. For some reason 11,810,000-yen is missing."

It was inconceivable that so much money could disappear from a bank safety box. Given the extraordinary sum of money involved, the media was quick to jump on the case with considerable enthusiasm. The shame was more than the poor bank manager could bear and he ended up committing suicide by jumping in front of a train in Shinjuku Station on December 7.

While we were trying to solve the case, an even more brazen felony occurred on December 14 when the remaining 20-million yen was swindled by a man pretending to be a detective from the No. 2 Crime Investigation Department. The conman, brandishing fake police ID, told the old lady that he needed to inspect the safety box. She dutifully handed the key and seal to the imposter. Before long, she was called to the branch as the depositor's presence was required to open the safety box. She went to the bank and waited together with the phony detective. A bank employee brought the safety box to a private room. The con artist ordered the bank staff out of the room and informed the lady that fingerprints would be taken from the bills. She opened the box and removed the money. He then put the bills into his shoulder bag and told her to stay put while he conferred with Investigation Director. He walked out of the bank with the bag and never came back. It was a truly audacious crime.

More than 30 detectives were assigned to the case at HQ. We examined the theft from all angles, but our Hoshi left us few clues to follow. Similar crimes started happening all over Japan in Fukuoka, Hiroshima, Miyazaki, Osaka, Kumamoto, Saga, and Okayama, and other places. The pattern was always the same. When big scandals like corruption, election violations, or tax fraud were plastered all over the news, the Hoshi would target those involved. He would approach them masquerading as the "lead investigator" and craftily obtain information such as the name of the bank where they deposited large sums of money. He would request bankbooks, official seals, and cash cards as evidence, and go to the bank and to withdraw all the money.

We continued our investigation for more than a year. A serious crime was committed at the Hokkaido Fisheries Cooperative Association's office in Tsukiji and this gave us the lead we were after. The director of the association's Business Division incurred a loss of more than ten-billion yen in a monumental breach of trust. An inquiry got underway at the Tsukiji Police Station amidst a media frenzy, so we knew the crook would be enticed by the news.

On December 28, we learned that the suspect was going from bank to bank in Tokyo. The next morning at the Tsukiji branch of the Hokkaido Development Bank, there was a phone call from someone claiming to be an attorney at law. He told the bank employee of an appointment with "Mr. A of the Hokkaido Fisheries Cooperative Association at 9:30am in the bank," but was going to be late because of a traffic jam. "Please ask Mr.

A to wait." This phone call was a cunning ruse.

Soon after, a man calling himself Mr. A showed up at the Tsukiji branch, but this was in fact the Hoshi himself. The very same man went to the Hokkaido Fisheries Cooperative Association office in Tsukiji the day before as "Police Detective Yokoyama." He talked directly with the Deputy Director of the Hokkaido Fisheries Cooperative Association's General Affairs Division and persuaded him to bring the association's bank seal and authorize a withdrawal form. The Hoshi then took this form to the bank pretending that he was Mr. A.

Unbeknownst to him, detectives from the Tsukiji Police Station were already there waiting. The Hoshi came in and started conversing with a bank employee. Noticing that something was awry, the Hoshi suddenly turned and ran out of the bank. He resisted arrest by throwing a handful of envelopes at the detectives but was duly restrained. In the envelopes were withdrawal slips for 7 million-yen, and one for 9 million-yen deposited in the Tsukiji branch of Fuji Bank.

Hearing that we had our man, I headed to Tsukiji Police Station. I interrogated the Hoshi who promptly confessed to 24 cases of 28 that we suspected he was involved in. Different to thieves, fraudsters tend to talk a lot. I questioned him on various matters concerning his offences and was confident that his confessions were veritable. I phoned the Metropolitan Police HQ and reported that his fellow was indeed the perpetrator and requested permission to hold a press conference the next day. He did not, however confess to stealing money from the old lady's safety-box at the Tokyo Mutual Bank, but this didn't stop the morning paper the following day reporting that the crook had been captured.

On January 4, the first work day of the year, we had a New Year ceremony in the morning and a toast with my colleagues in the office. I invited some of them to my house for a party. I received a call when I arrived home informing me that the Hoshi confessed to the safety-box con. At last! I let my men continue partying and headed to the station. I questioned him again to check the credibility of his confession. Convinced that it was reliable, I phoned Metropolitan Police HQ. The boss asked if I was sure.

To test authenticity in any admission of guilt, it is useful to ask the suspect things that only he could know. Things that were never reported in the media. For example, I asked him about his escape route, what transport he used, whether he used a taxi, how much it cost etc. As I said, fraudsters can't keep their mouths shut, and this Hoshi was no exception. Con artists usually observe the detective doing the questioning to see how experienced he is. If the questioner seemed like he knew what he was doing, they usually change their tune and get straight to the point. A professional thief is a different story. He typically won't say much at first and stares at the interrogator's face for hours on end.

Thus, we eventually charged the Hoshi after clarifying a multitude of other frauds he committed up and down the country. As for his victims, most of them were society's elite such as lawyers, doctors, professors, prefectural or municipal assemblymen who were ensconced in scandals of their own. The total amount of his ill-gotten gains exceeded 70-million yen, and his conviction earned us and the Tsukiji Police Station the National Police Agency Commissioner-General's and the Metropolitan Police Superintendent-General's Prize.

No Regrets

There are things that I still take pride in looking back on my career as a cop. Even after being promoted to Director of the Crime Investigation Division, or Vice Director of the No. 3 Metropolitan Police HQ, I refused to use the car at my disposal. I insisted on taking public transport instead. In important cases, I visited the victim's house and inspected the site personally even though the official crime scene investigation had been concluded. I would look around and deduce independently how and from where the criminal entered, how he escaped, and any other details.

I didn't record anything in my notebook when talking with the victims. I just paid attention to their eyes and listened to what they had to say. Notebooks tend to make people nervous and reluctant to open up. I wrote my observations down as soon as I left the scene.

Through my independent examinations I was able to double-check whether a crime was committed by one or more criminals, their idiosyncrasies, and their processes. I did this to decide whether the case warranted setting up an investigative HQ. We had so many crimes to solve, and once a special investigative HQ was launched, the lion's share of our resources would have to be poured into that. Given the shortage of staff, it was crucial that we produced results when taking this option. Because of our famous attention to detail we were inundated with requests from local police stations to set up investigation HQs so that their young detectives could learn from the best.

Strength from my Departed Brothers

I faced many hardships as a cop. No matter how tough it was though, I never forgot my deceased buddies. In times of adversity I would see visions of my dead friends remonstrating with me. "Hey! Kazu, get hard and deal with it!" Kasuya, Toyoda, and all my dead mates appeared before me just as they were when we fought together. Although I got grey over the years, they were still teenagers in my mind.

I had a career, got married and had a family. But they never had the chance. If ever I started feeling sorry for myself, I made sure I snapped out of it quickly. "I survived. I'm here, now. I have no right to be weak. I must live for them, too. It's my absolute obligation as one who was gifted life." I can't overstate how much this kept me going.

I was renowned for being strict on myself and my subordinates in the police. Some senior officers wanted to be seen as generous and gentle bosses, but I was never one of them. I was keenly aware of my sternness but couldn't bring myself to make compromises. My life was not one to be squandered in indulgence. I would be ashamed to face my dead comrades if I slacked off in a fog of comfort and laziness.

Sometimes, I heard rumors of complaints lodged about my exacting management, but I never paid attention. Each and every minute on the job was a matter of pride in doing the right thing, whatever it took. The faces of my long-departed brothers-in-arms were too vivid in my mind's eye to think any other way.

Of course, strictness alone is not the best way to run a team. Those in positions of authority must be able to judge the abilities and character of their subordinates and guide them accordingly. I used to partner up substandard detectives with excellent ones so that they could learn. I took young detectives to my independent crime scene inspections and imparted my knowledge first hand. When I was Director of the Crime Investigation Division at the Honjo Police Station, nine of my men passed the promotion examination to Sergeant even though they were far too busy to study.

I don't like to blow my own trumpet, but I can say with considerable satisfaction that those who stuck with me became exceptional detectives in their own right. I ascribe their successful careers, just as I do mine, to the guiding light that emanated from the souls of my deceased friends.

CHAPTER NINE

Life Goes On for the Living

Retiring from the TMPD aged 56, I started working for a major insurance company for a further 12 years. This was followed by another post in a different company. Working in insurance had some overlap with my detective days. I had to deal with a 300-million yen claim for a factory gutted by fire once. My detective skills told me that the fire was the result of arson by the claimant, so he decided not to pursue it any further.

I was placed in charge of assessing fraudulent claims at my first insurance company. The company had high hopes that my presence would in some way mitigate common gangster scams. Gangsters would summon insurance company employees to their offices and intimidate them into paying more money than they were insured for.

Many of the deceitful claims involved automobile accidents. Normally, calculation for an insurance payout depended on the contract and the ratio of negligence between both parties. Gangsters were known for driving expensive foreign luxury cars. Even if the onus of negligence in a collision fell primarily on the gangster, they typically made a big fuss and bullied the insurance company into reducing the measure of blame so they could claim more money. If the car was insured for 5-million yen, they would claim 8-million. If they were injured, they checked themselves into the most expensive hospital rooms even though their policy didn't cover it.

The usual method of intimidation involved calling insurers to the gang office and berating them for 20 minutes or so. Several goons would stand behind the boss with their arms crossed. The insurance man would be scared out of his wits and look timidly down at the table. It was my job to back these guys up.

I introduced myself by name only and sat upright in my chair staring silently at the boss gangster as he flew into his rant. After a while the thugs would start getting a little suspicious. While my colleague averted eye contact, I would finally say something along the lines of, "It must be tiring for your associates standing behind you. Why don't you let them sit down?" "Sitting or standing, what the hell does that have to do with anything?"

Their reservations would grow. "You said your name was Odachi. You wouldn't happen to belong to the Sakuradamon clan by any chance?" Sakuradamon is where the Tokyo Metropolitan Police Department Headquarters is located. "Indeed. Very perceptive of you." I continued, "Being such an astute man, you must understand how much of a payout you are really eligible for."

I would then encourage my colleague to speak up. "Your turn. Explain the relevant clause on page such-and-such in the contract." My colleague would nervously relay the details. The gangsters would ignore him and continue with their tirade of browbeating to which I would interject. "I'm assuming you understand what my colleague is saying. Do you still wish to persist with this façade? If so, then I will have no choice but to recuse myself. Is that okay with you?" The inference being that I would take the case to my "clansmen" in the police as a formal criminal investigation. This was enough to give them second thoughts. Suddenly they were making massive concessions reducing claims from 10 million yen to 2 million. The company kept me on for 12 years.

A Lid on the Past

From the time I entered the police force, I never told anybody about my Kamikaze past. I mentioned that I was in the Naval Air Service when I made my application to the police, but never alluded to the Special Attack Corps at all. Some of my close acquaintances only found out 30 years after we first met. Telling people about the war years would achieve nothing. If anything, I sensed that had people known, their estimation of me would have been quite negative. Soldiers were applauded and respected during the war, but public opinion shifted drastically once Japan was defeated. Military veterans were looked down upon coldly. It was wise for former Kamikaze pilots to be discreet. Although few in number, we were still perceived as being inordinately dangerous.

We entered the Yokaren as cadet pilots preparing to combat enemy planes. The whole premise for Kamikaze operations, however, was different. Japanese military leaders exploited us. We didn't want to be suicide pilots. We were not extremists in the mold of left or right-wing revolutionaries. We had no ideology driving us to martyrdom. We were not fanatics.

We were simply obeying orders to defend our country at all costs.

Kamikaze suicide missions were potentially a tremendously effective tactic; the sacrifice of one pilot could wipe out an entire carrier and its arsenal of 80 fighters and several thousand crewmen onboard. It was poles apart from conventional air combat where a skilled pilot claimed kills in hard fought dogfights. None of the pilots assigned to Kamikaze suicide missions wished for death, but they accepted their fates without complaint once ordered to sortie. When one of my brothers received his mission orders to die the next day, the typical response would be along the lines of, "Hey Kazu. I've got 10 cigarettes left. I can't smoke them all so they're yours." At times, we sat up until 3am engaged in casual chitchat. "This is probably the last time we'll see each other." "Let's go with grace and dignity...."

In the end, I never found a carrier with my name on it. Somehow, through some random inexplicable fluke, I got out alive. Through an intense feeling of empathy for their sacrifice, I never took liberties to talk about my brothers who died so courageously and with such poise in suicide missions. I just couldn't.

New generations in postwar Japan became affluent and preoccupied with personal wealth. They tended to criticize the past as an evil period of militaristic madness. People soon forgot that their peaceful and prosperous lifestyles were built on top of the bones of youth who also had great aspirations for peace and a zest for living. Postwar generations became incredibly shortsighted and selfish. "He bought a new car," "She purchased a big television set...." Veterans talking of their grim experiences during the war inevitably fell on deaf ears. Some listeners would even show signs of irritation, as if to say "Get over it! I really couldn't give a damn about what happened to you in the stupid war."

I didn't want the sacrifice of my friends to be forgotten, but sensed that talking about it was beyond the comprehension of those who had not suffered the calamity of war. They looked down on me, a Kamikaze pilot who somehow survived, as a pathetic a remnant of a time best forgotten. Given the postwar mood, I knew that arbitrarily speaking about my experiences would do the dead an immense disservice.

I only told my wife-to-be that I flew Zeros, but never disclosed to her that I was a Kamikaze pilot. After we married, I invited former associates from the 205th Air Group to our house for annual memorial ceremonies. Ten or more came, and we would drink together reminiscing on our adventures and friends lost in the war. My wife served them food and drinks and gradually came to know what we had been through.

She was only 15 or 16 during the final years of the war, a student at a girls' high school in Shinjuku ward. School girls were mobilized to work in factories like munitions plants to help the war effort. She told me that she too worked for the defense of the country. Apparently, she was deployed to a factory that assembled parts for airplanes. Young girls did not possess the physical strength needed to tighten screws sufficiently, and often the bolts were only squeezed half way in. Inspectors checked their work but were inclined to overlook "minor problems." I must admit to being rather miffed when I heard this. "It was exactly because of this negligent work ethic back home that our planes always had engine trouble and crashed." It drove home to me, yet again, how insignificant our lives were to them.

Prodding the "White Bikes"

The first and last time I talk at the TMPD about the Kamikaze is to members of the "White Bike" teams in the Traffic Bureau when I was Vice Commander of the No. 8 Traffic Mobile Unit. It was shortly before the crackdown on overloaded trucks, and after the introduction of the powerful new 750cc motorcycles. The officers were having trouble managing the sudden increase in horsepower. Accelerating too suddenly resulted in wheelies and spills. There were a few accidents at first, especially on rainy days, and superiors were reluctant to send bikes out on patrol when the weather was bad. I heard some officers rejoicing one day when they didn't have to go on duty thanks to the inclement weather. I summoned all members to the lecture hall.

"I heard some of you were happy that, because it is raining, the White Bikes wouldn't be patrolling today. I'm telling you all now, there is no way I'm going to let you slack off and shirk your responsibilities with those smug grins on your faces. You may think I'm being unreasonable, but let me tell you a little story...."

I talked to them for nearly two hours about Kamikaze missions. I told them how my brothers, younger than the traffic officers sitting before me, slammed themselves into the enemy without complaining in the slightest.

"You are all young men. But when you get on your White Bikes there will be times when you must face dangerous situations and put your lives on the line. Know this. You are not the only ones. My dead buddies fought for the future of our country. They did this by crash diving their Zeros into U.S. carriers. I carry their souls on my shoulders. I carry their spirit. Take your duty to protect and serve seriously. As proud members of White Bike teams you too must put your balls on the line. Protect and serve the people and keep them safe! Put your ponchos on and stand at dangerous intersections and roads on lookout. You might not like what I'm telling you, but know that I bear a bloody heavy load of souls."

My impromptu sermon must have seemed out of left field, but they kept quiet and listened respectfully. Later, some of them came to me wanting to hear more. I asked if they knew why I decided to tell them. "Yes" they said. "Please, tell us about it again." Hearing their pleas, I sensed they shared likenesses with my dead brothers, but I had to decline. "I don't want to turn it into a movie sequel. The deceased would never forgive me. Just be prepared to throw yourself into your work for the greater good." And, I never did talk about it again at work.

I think my message got through. White Bikers had many similarities with fighter pilots. They were spirited young guys who loved the wind in their faces as they rode. I had an inkling that they'd be able to relate in some small way to the courage of the Kamikaze. Other offices I worked in had a completely different mindset, and I never brought it up at all.

One time, a course was organized to improve motorcycle riding skills. I asked the instructor how much they had progressed, not technically, but mentally. He replied, "I think their techniques are okay, but I'm not sure about their spirit." I told him to leave that to me. I took all the White Bike trainees for a run on a mountain road. Mount Jimba (854 meters) happened to be in our region.

I rode my bike at the top of the line as the trainees followed. We navigated a narrow mountain path over a series of peaks. One screw up would mean a 30-meter tumble down a steep slope. I instructed the leader to ride at the end of the line and pick up anybody who came off their bikes. Riding over the mountain we traversed safely to the opposite side in Yamanashi Prefecture. They were as scared as hell, but they all made it in one piece. "Right you bastards. You have the technique, and now you've got the spirit. I'll vouch for you all."

Following their trial by fire, a lot of the young traffic cops used to come and visit me after work with drinks in hand. It was a good chance to drive home to them the responsibility they needed to embrace as officers of the law. The spirit of throwing body and soul into your work is something learned when young.

It was after this that we commenced our operation on overloaded trucks. As I mentioned, the truck drivers thought they could wait out the blitz in the highway parking areas. My officers kept a vigilant lookout for four days until the drivers folded and came to us with tails between their legs. I suspect that they managed this in no small part because of the kick up the butt I gave them with my war tales. The guys under me ended up to their chins in paperwork because of all the traffic violators they busted. More work for them, and more irate offenders, but their results were glowing compared to other divisions in the police. To protect and serve.

Testimony from a Junior Officer

I worked under Odachi-san at the TMPD No. 3 Investigation Department as a Subsection Chief. The kind of work we did wasn't necessarily big time like homicide cases, but burglary investigations and the like are fundamental for detectives. Odachi-san was an outstanding detective and superior. He didn't make a point of teaching us from above but led by example. We learned by following his lead. Although he was strict and uncompromising, once we'd finished for the day, he was a very friendly and jovial person and we enjoyed sharing a few beverages after work. He was kind boss. I didn't know until today that he was a Kamikaze pilot during the war. I am literally speechless to learn this. I never heard anything about it when I worked at the TMPD. Actually, my older brother was also a Kaiten suicide attacker during the war, but he escaped death by being hospitalized through illness. Knowing now that Odachi-san was also a suicide pilot moves me more than words can express.

Reunions and Memorials

Kamikaze pilots still alive at war's end boarded a train in Kagoshima and parted ways at various stops as it chuffed its way up the country. My close friend, Kagawa-san, alighted at Hiroshima. There were many soldiers on the same train who had returned from Rabaul, New Guinea, Saipan, Indian Sea, Borneo, etc. There were also graduates from the Naval Academy and student draftees, but Yokaren boys stood out. We were the only surviving Kamikaze pilots based overseas. Kazuo Tsunoda, whom I served together with, went as far as Chiba Prefecture. We said our goodbyes at Tokyo Station.

Everyone had a hard time making ends meet after the war, so there was little hope of getting together for a reunion. As things settled down in the early 1950s, there was finally a little leeway to have a ceremony for the dead. We continued our reunions for quite some time after. There were seven or eight survivors from the Yokaren, and we organized annual memorial gatherings at Yasukuni Shrine. I was tasked with organizing 205th Air Group vets. Tsunoda-san never missed a single observance. His daughter brought him by car when he could no longer move unaided.

Tsunoda-san was an ace pilot with considerable combat experience.[48] He was a calm and gentle man, and never boasted about the planes he shot down, nor did he reprimand his subordinates. He was not a graduate of the Naval Academy but was promoted right up the ranks to Second Lieutenant. Although qualified to hang out in the "Gun Room" for commissioned officers, he seldom did. He preferred instead to muck in with the rank-and-file in the barracks.

We held our reunions at a hotel and drank to the early hours harking back to those grueling days in the breach. We shared the same uncomfortable feeling that, in spite of what we went through, nothing good ever came of it. We had plenty to talk about when we got together, but this was not the case when people who had not been there were in our midst.

Vice Admiral Ohnishi's widow never missed a ceremony either. Kamikaze missions were carried out in various places, but the first involving Zeros was the Shikishima unit in the Philippines. The core of Kamikaze pilots later moved to Taiwan as the Taigitai of the 205th Air Group. Mrs. Ohnishi was acutely aware that her husband was a ringleader in initiating the Kamikaze tactic and that he was largely responsible for many fatalities. It was precisely because of this that she always attended our memorial ceremonies.

---

[48] Kazuo Tsunoda's memoirs *Shura no Tsubasa (The Wings of Struggle)* is one of the best and widely read chronicles of wartime air battles and Kamikaze operations. It is an unbiased and accurate account corroborated by documentation. He returned to his hometown after the war to take up farming. He encountered much suffering along the way, but devoted the rest of his life engaging in various activities to placate the souls of deceased comrades.

The number of us who could attend decreased over time as age caught up with us, so we started coming to the events accompanied by our wives. Mrs. Ohnishi used to sit with our spouses and engage in friendly banter with them. My wife became quite close to her. Mrs. Ohnishi said she knew that her husband would take his own life to follow the young pilots in death. The elderly Mrs. Ohnishi was later hospitalized near Yasukuni Shrine. Until then, she had been a regular attendee for nearly 20 years. One of our members, Hanakawa-san, owned a sightseeing business and assisted Mrs. Ohnishi to and from the hospital in his car.

Many books and movies have been published about the Kamikaze years after the war. Very few of them accurately communicate what we really went through. Very soon, there will be nobody left at all who knows the truth.

CHAPTER TEN

The Life-Giving Sword

Kendo became an integral part of my life when I met Mr. Kuroda in my childhood days. As I have already alluded to, one of the main reasons I became a policeman was because it would allow me to continue Kendo. When I was posted to Waseda Police Station, I was inducted into a special Kendo team on my first day of work. I trained every day on top of my regular police duties. Not long after I became a detective, I was transferred to Central Corps to specialize in Kendo. Because of the GHQ enforced prohibition on martial arts, however, and my gradual career shift to the field of crime investigation, I ultimately didn't become a fully-fledged Kendo professional in the police. I never really intended to become Kendo expert per se; I just loved to train. Until retirement, I crossed swords with my colleagues whenever I could find time, no matter where I was working, or what my position was. For me, "Kendo life" and "detective life" were one in the same.

From Waseda Police Station to the Central Corps

I practiced Kendo as an extracurricular activity at the Waseda Police Station when was residing at the Tokyo Women's Medical College dormitory. At the time, Saito-san, a former member of the Kendo squad at TMPD's Headquarters was also stationed in Waseda. I became acquainted with him through Kendo, but he transferred back to the Central Corps Kendo squad six months later. I had just become a detective, but Saito-san knew of my Kendo obsession. Before his transfer he asked me if I would consider moving to the Central Corps if there was an opening in the Kendo section. I was very amenable to the idea. I was slogging away as a detective when Saito-san rang me out of the blue about a new vacancy. "I talked to our Commander about you. He told me to call. Come to the Central Corps to be interviewed by the Vice Commander."

I went to the Central Corps the very next day without getting permission from my superior officer. I knew he would deny my request. I went to the Vice Commander's office. "Do you really want to specialize in Kendo?

What do you do now?" "I'm a detective." I replied. He seemed puzzled. Detective was something that all young police officers aspired to.

Detective work is exciting, but there was another reason why it was such a longed-for position. Detectives had what was referred to as a "Blue Pass," a small blue notebook with "Policeman Boarding Pass" written on the cover. The holder of such a prized possession could ride on any public transport and get into theaters and other establishments for free. Detectives needed these privileges in the pursuit of suspects. It was considerably more influential as a pass than the standard police notebook, but the number issued to police stations was limited and only detectives could carry one. The Vice Commander looked somewhat dumbfounded. "You're a detective and have Blue Pass. Do you really want to throw that all away to do Kendo?" "Yes Sir!" I replied.

It was an unthinkable career move, but the lure of Kendo was precisely the reason why I became a policeman. Detective duties kept me away from the dojo more often than not, and I longed to join a section in the police where Kendo was my main job. Meeting with Saito-san gave me hope. The Vice Commander advised that he would be in touch about the result of my impromptu interview.

Notification came about a week later. I was summoned by the Section Chief of General Affairs. As soon as I walked through the door, he reprimanded me in a loud voice. "There is a notice for your transfer to Central Corps. When did you decide to go and see them?!" The Vice Superintendent of Waseda Police Station sat beside him. I apologized immediately, but he also admonished me. "You obviously don't understand how this organization works. Why didn't you take the necessary steps beforehand?" I tried to explain. "A colleague suggested it, and I just went along without thinking too much of it." They were singularly unimpressed, but finally ordered me to go see the Superintendent.

He was waiting for me. "You've only just become a detective and now you're telling me you want to go back to wearing a uniform and wave bamboo sticks around?!" I explained my predicament as honestly as I could. "I had various aspirations when I became a policeman, and one of them was to practice Kendo. I trained hard in Kendo when I was a kid, and even won some local tournaments. After making detective, I get home late every night, cook my own meals, and don't even have time to sleep let alone go to Kendo. It dawned on me that I need to work in a section where Kendo can be a part of my life again."

A very rare and exceptional case, eventually my transfer was approved. The Vice Superintendent and Section Chief continued to fire sarcastic comments in my direction, but the Superintendent seemed much more understanding.

The Grandmasters of Kendo

I entered in Central Corps in the spring of 1949. At that time, there were four Corps: Central, South, North, and West. They were all under TMPD jurisdiction and were established to keep public order in Tokyo. The Central Corps was the only one that had Kendo specialists.[49] The formation of the Central Corps was divided into four working rotations and had seven sub-units each with 80 members. The third sub-unit was the one dedicated to Kendo, and that was where I was sent. The others specialized in sports such as Judo and baseball. Apart from daily physical training we also underwent formal studies in the classroom.

Although "Kendo specialists," our training was hampered by a shortage of protective equipment. The protectors that we did have were old and grungy, and there were no craftsmen around to repair them. There was always a mad dash to secure the nicest sets of training armor before each session in the dojo. This was our number one priority and we were competitive about it, checking where the better equipment was located before class.

The protectors were suspended from a steel bar set in the ceiling of the ground-floor dojo. As soon as our lectures finished on the second floor, we scrambled downstairs and grabbed one of the long wooden poles to unhook the best set of armor we could get to first. Even a few seconds delay meant enduring a tiring, sweaty Kendo training with an

---

[49] The TMPD maintained a riot squad before the war but this was disbanded by order of GHQ. These four corps were established to meet the need for maintaining security in postwar society and were later reorganized into the Police Reserve Corps spread throughout the seven wards of Tokyo. They were further restructured into the Riot Police that operates now. Their allotted task of preserving public security required members who were mentally and physically strong and martial arts such as Judo and Kendo and other sports were encouraged for this purpose. Their main duties revolved around crowd control and suppressing illegal and violent demonstrations. In politically volatile times they were mobilized at the first sign of trouble but spent the rest of their time undergoing harsh training in Kendo or Judo to maintain preparedness for duty. Many of the highest-ranked or competitively successful Kendo athletes today are policemen,

even more tired set of armor. Our training wear was also unkempt and held together with patches.

Most of our practices consisted of a grueling exercise called *kakari-geiko*. We would do this against the masters for about an hour, followed by sparring. *Kakari-geiko*, or attack practice, is an incredibly tough drill in which one relentlessly attacks target areas on the receiver. It is designed to build stamina and mental fortitude as well as improve technical ability. It is absolutely exhausting. Back in those days, violent thrusts to the throat and foot tripping were not prohibited like they are today, so if we weren't careful, we would be thrown to the floor and end up staring at the ceiling.[50]

Being the only police division specializing in Kendo in Tokyo, we were fortunate to have great masters teaching us. The most distinguished among them were grandmasters Moriji Mochida and Goroh Saimura, the most eminent Kendo teachers in all of Japan.[51] I used to practice with Mochida-sensei as much as possible. I tried to hit him with all I was worth, but he stood unperturbed and never gave an inch. The tip of his bamboo sword hardly moved, and he always had control of the centerline. I tried to push his sword out of the way to force an opening, but no matter what I tried his sword would just revert into an insurmountable barrier. All I could do was charge in with full power and speed to try and land a lucky strike on his head shouting *Me-e-e-n*! Although infrequent, every so often my sword would brush his head. When this happened, he would comment from under his mask, "Almost...." I wasn't exactly sure what he meant, but I got the hint that my strikes were insufficient. Still, "almost" was better than nothing. At least I was heading in the right direction.

"Sparring" with Mochida-sensei was essentially *kakari-geiko*. At the start of practice, he would politely urge me to make a move. The instant I

---

[50] The targets in Kendo are *men* (head), *kote* (forearm), *doh* (torso) and *tsuki*, a thrust to the throat. *Tsuki* requires pinpoint accuracy and is dangerous when it misses the protective flap in front of the throat. It is prohibited until high school level. Tripping an opponent up is also prohibited in Kendo now.

[51] Mochida and Saimura both held the highest rank in Kendo of 10th Dan. Only five people in the history of Kendo have even been awarded that rank. The current ranking system only goes up to 8th Dan. Both these men are referred to as "Kendo saints of the Showa era" and although they have long since passed away, they are still remembered and esteemed by Kendo players all over Japan. (See photos)

tried to push his bamboo sword out of the way, I would make one frantic hit after another, two or three times from the wrist to the head, or head to wrist. Mochida-sensei was tall man and his steadfast sword nullified every attack. I resigned myself to getting his sword tip lodged firmly in my throat as I extended out to strike in a flurry of desperation. Each bout with him only lasted a few minutes but it was physically and mentally shattering.

Saimura-sensei was just as formidable. Training with both men was hard, but they were never cruel to us. They did not kick our legs out from under us or try to hurt us with thrusts to the throat. Their level far exceeded that of other professional instructors who regularly resorted to nasty methods to keep us in our place. As I improved, I learned to develop mind and breath control rather than simply trying to prevail with speed and power; but these masters, so much older than us in our physical prime, were untouchable.

Kendo Prohibition

On May 20, 1949, we were thrashing it out in the dojo as usual when I noticed more than 20 GHQ officers with epaulets on their shoulders watching us from the entrance. Several U.S. military jeeps were parked in rows in the garden area. I wondered why and assumed they were high-ranking officers. One of our instructors gave the command to cease practice, and we were directed to the classroom on the second floor. We hurried upstairs drenched in sweat. Our leader informed us with a grim look on his face "From now on, by decree of GHQ, we can't practice Kendo anymore." We were terribly disappointed. Especially me, as I was the newest member and had only been there for a month.[52]

---

[52] GHQ prohibited all Kendo practice in schools on November 6, 1945, and in the police in November 1949. Kendo was deemed by the Allied Occupation Force as being symbolic of militarism. Kendo in modern times is not studied to kill or maim opponents but for the development of character through hard physical and mental training. In Kendo, it is important to esteem one's opponents and always act in a polite manner. Respect and humility are crucial elements of the Kendo mindset. For example, there is a common proverb in Kendo practice "*Utte hansei, utarete kansha.*" It means that when you successfully strike your opponent, it is not a time to boast, but to reflect earnestly on whether it was achieved with proper mind and posture. Conversely, when you are hit by your opponent, you should be grateful because of the opportunity to identify and rectify your shortcomings. Due to the efforts of Kendo masters, authorities gradually came to see that Kendo was not in itself militaristic, and the prohibition was eventually annulled in 1952. The official concept of Kendo now, as proscribed by the All

At the time, there was an office for the West Corps located in the annex of the TMPD Headquarters. Takei-san, former Superintendent of the Waseda Police Station was overseeing the establishment of the West Corps. He was a Judo player with the rank of 6th Dan, so understood my disappointment. "You can't practice Kendo now? That's a pity. Why don't you transfer to the West Corps. I can make you a messenger for the Commander." I thought there was no reason to stay with the Central Corps if Kendo was off the menu. "Thank you for the offer Takei-san. Yes please."

I transferred to the West Corps on May 26. It had been newly established in Shinjuku Ward with eight sub-units of around 80 members each. On my first day there I discovered to my delight that many of my new colleagues were actively practicing Kendo despite the prohibition under the pretext of training in the use of "batons." (60cm wooden staffs that officers used for crowd control.) The batons were much shorter than bamboo swords, but training with them required head and arm protectors, so there was a lot of overlap with Kendo. In fact, about 60 percent of West Corps members were experienced Kendo practitioners. At first, they trained with batons but became bored and replaced them with bamboo swords they had been hiding. Our superiors knew and gave us tacit permission to continue.

I later learned that this "baton training" was invented especially for us by like-minded superiors. Takichiro Yoshida, former director in the TMPD's Education Division was the main instigator. He had two aims: to prepare for the resurrection of Kendo in the future, and to create positions for Kendo instructors and specialists who had been made jobless through the GHQ directive. Yoshida-san surmised that GHQ would understand the importance of training officers in this most basic of police tools. Consulting with grandmasters Mochida and Saimura, Yoshida-san visited the GHQ office on several occasions to seek approval. Hooray for his efforts. Our main work in the West Corps was to guard busy areas and maintain public security. When we were not on duty we trained in "baton" Kendo.

Japan Kendo Federation in 1975 is "to discipline the human character through the application of the principles of the sword."

Grandmaster Chutaro Ogawa

When I worked at TMPD's No.1 District HQ a few years later, my desk was positioned next to that of another Kendo grandmaster, Chutaro Ogawa.[53] He and Hajime Kudo, a master of Judo, oversaw the coaching of Kendo and Judo to special units in the police. They usually went out to teach in the afternoon, so I would see them in the office during the morning.

It was interesting and often amusing to listen in on their conversations. For example, Kudo-sensei once boasted in a loud voice "I drank and ate myself silly last night. I knocked back 80 skewers of grilled chicken!" Ten to 20 skewers of grilled chicken are usually more than enough for the average person. Ogawa-sensei replied, "My goodness! That's a tad gluttonous. Hahaha...." One of greatest Kendo masters of the postwar era, he had a wonderfully innocent temperament.

Unfortunately, I never had a chance to ask Ogawa-sensei for Kendo lessons. However, one afternoon when I was practicing in the TMPD dojo, he happened by and observed me in action. When the session finished, he offered me some timely advice. "Odachi-san, I don't think you need to strike the *kote-men* technique anymore." This is a rapid two-step strike from the wrist to the head. I remember his words well. He was encouraging me to seek the true mind and heart of Kendo through a single, spirited, decisive blow instead of relying on technical agility and speed. Ogawa-sensei was also a practitioner of Zen Buddhism and advocated a mental approach to Kendo.

MPD Morning Training

The "Morning Kendo Club" which trains at the TMPD HQ in Sakuradamon started in 1970. It was not a compulsory training session for the Kendo professionals, but a voluntary gathering for all TMPD staff. Regular practices were, and still are, conducted on Monday, Wednesday and Friday from 6:30am to 8am. When it started, I was stationed with the No. 8 Traffic Unit and was unable to take part, but I rarely missed a training after I was transferred to the TMPD HQ.

Tsuchida-san and Kageyama-san were stalwarts of the Kendo sessions. It made no difference that they were very high up in the police

---

[53] Chutaro Ogawa (1901–92) was a 9th Dan Kendo master and served as the Honorary Kendo Master of the TMPD. He was a long-time student of Mochida-sensei. (See photos)

hierarchy. They simply enjoyed crossing swords with police staff of all ranks and ages. A large man, Kageyama-san's Kendo was calm and had a solemn quality. An alumnus of Tokyo University Kendo Club, Tsuchida-san was born in Akita Prefecture in the north of Japan. His style of Kendo was simple, powerful, and distinctive.

Tsuchida-san was not particular about promotion examinations being quite content with his current rank of 5th Dan. "It's enough for me just to be able to train. That's the only way to find out what true Kendo is...." I understood exactly where he was coming from and decided that I wouldn't bother with promotion examinations to go up the ranks in Kendo either. I did not take the examination for 6th Dan for a long time, but later came to think that possession of this senior rank would be meaningful for coaching children. I eventually took 6th Dan and then 7th Dan, but never tried out for the highest grade of 8th Dan.

Tsuchida-san was kind to me. He was promoted to Superintendent General of the TMPD and would often call into my office. "Hi Odachi, this is Tsuchida. Do you have time tonight? Come to my place after work. Let's have a few drinks and talk about Kendo." There was always a policeman standing guard outside his house. I would have to state my name and business before I could enter, but it became a regular fixture before long.

Tsuchida-san talked of how he desired to return to Akita after retirement. We had many things in common, and plenty to chat about concerning Kendo and the war. He had been a Lieutenant in the Navy. His ship was bombed, and he was rescued after spending quite some time bobbing around in the ocean. I decided to confide in him about my experiences as a Kamikaze pilot. He was quite taken aback. "Are you serious? Wow, what an extraordinary life you've had!"

Foreign Kendo practitioners sometimes joined our morning trainings. The Metropolitan Police used to dispatch young instructors to European countries such as France, Britain and Germany. Their foreign charges would follow them back to Japan on occasion, and we welcomed them to join our practices. Around 1981, a French Police Superintendent-General from Paris came to train with us for 50 days. He rented an apartment in Ohta Ward and frequented the MPD dojo almost every day. He held the grade of 3rd Dan and was eager to learn.

We became good friends, and he was invited to a police social gathering at some resort. He got terribly drunk and passed out in the entrance as we were about to return. A jovial man, I asked him through a translator how he was able to take such a long time off work. "Aren't Superintendent Generals in Paris busy?" I asked. "That's why I have a deputy." he replied. Japanese policemen could hardly ever take paid leave. It was frightening just asking for one day off. Apart from him, seven or eight Kendo practitioners from England and Germany came for several days at a time.

My work in the No. 3 Crime Investigation Bureau was hectic, but I never missed the three morning trainings each week. I worked until midnight nearly every day, so early morning trainings left me susceptible to bouts of drowsiness at times in the afternoon. I tried to make the Saturday trainings as well if my schedule permitted.

I have not missed many trainings in the 33 years since my retirement, except when I was hospitalized for stomach cancer and cataracts. For all these years, my daily routine has basically remained unchanged. I get up 4:30am, have breakfast, read the newspaper, and leave home around 5:50am for morning practice.

Coaching Kids

There are many advantages to starting Kendo in one's childhood as I did, I thought that someday I would coach children and carry on the tradition of giving back to Kendo. That was not possible when I was in the police, so I decided to start the very day I retired.

When that day came, I visited a primary school within walking distance from my house. I knew that Kendo lessons for children were conducted there two days a week after school. There were a few voluntary instructors who were also retirees, but they were not of such a high level. I introduced myself and asked if I could observe the training. The instructor politely asked if I was experienced in Kendo. I told him that I had 7th Dan. At once he called the children over and introduced me as their new instructor. It was a little hasty, but I started coaching the kids from that moment, and have done so for the last 33 years (see photos).

Good teachers are needed to instruct children, but this is not easy if qualified instructors are still in the work force. They are busy with their careers and it is difficult to attend evening trainings regularly. I intend to keep teaching for as long as I can. No one turns up to training more than I do. Children know that if I'm not there, then it must be because of a very special reason.

I remained a member of the Metropolitan Police Kendo Association for a while, but the Secretary of the Nakano Ward Kendo Association requested me to transfer my membership in the autumn of 1994. He also asked that I participate as captain of the Nakano Ward team in the Kendo tournament contested among the five wards of Tokyo. The five wards were Shinjuku, Suginami, Setagaya, Nakano, and Shibuya. The strongest team had traditionally been Setagaya.

In Setagaya is the powerhouse of collegiate Kendo, Kokushikan University, and it boasted the biggest Kendo population. From the first of the 5-man team matches, my job as the fifth fighter, the so-called "General," was to break the tie and win the decisive bout. Eventually I won all my bouts, thereby contributing to Nakano Ward's tournament victory. Since then, I have participated in this championship as Nakano's "General" every year for a decade.

My wife was four years younger than me. She passed away ten years ago. About four years before her passing she started suffering from dementia. As her symptoms worsened, she sometimes left the house at night and wandered around outside. I would frantically search for her and occasionally had to ask for police assistance. When I headed out to Kendo, I had to lock the door from the outside to ensure she didn't go missing in my absence. Sometimes she still managed to open it and went walkabout.

I was grateful when some parents of the children I was teaching kindly offered to look after her during the day. They came and took her out until evening so I could continue going to the Metropolitan Police for morning trainings three times a week and teach the kids in the afternoon. I didn't want to burden them too much, so for the other four days, I took care of everything myself doing all the housework and making the meals.

As her symptoms worsened, I consulted administrative offices to find a suitable facility to care for her. There was a waiting list, and it took a long time before spare beds became available. Notification of an opening came just one month before her death. She was hospitalized and I was worried she was lonely even though she was barely conscious by this stage. I received a phone call telling me that her condition had become critical. I rushed to the facility, but she had already passed by the time I got there.[54] Now it's just Kendo and me.

I am not concerned with matters of rank or success in the competitive arena now. I think that first and foremost Kendo is a fight with the self. Improvement in Kendo requires the discipline to always turn up for training, even if you feel tired or under the weather. Human beings are typically weak in nature, so Kendo provides a vehicle for overcoming personal shortcomings. Even the simple act of mustering the willpower to get up early in the morning to go to the dojo poses the first challenge.

When faced with an opponent, you must not be disrupted by idle thoughts or by the desire to win and not be struck. You need confidence in your ability and the fortitude to never retreat, and this only comes from consistent effort through years of rigorous training. Stepping back when your opponent applies pressure shows that you are already defeated. In this sense, having an immovable mind is crucial to the outcome of any bout in Kendo.

When I was young and considerably more agile than I am now, my approach was to simply enter the optimum striking distance and jump in with abandon. This mindset has many similarities with that of the Kamikaze pilot. That is, to launch into a sacrificial attack with no thought to the outcome. As I got older and my body weaker, I was no longer able to make such speedy and powerful strikes. To compensate for this, I had to master the timing known as "*go-no-sen*."[55]

I am not fond of arrogant, rough-and-tumble style of Kendo which has no grace. The kind of Kendo I aspire to is calm and unpretentious.

---

[54] Odachi seldom talks about his wife. One of his close friends at the TMPD morning practice recalls that Mrs. Odachi was a graceful lady who supported him greatly when times were tough.

[55] "*Sen*" is the term used in Kendo and other martial arts to represent taking the initiative and striking faster than the opponent. Young Kendo practitioners are encouraged attack their opponents relentlessly with the timing of *sen*. To win this way requires alacrity and strength built up through arduous training. As there is no concept of retirement in Kendo, older practitioners naturally see a demise in their physical dexterity, and their style of Kendo evolves through necessity. Over time, Kendo practitioners learn how to observe their opponent's physical and mental movements and learn to entice them into a false sense of security surreptitiously relieving them of the initiative. What looks like an easy striking opportunity is in fact a trap, and the speedier, younger challenger will be struck before he or she realizes what is happening. This timing is referred to as *go-no-sen*–that is, taking the initiative after seemingly surrendering the initiative to attack. To master this timing takes decades of training. The *kiri-otoshi* mentioned by Hiroyoshi Nishijima on page 167 is s fine example of a technique performed with *go-no-sen*.

I developed this ideal though the hard training I underwent during the war. This experience guides me in my Kendo.

When I joined the police after the war, I practiced Kendo in the mornings, afternoons, and even after work at local police stations. Sometimes I trained three or four times a day. I was also fortunate to learn from the grandmasters mentioned before.

Studying Kendo made me think about my ancestors once in a while. This took on more meaning after becoming a fighter pilot when constantly faced with life and death. As my ancestors were samurai of historical repute, I was proud that genuine warrior blood flowed through my veins. One of the pivotal wars in Japanese history was the Genpei Disturbance (1180-85) in which my ancestors in the Nitta-Genji clan fought against the Heike warriors. Many Genji samurai were killed, but their names lived on because of their prowess and honor demonstrated in battle. In fact, both sides saw many casualties, even young boys who had barely come of age. These historical events are lore in Japan, and I knew that as a descendant of an illustrious samurai family, I must never die disgracefully in battle.

People in Japan today no doubt think that such sentiments are outdated and irrelevant, but this was not the case when I was a young man. It was a matter of pride, and it was rooted deeply in my consciousness even though I did not talk of such matters openly. All of my friends had their own family backgrounds, so I never told them that my ancestors were of the Nitta-Genji clan.

When I applied for Yokaren, I was determined to follow the warrior "Way." I was young and believed that fighting for one's country, like the samurai of old fighting for their lords, was a righteous cause. I never regretted it, but after becoming a policeman and through teaching Kendo to children for over 30 years, I started to ruminate on whether my "Way" was right or not.

The young people in Japan now do not seem to have much attachment to their country of birth. The kind of things we were concerned about in my youth would not be accepted today. Modern youth have been brought up in a society that is affluent and full of interesting things to occupy their minds and time. They have so much to do, but little time or incentive to reflect. Teachers are overrun by work responsibilities and have no chance to truly connect and communicate with their students. If anything, I feel quite sorry for them.

When I began coaching children, most of them showed no inhibitions in facing me directly and greeting me in a loud voice or, looking into my eyes when I was teaching them something. For the most part they were able to make up their own minds about what they should or should not do without having to be told. Recently, however, children avoid looking into my eyes and just stare down at the floor. They seem despondent when they come to the dojo. I do not bring these points up to criticize. Rather, I feel for them. They are affected by a negative mood that seems prevalent in society today.

I always say a few words after teaching. For example, "You might feel that school or Kendo is hard at times, but don't get too down in the tooth. In one year's time, you will all be one year older. In ten years, you will be ten years older. It seems a long way off, but it will come quicker than you can imagine. Trust me when I say that the efforts you make today will make you happier in the future. When you go to bed at night, just think to yourself, 'Did I try my best today?' I also do this every day. At the end of each Kendo practice, we all sit quietly and meditate for a while. This is when you are supposed to reflect on whether you had a good training, right? Life is the same. Take time out each day to think about how your day was."

To my juniors in the police force, so much time has passed since I was in the front line that my advice to them may not be pertinent any more. Society has changed so much in the last three decades, and the struggles police face now are very different than they were in my day. There is one thing that hasn't changed though: the most important police work should not be left up to machines or technology. The human aspect is crucial. To be an effective policeman, you must be respected by your adversaries. Human being versus human being is the beginning, the middle, and the end of all interaction. Only a strong heart and an honest, graceful attitude in any situation, good or bad, will enable one to prevail. To me, this is precisely the ideal mindset of a fighter pilot, a police officer, and a student of Kendo.

EPILOGUE
by Kazuo Odachi

Over seventy years have passed since the end of the war. My Kendo friends Shigeru Ohta and Hiroyoshi Nishijima proposed I introduce my experiences to the general public. Being a survivor, I began viewing it as my duty to make known some of the astonishing exploits of my deceased friends, who fought bravely and with equanimity as honorable warriors. I made up my mind to speak openly to Ohta-san and Nishijima-san so that they could record it for posterity.

Whenever I ask myself if I have fulfilled my duty to society on behalf of my deceased companions, I still become overwhelmed by a sense of inadequacy and shame. Nonetheless, keeping in mind that this book may become a requiem for the dead, I am grateful that the encouraging words of Messrs. Ohta and Nishijima thawed my long-held resolve to never talk of those fateful days.

I would be greatly appreciative if the reader interprets the experiences and sentiments expressed here without judgment.

The Sky Requiem

by Shigeru Ohta

I have close ties with the police thanks to my longtime career as a public prosecutor, and I was permitted to join the morning Kendo trainings held at the Metropolitan Police Department Headquarters. This gathering of Kendo aficionados also meets each month to clean the dojo. It has long been our custom to engage in friendly banter about Kendo and other things after cleaning as this is impossible during weekdays because of work commitments. Kazuo Odachi-sensei is the esteemed elder of the club. Around ten years ago, Odachi-sensei started touching on his experiences as a Kamikaze Special Attack pilot during the war. Being of the postwar generation, I found his reminiscences simultaneously shocking and inspiring.

Odachi-sensei kept silent about this for nearly seven decades. Thinking that such an important chapter in his and Japan's history would be of great interest to the general public, I confided with my Kendo associate and newspaper man Hiroyoshi Nishijima about recording his experiences for posterity. He was on board straight away. Other members expressed that they would gladly assist in bringing this remarkable story to a wider audience. Fortunately, Odachi-sensei, our senior in Kendo as well as in life, graciously agreed to cooperate.

In Clark Field, under the shimmering glow of the Southern Cross, the young Odachi and his comrades were encouraged to 'volunteer' for the Kamikaze Special Attack Unit. They acquiesced to the bidding of superior officers not as fanatics or through some tragic resolution, but with a calm, solemn acceptance that they had already bequeathed their lives to the nation when they became cadets in the elite Yokaren Naval Preparatory Flight Training Program. These young aviators did not convey their last wishes for the likely event of their demise, for graduating from the Yokaren meant that a final will and testament was meaningless.

This book is not chronicle of war, nor is it a collection of research papers compiled by scholars. It is a transcript of Odachi's words. We corroborated points of historical accuracy as best we could in books and historical documents, but given the unique firsthand experiences of the orator, we also suspected that new information would come to light concerning the Kamikaze Special Attack Unit. We were not disappointed.

In the Appendix, we have included our research on a hitherto unknown episode based on Odachi's recollections of an escort mission to Shanghai for none other than the emperor's brother, Prince Mikasa, in February 1945. Odachi's testimony provides important clues to the hidden history between Japan and China's peace negotiations.

We were constantly amazed by Odachi's lucid recollection of events that happened so long ago. Perhaps we shouldn't have been, considering the training that he underwent to sharpen his senses and nerve. He had to remain calm and collected enough in the cauldron of battle to find his way back to base should he be separated from the other pilots. He also had to identify small dots in the distance to get an advantage over the encroaching enemy. Attention to detail was the difference between life and death.

His cool demeanor served him well after the war in his career as a detective. He would listen intently to witness testimony and record it in his notebook only after parting so they would not become nervous. He made thorough inspections of crime scenes and pieced together what happened with piercing foresight and precision. No matter how taxing the day was, he would once more make notes riding the midnight train home. This diligence and dedication is still evident in his nineties as he joins our morning Kendo sessions without fail.

In the final months of the war, one of Odachi's superiors tried to convince him to remain at the Kasanohara Airbase as an instructor to newly drafted student soldiers. Accepting this post would have all but guaranteed survival. Nevertheless, he declined the offer and returned to Taiwan determined to die with his friends, and join with those who had already fallen.

Times were tough for him after the war and he contracted tuberculosis as a junior policeman. He was hospitalized for a significant period of time, but with the patience of a man who had already been to hell and back, he remained single-minded in intent. Instead of wallowing in self-pity, he pondered how he could return to the dojo to practice his beloved

Kendo, and also make a contribution to Japanese society which was reeling in the aftermath of defeat.

In his hospital bed he composed a Haiku. "*Akibare no hate ni, hirogaru Kumo-no-shima.*" (On a fine autumn day, I gaze at bands of white clouds, swelling in the blue sky above.) I imagine him looking up and remembering his fellow "Cherry Blossoms" from the Yokaren who scattered from the sky in the southern Pacific. To Odachi, the pages of this book represent a requiem for his departed friends. There are many books pointing to the stupidity and mistakes made by Japan's leaders in this tragic war. Their failings aside, how can we not be moved by the selfless dedication demonstrated by these young men who sacrificed themselves for their country.

I visited Tokorozawa Aviation Memorial Park to confirm some historical facts as we prepared this book for publication. The park is spacious with thousands of houses around the perimeter. It was Tokorozawa Airbase during the war years and was once surrounded by grassland and trees. Standing in the park I recalled Odachi's childhood memories of sneaking into the base and gazing at the Red Dragonfly trainers buzzing in the sky above.

This area also happened to be a battlefield hundreds of years before when Nitta-Genji clansmen fought against the Kamakura shogunate in a momentous event in Japanese history. Odachi is proud of his family connection with the Nitta-Genji clan who were destined to fall defending the Southern court way back in the 14th century. This "samurai spirit" has always been a constant in his life, starting in his childhood days studying Kendo, followed by his time as a knight of the sky, and then as a protector of the people in the police.

I hope that this volume will serve as an inspiration for generations to come. Kazuo Odachi, a man of incredible humility, has lived a life that is inconceivable to most of us. A Kendo man, a pilot, and a policeman, he holds the key to help all of us make sense of where we have come from, and where we are heading.

The Weight of Seventy Year's Silence

by Hiroyoshi Nishijima

"Now's my chance!" I tried to strike Odachi's mask, the head target in Kendo, but the moment my bamboo sword was about to land on its mark, his mask disappeared before my eyes. Instead, he thwacked me in the head before I knew what was happening. Coaxing me into making a move, he countered with devastating accuracy using the old secret striking-down technique known as "*kiri-otoshi*."

This was my first encounter with Odachi-sensei. It was about thirty years ago at the Metropolitan Police Headquarters dojo. I was in my early 30s and held the 4th Dan grade in Kendo. I knew of such legendary techniques as *kiri-otoshi* from the days of the samurai, but had no idea that it could be executed with a bamboo practice sword. I was in awe.

I am considerably older now, and hold the rank of 7th Dan. I have yet to master the *kiri-otoshi* move, but Kendo occupies a big part of my life. It was my senior colleague at the Yomiuri Daily Newspaper, Kunio Yasuyoshi, who first guided me back down the path of Kendo after years away from it. He was a man with a sharp tongue, but his simple and honest nature was a beloved trait. Yasuyoshi helped me find myself in Kendo again at a time when I was prone to drinking self destructively in pubs to deal with the pressures of the fourth estate. Around ten years ago, Yasuyoshi asked Odachi-sensei if he could write of his experiences as a Kamikaze pilot. Odachi declined. "I am not ready yet," he said. Before long, Yasuyoshi passed away. He was only 54 years old.

Although I had been in a close relationship with Odachi on the end of his sword in Kendo, his history as a Kamikaze pilot fell out of my mind. More than ten years passed when another Kendo friend, Shigeru Ohta, mentioned to me his desire to write about Odachi-sensei's life. "Why don't we do it together?" he suggested. It reminded me of my old friend Yasuyoshi, and I immediately agreed to help.

It was in the spring of 2014 when Odachi-sensei accepted our proposal. Sixty-nine years had elapsed since the war's end. Odachi-sensei was already 89 years old. It took him a long time to open up about his experiences, but the more we spoke with him, the more we came to understand the gravity of this project.

"What is the '2nd Naval Air Fleet?'" Right from the outset there were so many things we had no understanding of. My father was drafted as a student soldier and I used to make plastic models of fighters as a boy, so I thought I was reasonably familiar with the war. It soon became apparent that I knew nothing. I had some work ahead of me to do Odachi's story justice, so picked up and read as many books as I could get my hands on.

Over three million Japanese alone died in the war. It was an unprecedented time of darkness in Japan's history, and of the countless tragic episodes the Kamikaze is most notable for its futility. Many of the pilots were Yokaren graduates or student draftees. In other words, they were incredibly young, and in the case of the students, amateur soldiers. They sortied with the call sign "Ten dead, Zero alive."

How can we reconcile this? A famous nonfiction novelist, Masayasu Hosaka, wrote the following:

> "It is outrageous that the state, which one-sidedly instigated war, should lay the load of responsibility on the shoulders her youth. The Kamikaze Special Attack Units were comprised of young men who directly bore this perverseness.... Therefore, by sharing in their sorrow do we not have a gage to determine the age we live in now?"

Odachi was only 16 when he joined the Yokaren. He was 18 when the war ended. As I write this draft, I can hear the TV in the adjoining room broadcasting the All-Japan High School Baseball Championship. Odachi was the same as these boys on TV when he was fighting the enemy in mortal combat. It makes me reflect deeply on the ages of those who fought and laid down their lives. War is war, and countless innocents are thrust into the fray. Throughout history, military leaders everywhere have sent young soldiers to their deaths, but few have been held to account.

Talking with Odachi, there was something in particular that stuck with me. A mere ten days after returning to his family home following Japan's surrender, Odachi engaged in activities to inject some vitality in the community. His mind and actions were at odds with most people who had become confused and somewhat nihilistic following defeat. He told us that people were broken, and he resented the thought that he and his companions sacrificed so much for such a shoddy, meek society. "It made me mad" he said, "but gave me the impetus to kick some life back into the country."

Having experienced so much at such a tender age he knew first-hand the overwhelming differences in military might and power between the United States and Japan. He lost many friends and was obliged to obey the perverse orders of his superiors. He was under no illusion of the monumental failures made by Japan's leaders. For that reason, learning Japan had surrendered on August 15, 1945, rather than a feeling of "defeat" his only sentiment was that it was finally over. Returning home, he promptly discarded his "alter-ego," the short-sword awarded to him in honor of volunteering as a suicide pilot, by throwing it on the fire. He thought that he did not need it anymore demonstrating how his transition from war to peacetime was seamless. Remarkably so, in fact. With that, he set his sights on navigating the new postwar world.

It impressed me greatly how lucid his memory was. Listening to him reminisce, the scenes he described were so vivid it was as if we were watching a motion picture. He mentioned that his wartime experiences still haunt him today. When drifting off to sleep, for example, he sometimes awakens to the sound of an approaching Hellcat. He recalls the moment under the Southern Cross when he volunteered for the special attack unit as if it were yesterday. He remembers clearly the white wave tops tickling the undercarriage of his Zero. The orders of his superiors and the consequences play like a movie on loop in his mind.

We attempted to keep the tone of the book as close as possible to the way he orated the events. Interestingly, he conveyed his stories in the present tense. We don't really know why. It might have been just out of habit as he relayed events in real time in his mind, but we ended up writing in the past tense. Maybe, with some closure he will come recount this time in the past tense. Then again, maybe not. In any case, perhaps this opportunity to open up has in some way lightened the burden he has carried all these years as a survivor when so many of his companions never came back.

I cannot begin to express how grateful I am to have been a part of this project. There are many people who assisted us along the way. With the mystery of Prince Mikasa, Fumio Ohta (former Admiral in the Ministry of Defense), Michiyuki Hirabuki (Research Institute of the Ministry of Defense), and Michihiro Kudo (prominent war scholar) helped us immensely. In addition, friends at the Metropolitan Police Headquarters morning Kendo session, and newspaper acquaintances were extremely supportive, as was Kimihiro Hirasawa, president of Fuyoshobo Publishing. We thank you all.

It's 7:15am in the Metropolitan Police dojo in Sakuradamon. "Practice time! Let's start with a warm up." Odachi's powerful voice resonates through the dojo. He is vital and cheerful today, as he always is. What an incredible privilege.

Lest We Forget
by Alexander Bennett

The irony is not lost on me as I start writing this afterword on 11th day of the 11th month, 2018. It has just turned 11:00am. This marks the centenary of Amnesty Day when the Great War, the so-called "war to end all wars" was ended. The First World War was a defining episode in the young history of my country of birth. Every little town you pass through in New Zealand has a cenotaph for scores of local lads who laid down their lives fighting for the British Empire in far-away lands on the other side of the world. "Lest we forget" is the call sign for remembering those who made the ultimate sacrifice in the prime of their lives. One-hundred years on, and the tragedy of so many lives lost, and the immense courage demonstrated by those sent to their deaths is kept fresh in the collective memory of New Zealanders, as it is in many countries.

Of course, this was not the war to end them all. The world has been forever in the throes of chaos and sanctioned slaughter for one cause or another since then, with no sign of respite on the horizon. What we hear about any given conflict is typically crafted by the 'victors,' and tempered with political and ideological justification. The stories created about war, however, are seldom written by those who were taking fire in the thick of it. More than the official histories of conflict, it is the humble piece of poetry penned in despair by lowly rank-in-file soldiers stuck in trenches that give us glimpses into what it really is. It is their words that resonate and induce an uncomfortable sensation in the pit of the gut. A verse from the Canadian physician John McCrae's timeless poem, "In Flanders Fields" should demonstrate my point.

We are the Dead. Short days ago
We lived, felt dawn, saw sunset glow,
Loved and were loved, and now we lie,
In Flanders fields.

One can sense the sickening futility of it all. Pawns on chessboards of large-scale destruction and carnage are kept as much in the dark as those who observe helplessly from afar. Those at the front live each day not knowing if it will be their last. They not only fight the enemy but also the self as they negotiate a balance between survival instincts and a measure of resignation to the stark reality of their mortality.

Glory and honor are nebulous virtues contrived to give the perception of war as a necessary evil in some noble but subjective pursuit of justice. To the grocery shop clerk, the high school graduate, or the physician indifferent to the tsunami of geopolitical machinations far beyond their comprehension but find themselves thrust into the armory of a blood-lusting war machine, such awakening comes after the point of no return. The only voice that they have in the matter is a frenzied battle cry before their charge into oblivion. Oblivion is later expressed to future generations as the heroism and sacrifice that contributed to the greater good. We may very well be shaken to the core by the loss of a loved one, or moved to tears upon hearing of the horror and insane wastefulness, but we remain oblivious to the true meaning of their oblivion.

Only in the prose of those wretched souls who were there do we get glimpses of that oblivion, and firsthand insights into the darkest reaches of the human spirit. It is their words that cut through the jingoistic rhetoric of glory and national honor. It is their words that hint at moments of sublime tranquility achieved only through facing an unthinkably violent demise head-on. And, it is their words that present us with the ultimate paradox: how the stench of death evokes a veritable appreciation for the gift of life in the most profound way. What is more, at its core, this paradox has no borders. It is a universal truth. For those of us who have been spared the hell, we must simply take their word for it and be grateful for the bequeathal of their bloodstained wisdom.

How many of us really are, though? It is precisely for this reason that Kazuo Odachi's book is so immensely valuable. His story almost defies belief. By all estimations he should have been another abject casualty of war. Astonishingly, he survived when so many of his brothers-in-arms did not. For most of his life he refused to tell his remarkable tale. The tiny number of Kamikaze pilots who made it home were unjustly shunned as deranged fanatics. To add insult to injury, possessed by consumerism and hedonism, postwar generations in Japan tend to be somewhat ignorant to the events of the Second World War. Perhaps it is because such an epic defeat and humiliation was just too difficult to glorify. Instead of "lest we forget," "best we forget" seems to be the prevalent attitude.

The purpose of this book is certainly not to extol Japan's actions in the war. If anything, the opposite is true. As I translated the pages, I found myself daring to imagine the torment Odachi must have endured. In a perverse kind of way, at times I was almost envious of him for having seen and experienced so much at such a young age. I was drawn to the allure of "heroism" and a yearning to know what it was like to soar through the sky in a fighter plane engaged in life-or-death duels. An uncomfortable throbbing sensation in the pit of my stomach would inevitably bring me back to my senses. Odachi-sensei for one does not consider himself a hero. Far from it. What he tells us is that war is a miserable abyss. It is vile, inhumane, and just wrong.

Why did he finally open up about it in the twilight years of his life? It is because he has carried the ghosts of all his friends who perished around him. He wanted to remind us that the peaceful existence we enjoy now came at a terrible, terrible cost. He lived when so many did not, and he owes it to them to keep their memories alive, lest we forget. To this end, he made sure to live his life as best as he possibly could. To squander the gift and wallow in self-pity or languor would be an unpardonable insult to those who were not so lucky.

As I became involved in the production of this translation, I was privileged to go and train with Odachi-sensei at the Tokyo Metropolitan Police Department Kendo dojo in Sakuradamon. We share the same passion for Kendo, the traditional martial art of Japanese swordsmanship. With all my might, I launched myself at him with my bamboo sword in hand as we sparred, only to be completely overwhelmed by his spirit. He transfixed me with what I can only describe as an "aura of compassion." Although 94 years of age and of diminutive stature, there was nothing I could do to defeat him. For he is a man with absolutely nothing to prove. He only has something, everything, to give.

I know that crossing swords with Odachi-sensei will remain a cherished memory. He conveyed something on to me, a feeling, a sentiment of humanity that I do not fully understand yet. Suffice it to say getting to know him through the pages of this book and on the dojo floor encouraged me to contemplate the meaning of my fleeting existence. It is an inconvenient truism that we all die one day. We try not to think too much of our impermanence, preferring instead to cross that baleful bridge when the time comes, hopefully a long way off in the future. In the meantime, we are inclined to neglect living each moment to its fullest, not daring to think that today might be our last. We misunderstand that the greatest peril we face is not death per se, but not appreciating being.

Odachi-sensei knows exactly what this means. It is the underlying moral conveyed in his book. Although impossible to see them as he does, I do feel the weight of the ghosts he carries. Such is the weight of his message. I am eternally grateful for this conferral of wisdom, and his timely reminder of life's ephemeral beauty.

Escorting Prince Mikasa to Shanghai

In late February 1945 when Japan's defeat was inevitable, a man who may have been Prince Mikasa-no-miya Takahito, younger brother of Emperor Hirohito, apparently made a secret journey from Kagoshima to Shanghai by plane. If true, this is an interesting chapter in the final days of the war that was revealed for the first time through Odachi's recollections. Given the historical significance of such an event, the authors spent considerable time researching source materials to corroborate Odachi's testimony.

As outlined in Chapter 5, when Odachi and his fellow airmen were preparing to return to Taiwan following a visit to the mainland to procure Zeros for suicide missions, they were asked by a former superior of Odachi's to remain in Kasanohara Airbase to train student pilots. As they were discussing this unexpected proposition in their barracks, a distinguished looking officer claiming to be "Chamberlain of Prince Mikasa" appeared and asked for their assistance in escorting the prince to Shanghai. The pilots eventually acquiesced to this extraordinary request and took off from Kasanohara the next morning accompanying the Mitsubishi Navy Type-1 Attack Bomber (G4M) assumed to be transporting the imperial passenger. When Odachi's Zero drew near the bomber, a man whom he believes was Prince Mikasa waved at him from the window.

Odachi never met Prince Mikasa face-to-face. The Zeros took off from Kasanohara first and circled the skies as they waited for the G4M to depart from nearby Kanoya Airbase. They remained airborn on lookout as the aircraft landed safely below in Shanghai. As fascinating as the story is, the man Odachi identified in the bomber window as Prince Mikasa is an assumption based solely on the words of mysterious man who introduced himself as the Prince's Chamberlain.

The episode warranted verification before including it in the book but none of the sources that we scanned through made mention of it. As for the possible motivations for Prince Mikasa to fly to Shanghai, we first thought it may have been a secret mission undertaken by the prince to engage in peace talks with China. In this sense, the trip may have been part of a greater covert plan. We also had reservations about the identity of the man seen in the Mitsubishi Navy Type-1 Attack Bomber. It could have been an entirely different person to the Prince, albeit very high up in the military hierarchy.

We were determined to get to the bottom of this curious affair and sought to establish the following points:

1. Did Prince Mikasa have any openings in his schedule at that time to fly to and from Shanghai? Did he have an alibi?
2. Did Prince Mikasa have a strong enough reason to embark on such a dangerous mission at the end of the war.
3. Prince Mikasa was affiliated with the Army. Why was it that he boarded a naval aircraft? Furthermore, why were no escort fighters provided for him? Again, why did his chamberlain, a high-ranking officer, ask the pilots directly instead of going through official channels?

Finding answers proved to be like searching for a needle in a haystack, and regrettably we were unsuccessful in our quest to uncover irrefutable evidence to back up Odachi's claims. Nevertheless, with the circumstantial evidence that we did procure, we feel confident in concluding that Odachi's account of events stacks up and was most likely true.[56]

The Escort Flight was on February 26. Prince Mikasa's Attendant was Lieutenant Colonel Akijiro Imai

We checked various primary sources such as Emperor Hirohito's memoirs, the diaries of Prince Takamatsu, Fumimaro Konoe (former wartime Prime Minister who took his own life after Japan's defeat), Koichi Kido (Minister of the Interior who served the Emperor directly during the war), Hisanori Fujita (Lord Chamberlain for Hirohito). We also checked the documents titled "True Records of the Showa Emperor" which were made public recently. Careful scrutiny of these materials revealed pos-

---

[56] All the documents and materials we unearthed are written in Japanese. Readers who wish to see a more detailed analysis are advised to refer to the original Japanese volume of this book.

sible days in which Prince Mikasa could have gone to Shanghai. These were from February 26–28, 1945.

In addition, we were able to corroborate the following facts through records of the 205th Air Group which Odachi belonged to, and the diary of Matome Ugaki (Commander-General of naval air bases in Kagoshima) stored in the Research Institution of Defense at the Ministry of Defense in Tokyo.

1. Odachi and his colleagues left Taiwan for Kanoya Airbase in Kagoshima on February 10, 1945 to procure Zeros for Kamikaze missions.
2. After acquiring Zeros, Odachi and the other pilots took off from Kasanohara Airbase at 9:30am on February 26 and escorted a plane which Chamberlain Officer Akijiro Imai boarded for Shanghai. Sixteen planes departed for Shanghai, of which eight Zeros were designated as escort fighters.
3. At 2:30pm on February 27, Chamberlain Officer Akijiro Imai departed Shanghai and headed for Taiwan with five escort Zeros.
4. Ten Zeros bound for Taiwan remained in Shanghai for a few more days.
5. The Zero piloted by Odachi was one of the escorts. After landing, Odachi was one of the airmen who remained in Shanghai before returning to Taiwan later.

Based on this information, it is reasonable to assume that the officer who appeared in the barracks on the evening of February 25 was Chamberlain Officer Akijiro Imai. Odachi recalled the officer "wore a uniform we had never seen before and had an epaulet that was a white-silver color." This matches the uniform of chamberlain officers. However, chamberlain officers served directly under the emperor, not princes. No chamberlain was posted as an aide to Prince Mikasa's family at the time. Furthermore, records indicate that an official trip was made by Akijiro Imai around mid-February, but the original plan was to travel to Taiwan, not Shanghai.

Why then did an aide to the Emperor call himself Chamberlain officer of Prince Mikasa? And, why did he request an escort? Maybe it was that Akijiro Imai was indeed originally bound for Taiwan but was informed of a change in plan after arriving in Kagoshima. Perhaps it was there that a directive ("Heavenly Command") was issued for him to accompany Prince Mikasa to Shanghai. Obliged to follow orders, he may have flown to Shanghai with Prince Mikasa, and then to Taiwan as planned beforehand.

Prince Mikasa Had Reason to Visit Shanghai

Prince Mikasa was affiliated with the Army and served as a staff officer at the Nanjing General Headquarters from January 1943 to January 1944. He saw firsthand the atrocities committed by Japanese troops, and later wrote an article titled "Japanese Regret over the China Incident" where he strongly admonished the Army for its inhumane actions. As a result, the Army came to view Prince Mikasa as a dangerous agitator. In a book Prince Mikasa wrote in 1956 on his experiences he states, "I completely lost confidence that the war was being waged for any righteous cause, and began to seek only peace." He also told a reporter in 1994, "I was convinced that the war must be stopped somehow. I had compelling reasons for wishing so."

In spring 1944, Prince Mikasa was connected to a planned coup d'état to topple the Tojo Cabinet. The plot was led by Lieutenant Commander Tadashige Tsunoda of the Army. In July 1944, Tsunoda wrote of the necessity to quickly bring the war to a conclusion. He advocated negotiating with Chiang Kai-shek and withdrawing all military forces from the continent. He also promoted a plan to hammer out a deal with the United States through Chongqing (Republic of China's wartime capital). Had the coup d'état been successful, Prince Mikasa would have assumed the position of Commander-General of the Japanese Army in China.

When Prince Mikasa served in Nanjing in the early days of the Sino-Japanese War, he cooperated with Colonel Masanobu Tsuji in conducting a memorial ceremony for Chiang Kai-shek's mother.[57] Apparently Prince Mikasa proposed an idea to Tsuji of enshrining Chiang Kai-shek's mother. Chiang Kai-shek was impressed when he heard about this act of

---

[57] Masanobu Tsuji was a controversial figure who was known as an outstanding military officer but was criticized in some quarters for his peculiar character and behavior. Prince Mikasa had been a student of Tsuji in the Military Academy. Just like Prince Mikasa, Tsuji was also critical of Army corruption in China. Thus, despite his questionable reputation, the Prince found a kindred spirit in Tsuji. With his own close connection to Chiang Kai-shek, Tsuji also took liberties in negotiating peace with Chongqing. Tsuji disappeared for a long time after the war hiding somewhere in Asia to avoid the Tokyo war criminal trials.

respect to his mother.

Thus, even at such a tumultuous time with the bombing of Tokyo in full swing, Prince Mikasa had a possible communication pipeline with Chongqing, and enough reason to visit Shanghai for the goal of promoting reconciliation.

Peace Negotiations

Negotiations between Japan and China had been conducted through various avenues from early on. Several were held from 1944 to 1945 but with little effect. The initial basic policy of the Imperial Headquarters and Supreme Council for the Direction of War was not to negotiate, but to force China submit to pressure. As the war situation worsened for Japan, the government changed tact and jostled to hold peace talks on equal footing. The path for negotiation was facilitated through the Wang Jingwei regime (Reorganized National Government of the Republic of China) in Nanjing, being a puppet state of Japan, rather than directly with Chiang Kai-shek's ROC in Chongqing.

Even though the Army outlawed negotiating with Chongqing until late Spring of 1945, talks were attempted behind closed doors. It was a highly confidential effort led by Fumimaro Konoe (former Prime Minister) who possibly had the Emperor's ear. The central figure operating under Konoe was his younger brother, Baron Tadamaro Miyagawa (House of Peers). Miyagawa made frequent forays into China to discuss a resolution to the conflict despite the Army's resistance.[58]

As for the Chongqing side, even when Japan's defeat was inevitable, they continued seeking reconciliation with Japan right up until surrender. There were two reasons for this: Chongqing wanted to prevent fighting between Japan and U.S. forces in mainland China, and should Japan be completely defeated by the United States and Russia, there would be

---

[58] Konoe served as Prime Minister for three times during the war and has been criticized for his part. In January 1938 he announced, "Japan will not recognize Chiang Kai-shek's government" causing a serious deterioration in the relationship between China and Japan. The Tripartite Pact between Germany, Japan and Italy was realized under his cabinet in September 1940. He has also been criticized for his indecisive nature at crucial stages, and was against an Army-led government, and is known to have started negotiations with China from early on. He killed himself with poison before detention in Sugamo Prison for war crimes. In his will and testament he wrote, "I am guilty of committing grave errors from the outset of the China Incident. My top priority now is to take responsibility for my actions."

a power vacuum that would work against Chiang Kai-shek. He did not trust the puppet government in Nanjing or the Japanese Army in China, and sought a direct channel outside the government which would connect him with the Emperor.

The option presented by Konoe and Miyagawa was the most convenient for Chiang Kai-shek's aspirations, and records show that Miyagawa went to China four times to parley directly with Chongqing in an operation referred to as "He Shi-zhen." In October 1944, correspondences from He Shi-zhen and Xu Ming-cheng in Chongqing conveyed to Miyagawa and Makoto Doi (Manchu Railway Company) three conditions for peace: 1. Direct rule by the Emperor; 2. Punishment of war criminals; 3. Immediate withdrawal of Japan from China. Miyagawa and Doi reported these to Konoe who then proposed that Foreign Minister Mamoru Shigemitsu give the proposal formal consideration. He declined, however, because direct negotiation with Chongqing contravened official policy of going through Nanjing.

Konoe subsequently stopped relying on formal channels, making all further attempts at negotiation behind closed doors. Miyagawa went to Shanghai again in January 1945, but to no avail. The mission failed on January 31 because of Army interference.

Zhou Fohai, successor of Wang Jingwei in Nanjing, left a detailed diary and it is an invaluable source of information about the peace negotiations. He was a powerful leader in the Nanjing government, but kept communications open with Chongqing as he shared a similar stance. Through entries in his diary, we know that direct truce discussions held with Chongqing were known about by Zhou Fohai. For example, the entry for February 15, 1945 states the following:

> "Yang Jienwei came. He said he will meet with Wo Zhaoshi and they would come to Shanghai soon with the provisos for peace. I am not sure if this information is reliable or not. However, he said that Chongqing does not want to negotiate with the Japanese Army, but is willing to meet with non-government leaders of Japan. This matches what He Shizhen told me previously, so I suspect it is not groundless."

Zhou Fohai was suspicious of direct negotiations between Chongqing and Japan, but this entry was quite specific. Furthermore, he wrote on

March 31 that "Zhang Ziyu came with Xu Mingcheng today and we discussed the issue of peace with Japan."[59]

As Zhou Fohai mentioned "negotiation with non-government leaders of Japan," it cannot have been a formal meeting facilitated by the Nanjing government under the auspices of Zhou. In addition, although he had connections with influential people in the government, army, and other groups involved in negotiations, the names of Miyagawa and Doi do not appear in his diary at all. That means talks promoted by Konoe, Miyagawa and Doi had no relation whatsoever to the Nanjing government. There is little doubt that these were conducted in secret with Chongqing.

Although Miyagawa's efforts were obstructed by the Army on January 31, Zhou wrote on February 15 that envoys from Chongqing were arriving in Shanghai with conditions for a truce. Who it was that came to Shanghai to meet the Chongqing representatives in February? Miyagawa was already being watched by the Army, and would not have been able to travel. It is reasonable to deduce that Prince Mikasa, who was close to the Emperor, went in Miyagawa's stead.

Additionally, from May to July 1945, Masaru Nakayama, an advisor to Konoe and a professor at Manchu Jianguo University, met with Fu Jingpo, a trusted aide of Chiang Kai-shek, and talked about negotiations in Beijing. This suggests that Konoe's involvement continued right up until the end of war.

Prince Mikasa's name does not appear in any records, but he too was considered as suspicious by the Army, and any open involvement in amity discussions would be perilous. Anybody who even mentioned of making peace with Chiang Kai-shek would be a target for assassination. Those in attendance of Prince Mikasa would have covered up his involvement and avoided recording anything that may incriminate him.

The most plausible reason for Prince Mikasa's visit to Shanghai was to meet with envoys from Chongqing following Miyagawa and Doi's failed efforts. There is another reason related to the "Miao Bin" operation. At that time, Prime Minister Kuniaki Koiso was in favor of peace with Chongqing through Miao Bin as a direct link to Chiang Kai-shek. This was a cabinet-led negotiation but was strongly opposed by Foreign

---

[59] He Shizhen, Xu Mingcheng, Yang Jianwei, and Zhang Ziyu were officials in Chongqing involved in negotiations with Japan through unofficial channels.

Minister Shigemitsu.

Both the Army and Navy Ministers were also reluctant to endorse it, and it became a highly controversial issue in cabinet. The credibility of Mian Bin as a go between was crucial. The timing of Prince Mikasa's flight to Shanghai preceded a fruitless visit by Miao Bin to Japan in March 1945, so it is plausible that he went to gather information about Miao Bin. In any case, Emperor Hirohito was against the idea and told Koiso in early April that this line of negotiation should be ceased. This was one of the main reasons for Koiso's resignation and the fall of his cabinet.

Another possibility concerns negotiations attempted by Colonel Tsuji. He was serving in Burma rather than China at the time, but was communicating independently with Chongqing. Although he has been condemned for his wartime activities, Prince Mikasa cites only Tsuji's name favorably in his books and interviews as someone who assisted peace negotiations. This implies that Prince Mikasa may have been helping Tsuji.

Emperor Hirohito's Pursuit of Peace with China

There are records that indicate Emperor Hirohito was secretly pursuing amity with China from late 1944 to 1945. In the book "Reminiscences of the Lord Chamberlain" by Hisanori Fujita, the author claims that he was informed by Shigeru Yoshida that negotiations were imperative.[60] "I heard him talk about this, but did not proffer my own opinion. Still, Mr. Yoshida returned in good spirits. At the time, planning for peace negotiations was recommended behind closed doors by Marquess Konoe (Fumimaro), Inner Minister Kido and others."

He also wrote,

"At one time, His Majesty summoned me and said 'Koiso (Prime Minister) suggested that I meet with Ugaki (Issei Ugaki, Army General) about the current situation in China. Ask Kido what he thinks about this and let me know.' This suggests that General Ugaki had recently been to China and was willing to inform the Emperor of his ideas for a

---

[60] Shigeru Yoshida was Japan's Prime Minister after the war and was arguably the most important statesman during the GHQ occupation. He was a diplomat during the war, but was placed in custody in the later stages for his opposition to the Tojo cabinet.

peaceful resolution. His Majesty knew well of Yoshida's movements for peace at that time, and I assume was thinking positively on the matter.

I went right away to see Minister of the Interior Kido to convey the message from His Majesty. Kido, hearing this, meditated for a while and told me, 'I think it might be better for His Majesty not to reply to Prime Minister Koiso about this matter at all. Please tell His Majesty so. As for negotiations, if His Majesty mentions it his words will exert significant influence. We must be very careful and choose our timing well.' I conveyed Mr. Kido's words verbatim to His Majesty who replied only with 'Thank you.' However, I sensed that preparations for peace had been going ahead privately."

Fujita was an honest and sincere Chamberlain, and not one to speculate lightly. The episodes Fujita outlines in his memoirs carry weight. Emperor Hirohito decided to receive counsel from senior advisors, most of whom were former Prime Ministers. Konoe tendered his views on February 14, 1945. Lord Chamberlain Fujita was expected to attend all advisor presentations, but he did not on this occasion. Minister of the Interior Kido requested that Fujita not be present so that Konoe and the Emperor could talk frankly. Thus, Kido was the only person in attendance at Konoe's presentation to the Emperor. The session lasted for quite some time, and although the content of Konoe's address was documented, some of the ensuing discussion was likely expunged from the record.

It is conceivable that Konoe mentioned negotiations with Chongqing that he had been pursuing with Baron Miyagawa. If so, such matters would certainly not have been recorded for it would have made him a target of assassination. Yoshio Kodama, who had established the Kodama Agency in Shanghai to procure military supplies for the Army and Navy, wrote the following in his memoir.[61]

"The Emperor decided to propose peace with Chiang Kai-shek in

---

[61] Yoshio Kodama was born in to a poor family. Frustrated at all the social injustices he became politically active, and eventually became a radical right-wing agitator. He was imprisoned several times before the war, but later went to China and forged a strong relationship with Army and Navy officials. After the war he became a powerful 'fixer' behind the scenes in politics and the underworld. He was indicted in 1976 for taking kickbacks from Lockheed Company in the infamous corruption scandal involving Prime Minister Kakuei Tanaka.

Chongqing. Baron Miyagawa was sent to Shanghai for this mission, but as the Army was opposed he barely escaped arrest when returning to Japan."

This memoir was written in 1949 while Kodama was detained in Sugamo Prison waiting trial as a war criminal. Kodama had his ear to the ground in China, but the Emperor was cautious about being seen to sway political and military affairs because of the principles underlying constitutional monarchy. He requested Prime Minister Giichi Tanaka resign to take responsibility for Kwantung Army's assassination of Zhang Zuolin in 1928. As for talks with China during the war, his hands were tied because of the policy of negotiating with the Nanjing government.

It might be an exaggeration to say that the Emperor fully endorsed Miyagawa's activities. It is plausible, however, that hearing of undertakings to negotiate with Chiang Kai-shek, the Emperor permitted Konoe to pass on his support. This did not mean direct advocacy, but it would be a considerable help in enabling movements for peace in both Japan and China, and in encouraging Chiang Kai-shek to overcome his suspicions regarding the true intentions of the Emperor. This adds context to Fujita's comments that the Emperor was positive about the matter, and that preparations for peace seemed as if they were making progress in private.

The Navy's Motivation to Help Prince Mikasa

The airplane which Odachi escorted was a Mitsubishi Navy Type-1 Attack Bomber. Why was it that Prince Mikasa, an Army man, was transported on a naval aircraft? We believe this mystery has been solved. As the Army forbade negotiations with Chiang Kai-shek and deemed Prince Mikasa as a threat, they would never have allowed him to go to Shanghai. On the other hand, the Navy sought peace with China much earlier than is usually thought.

Some interesting comments can be found in the diary of Zhou Fohai. Before Tojo's cabinet fell in July 1944, "Navy Colonel Horii[62] took back peace conditions proposed by Chongqing." Also, "The Navy proposed peace with Chongqing with toppling of the Tojo Cabinet being a prem-

---

[62] Possibly Colonel Michio Horii. He was a classmate of Chamberlain Akijiro Imai in the Naval Academy and was close to Prince Takamatsu, who also was party to the plot to oust Tojo.

ise for negotiations." Furthermore, Navy Major-General Sokichi Takagi plotted to depose the Tojo cabinet and assassinate Tojo himself, but this never eventuated because of Tojo's resignation in July 1944.

Shortly after this, Takagi was ordered by Naval Ministry Vice-Minister Shigeyoshi Inoue to secretly plan an end to the war. There were only four people who knew of this: Navy Minister Mitsumasa Yonai, Commander-General of Navy Headquarters Koshiro Oikawa, Vice-Minister Inoue, and Takagi. Takagi devoted himself to the mission under the pretense that he needed medical treatment. There are many records detailing Takagi's labors, and convincing chief aides of the imperial family was also a part of his undertaking.

There is yet another episode which indicates Konoe and the commanders of the Navy sharing same the intentions to end the war. On January 25 1945, shortly before Konoe's presentation to the Emperor, Konoe invited Admiral Keisuke Okada (former Prime Minister) and Navy Minister Mitsumasa Yonai to his villa in Kyoto. Konoe informed those gathered of the following:

> "The war is the worst it has ever been. Japan's eventual defeat cannot be questioned now. The gravest issue for is how to preserve the structure of state.... We must find a way for peace.... The Army will certainly not agree to this readily.... If we succeed in preserving the Imperial Family, however, that would be enough. If the territories of Japan are limited only to the mainland, we should accept it.... To this end, we should ask the Emperor to relinquish the throne and become a monk in the Ninnaji Temple [as was the tradition to remove an emperor from positions of political influence]."

They discussed this proposal for hours. The next day Konoe also invited Prince Takamatsu to his villa. All employees of the villa were kept away to maintain secrecy, and only Konoe's direct family members were present, as well as the wife of Baron Miyagawa. Konoe and other government officers seeking reconciliation with China were under surveillance by the Military Police, so they had to take the utmost care.[63]

---

[63] Although Tojo resigned as Prime Minister the previous summer, he still wielded considerable power over the Military Police. Konoe consulted with Shigeru Yoshida about his presentation to the Emperor. Yoshida was later arrested and interrogated about what he had heard.

It is thus plausible that a small group of Navy elites were asked by Konoe or related persons to help Prince Mikasa go to Shanghai, and that they cooperated by supplying a Mitsubishi Navy Type-1 Attack Bomber. However, it would not have been carried out as an official Navy operation as it was in contravention of the Army and Supreme Council for the Direction of the War policies stipulating that negotiations only go through Nanjing. As such, this mission was kept out of official records.

Our Conclusions

Although our conclusions contain a degree speculation, we believe that Prince Mikasa needed to go to Shanghai to engage in discussions with Chongqing, and a small group of top-level officers in the Navy agreed to assist him. The timing coincides with the previously scheduled flight of Chamberlain Akijiro Imai to Taiwan.

Imai had already arrived at Kanoya Airbase on February 24 to charter a flight to Taiwan (as recorded in Matome Ugaki's diary). Imai received a "Heavenly Command" to alter his schedule and escort Prince Mikasa to Shanghai first, and then go to Taiwan from there. Imai must have been surprised to receive orders to escort a member of the imperial family at such a risky time. If it was only a matter of accompanying Imai to Taiwan, Odachi and his comrades would not have thought anything of it, and they would have received orders from their superiors. The fact that the Chamberlain himself asked Odachi and the others by visiting their barracks was a bizarre situation.

Imai must have thought it prudent to ask the pilots in person and let them know the true purpose. Odachi and the others were highly experienced air combatants. Nobody could be more suited to the task.

Incidentally, a luncheon for the Emperor and Prince had been scheduled for February 25. On that day, however, Tokyo was subjected to heavy bombing and the Imperial Palace was damaged. It is mentioned in Prince Takamatsu's diary that Prince Mikasa visited the palace at 8pm. Prince Mikasa was originally scheduled to fly to Kagoshima after this luncheon but presumably had to postpone his flight because of the raid. He took off before dawn the next morning from Atsugi Airbase (Kanagawa Prefecture) for Kanoya. Prince Mikasa joined Imai there, and both departed for Shanghai, escorted by Odachi and his fellow airmen.

After telling Odachi of our findings, the lingering doubts he harbored over the years seemed to melt away. It all seemed to make perfect sense many decades later. "Then, the person I saw in the window who I suspected was the Prince actually was him? He smiled and waved at me. It was a gentle smile, and he seemed to be in good cheer. We were only separated by 30 or 40 meters, and I was sure it must be him. I bowed in respect and was determined to get him to his destination safely...."

On the evening of February 25, Chamberlain Officer Imai made the necessary arrangements with the Kasanohara Airbase officers and 205th Air Group leaders in Taiwan after asking Odachi to accept the mission. Odachi followed up by informing his former superior, Flight Lieutenant Asai, that they were unable to accept his offer to remain in Kasanohara as flight instructors. "Flight Lieutenant Asai already knew and gave me a wry smile. It was all very awkward." The mysteries surrounding why the Prince's Chamberlain would approach NCOs to make such a request, why the Navy would assist Prince Mikasa when he was affiliated with the Army, and why the Navy would provide a transport plane, but no fighter escorts finally made make sense to Odachi.

Letter to Prince Mikasa

To corroborate our findings, we decided to ask Prince Mikasa directly. After all, we had used the Prince's name in the book in what might be construed as a somewhat controversial theory surrounding peace negotiations between China and Japan.

On November 5, 2015, we sent a letter to Prince Mikasa through the Imperial Household Agency. In the letter, we wrote about the purpose of this book, attached related materials pertaining to this episode, and included a draft of the section outlining the flight to Shanghai. We asked if he remembered flying to Shanghai, and if so, what was the purpose of the visit and the outcome.

A reply came earlier than we expected. Six days later, an official in charge of the Mikasa family relayed the following:

"His Highness (Mikasa) is doing well but will soon be 100 years old. His Highness read the letter with Princess Mikasa. However, His Highness says that he cannot recall [much about those days]. Princess Mikasa looked for any related documents that could be of help, but there were none to be found. It might be that relevant records were lost when the house of Mikasa was burned during the wartime air raids. At the time, the official diary of the official in charge of the Mikasa family was also burned, and it is not possible to check. Related personnel have all since passed away, and there is nobody left to ask."

We had hoped for an answer from the Prince saying that he had in fact flown to Shanghai. At the same time, we were afraid that he might refute the theory outright, or send no reply at all. The news that he "could not recall" what happened was neither affirmative nor negative, which is not insignificant. Barely a month after our correspondence with the Prince, he became a centenarian. It is hardly surprising that a gentleman of this age had difficulty recalling exactly what happened seven decades before. Furthermore, the Prince read our letter with the Princess and made efforts to find locate any surviving records. If the Prince was adamant that such a flight never took place, he would hardly have wasted time looking for documentation. We are grateful for their sincere and kind response to our letter. He passed away on October 27, 2016.

Remaining Questions
We are confident that the flight of Prince Mikasa to Shanghai did take place. Even so, there remain many unanswered questions. What was the purpose of the flight? Who gave the "Heavenly Command" to Imai, and through what channels? Who did Prince Mikasa meet with in Shanghai? What did it achieve? Did the Prince report back to the Emperor? It may well be that these questions remain forever unanswered.

Nevertheless, a book titled the *True records of the Showa Emperor* published last year mentions countless records and documents still closed to the public. Our access to documentation at the time of writing this book was limited, but it is our sincere wish that the ripple created from the tiny pebble we cast in the ocean of history will become a wave for further research by specialists in the field.

ACKNOWLEDGMENTS

Many people have been involved in making the publication of this volume possible. First, thanks must go to Kazuo Odachi who agreed to publish an English translation from the original Japanese. After seven decades of silence regarding his wartime experiences, he graciously allowed us to interview him for the Japanese edition of this book. He sanctioned the English translation so that more people around the world could learn the truth about the tragic events surrounding the Kamikaze Special Attack Corps and his close friends who perished in the war.

Thanks also to Hiroyoshi Nishijima who was my co-author for the Japanese book and to colleagues in the TMPD morning Kendo training sessions. Daisuke Namioka (Director of Second Africa Division, African Affairs Department in the Ministry of Foreign Affairs, and All Japan Kendo Federation International Committee), Yukio Sato (Former Director General, Science and Technology Agency and current Secretary General of the International Kendo Federation) were extremely supportive of this undertaking, and Alex Bennett as co-translator.

I also owe a debt of gratitude to my longtime friend Daniel Foote (Professor of Law at the University of Tokyo). Professor Foote introduced me to Jay Rubin, Professor Emeritus at Harvard University and one of the preeminent scholars of Japanese literature in the United States; and Michael Cooney of Westport, CT, a freelance translator and former longtime resident of Japan. These gentlemen have offered valuable advice and assistance in the publication of this English translation. Finally, I would like to thank Eric Oey of Tuttle Publishing and Kimihiro Hirasawa of Fuyushobo Publishing for their support in bringing this project to fruition.

—Shigeru Ohta

ENGLISH EDITION TEAM

Shigeru Ohta

Born in 1949, Shigeru Ohta is a lawyer (Toranomon General Law Office), Auditor for WWF Japan, and is on the All Japan Kendo Federation Disciplinary Committee. He graduated from Kyoto University, and was appointed as a prosecutor in 1977. Ohta worked for 34 years at the Ministry of Justice in Tokyo, Osaka, and other localities. He served as the Deputy Director of the Criminal Division, Tokyo District Public Prosecutor's Office, Ministry of Justice Secretarial Division Director, and Supreme Public Prosecutor's Office Chief of General Affairs. After retiring from the Kyoto District Prosecutor's Office in 2011, Ohta took up a professorial post for five years at Waseda University's Law School, and three years as a professor at Nihon University's College of Risk Management. Holds the Kendo rank of Renshi 7th Dan.

Hiroyoshi Nishijima

Born in 1948. Graduated from Waseda University. Entered the Yomiuri Newspaper Tokyo headquarters in 1975 and worked in various departments including the Akita Branch, Tokyo HQ Community Division, Lifestyle Information Division, Investigation and Research Department, Newspaper Auditing Committee before retiring after his last post as Chief of the Editorial Bureau. Currently a member of the Japan National Press Club, and Editorial Committee of the Shibata Ryotaro Memorial Foundation Magazine "Ryo". Holds the Kendo rank of Renshi 7th Dan.

Alexander Bennett

Born in New Zealand in 1970. Graduated from the University of Canterbury in 1994, and the doctoral program at Kyoto University in 2001. Received a second doctorate from the University of Canterbury in 2012. Currently professor of history at Kansai University. Recent publications include *Hagakure: The Spirit of the Samurai*, (Tuttle Publishing 2014), *Kendo: Culture of the Sword* (University of California Press 2015), *Bushido and the Art of Living: An Inquiry into Samurai Values* (Japan Publishing

Industry Foundation For Culture 2017), *Japan: The Ultimate Samurai Guide* (Tuttle 2018), *The Complete Musashi: The Book of Five Rings and Other Works* (Tuttle, 2018), *Bushido Explained: The Japanese Samurai Code* (Tuttle 2019). He holds the Kendo rank of Kyoshi 7th Dan.